Disaster Management and Emergency Medicine in the Asia-Pacific Region

Disaster Management and Emergency Medicine in the Asia-Pacific Region: Current Practices and Future Directions

Edited by
Kenneth N. K. FONG and Ben Y. F. FONG

香港城市大學出版社
City University of Hong Kong Press

Donation

All the authors' royalties from this book, if any, will go to the Hong Kong Red Cross for the purpose of disaster relief.

Acknowledgements

This study was fully supported by an internal grant: "A preliminary study for post-disaster rehabilitation, management model building and validation: A 10-year systematic review of the Wenchuan, Ya'an and Ludian experiences" (Ref. no.: ZZHH) from the Dean's Reserve (Faculty of Health and Social Sciences and Faculty of Engineering), The Hong Kong Polytechnic University.

ISBN: 978-962-937-653-6

Published by
City University of Hong Kong Press
Tat Chee Avenue
Kowloon, Hong Kong
Website: www.cityu.edu.hk/upress
E-mail: upress@cityu.edu.hk

Printed in Hong Kong

This book is dedicated to all the families who have lost loved ones in natural disasters and the COVID-19 pandemic.

Table of Contents

**Part I—Disaster Risk Management and Reconstruction:
What We Can Learn from Earthquakes**

Part II—Health and Emergency Medicine: Considerations for Hong Kong

Part III—Looking Forward: Policy and Technology Systems Thinking

List of Tables and Figures

Tables

Figures

Abbreviations

3D	three-dimensional
AAMI	Association for the Advancement of Medical Instrumentation
ACH	air changes per hour
ACLS	Advanced Cardiac Life Support training
A&E	accident and emergency department
AED	automated external defibrillator
AGP	aerosol-generating procedure
AI	artificial intelligence
AIDR	Artificial Intelligence for Disaster Response
AIIR	airborne infection isolation room
AMP	amputee mobility predictor
AMS	Auxiliary Medical Service
ASTM	American Society for Testing and Materials
ATS	Australasian Triage Scale
CCIDER	Central Committee on Infectious Diseases and Emergency Response
CCOUC	Collaborating Centre for Oxford University and the CUHK for Disaster and Medical Humanitarian Response
CDC	Centers for Disease Control and Prevention
CEPS	California Earthquake Preparedness Survey
CHP	Centre for Health Protection
CLP	CLP Power
CMAB	Constitutional and Mainland Affairs Bureau
CMO	chief medical officer
CoV	coronavirus
COVID-19	coronavirus disease 2019
CPR	cardiopulmonary resuscitation

CTAS	Canadian Triage and Acute Scale
CUHK	The Chinese University of Hong Kong
DIS	disaster inventory system
DMIS	disaster management information system
DORSCON	Disease Outbreak Response System Condition
DPSIR	Driver-Pressures-States-Impacts-Responses
DRR	disaster risk reduction
EADRCC	Euro-Atlantic Disaster Response Coordination Centre
EM Model	Model of the Clinical Practice of Emergency Medicine
EMS	emergency medical services
EMSC	Emergency Monitoring and Support Centre
ESI	Emergency Severity Index
ESU	Emergency Support Unit
FIA	Fédération Internationale de l'Automobile
FSD	Fire Services Department
GDP	gross domestic product
GIS	geographic information system
GLD	Government Logistics Department
GOPC	general outpatient clinic
GPRS	general packet radio service
GPS	Global Positioning System
HA	Hospital Authority
HADR	humanitarian assistance and disaster relief
HEDRM	Health Emergency and Disaster Risk Management Framework
HEPA	high-efficiency particulate air
HIV	human immunodeficiency virus
HKAA	Hong Kong Automobile Association
HKAAA	Hong Kong Association of Athletics Affiliates
HKDMA	Hong Kong Disaster Medicine Association
HKICC	Hong Kong Infection Control Centre
HKJC	Hong Kong Jockey Club

HKJCDPRI	Hong Kong Jockey Club Disaster Preparedness and Response Institute
HKPF	Hong Kong Police Force
HKRC	Hong Kong Red Cross
HKSAR	Hong Kong Special Administrative Region
ICC	Incident Coordinating Centre
ICN	International Council of Nurses
ICRC	International Committee of the Red Cross
ICU	intensive care unit
IDMR	Institute for Disaster Management and Reconstruction
IES-R	Impact of Event Scale–Revised
IFRC	International Federation of Red Cross and Red Crescent Societies
IMS	information management system
IoT	Internet of Things
IPAWS	Integrated Public Alert & Warning System
IT	information technology
ITU	International Telecommunication Union
LAN	local area network
MCI	mass casualty incident
MCS	SF-12 mental component score
MIT	Massachusetts Institute of Technology
MMSE	Mini–Mental State Examination
MOOCs	Massive Open Online Courses
MPCOME	Medical and Professional Committee on Major Events
mRNA	messenger ribonucleic acid
MTR	Mass Transit Railway
MTS	Manchester Triage Scale
NASA	National Aeronautics and Space Administration
NATO	North Atlantic Treaty Organisation
NGO	non-governmental organisation

NHS	National Health Service
OCHA	UN Office for the Coordination of Humanitarian Affairs
OOP	out-of-pocket
PCR	polymerase chain reaction
PCS	SF-12 physical component score
PEQ	Prosthesis Evaluation Questionnaire
PFE	particle filtration efficiency
PHC	primary healthcare
PHEP	public health emergency preparedness
PHQ-9	Patient Health Questionnaire – 9
PolyU	The Hong Kong Polytechnic University
PPE	personal protective equipment
PTC	International Commission for Primary Trauma Treatment
PTSD	post-traumatic stress disorder
QoL	quality of life
RAT	rapid antigen test
RNA	ribonucleic acid
RT-PCR	real-time polymerase chain reaction
SADC	Southern African Development Community
SARS	severe acute respiratory syndrome
SARS-CoV-2	severe acute respiratory syndrome coronavirus 2
SATS	South African Triage Scale
SB	Security Bureau
SCHKM	Standard Chartered Hong Kong Marathon
SDG	Sustainable Development Goal
SF-12	12-item Short Form Health Survey
SMART elements	specific, measurable, achievable, relevant, time-bound
START	simple triage and rapid treatment method
TUG	Timed Up and Go Test
UHC	universal health coverage
UK	United Kingdom

UN	United Nations
UNCRD	United Nations Centre for Regional Development
UNDAC	United Nations Disaster Assessment and Coordination
UNICEF	United Nations Children's Fund
US	United States
VAS	visual analogue scale
VR	virtual reality
WAN	wide area network
WHO	World Health Organisation

Foreword

Due to its geographical features and large population, the majority of natural hazard-related disasters, fatalities, and people affected by natural disasters occur in Asia than in any other continent. According to the United Nations report "Human Cost of Disasters 2000–2019" by the University of Louvain's Centre for Research on the Epidemiology of Disasters, Asia was hit by 3,068 major natural disasters from 2000 to 2019, while the continent with the next highest total was the Americas with 1,756 disaster events, followed by Africa with 1,192.

China tops the global league table for countries that experience the highest number of natural disasters. With our region and the world facing an ever-increasing number of natural disasters, and with the coronavirus disease 2019 (COVID-19) pandemic claiming millions of lives and affecting billions more, this new book is a welcome collection of insights into disaster-related topics by scholars and medical and health professionals in Hong Kong and mainland China. Notably, some of the authors have first-hand experience of conducting disaster relief in Sichuan province during the immediate aftermath of the 2008 earthquake in which some 90,000 people lost their lives or went missing and hundreds of thousands were injured, not to mention the millions who were displaced.

The topics in the book range from the macro level of systems thinking for disaster management policy to the institutional level of emergency protocols in Hong Kong and disaster education and training in mainland China. At a more personal level are investigations of lower limb amputee survivors' quality of life and people's disaster preparedness after the 2008 Sichuan earthquake. Technology, humanitarian and emergency logistics, prosthetic services, and public health and healthcare issues arising from the COVID-19 pandemic are also covered.

Anyone who wishes to learn about different aspects of disaster risk reduction and management in action will find this book extremely useful.

Prof David H. K. SHUM

Yeung Tsang Wing Yee and Tsang Wing Hing Professor in Neuropsychology

Chair Professor of Neuropsychology

Dean, Faculty of Health and Social Sciences

The Hong Kong Polytechnic University

Foreword

This new book is, as far as I know, the first of its kind in Hong Kong on the topics of disaster management and emergency medicine in the region. In the past decades, some major disasters in our region have caused serious calamities threatening and claiming human lives and causing destruction. As one of the key members in establishing the Institute for Disaster Management and Reconstruction in response to the earthquake in Sichuan on 12 May 2008, I personally witnessed how disaster management and reconstruction could provide effective and humane responses. Opened in 2013, the Institute is the first of its kind in mainland China to specialise in disaster preparedness, disaster risk reduction, and disaster reconstruction. The Institute is a pioneer as well as an exemplified model in the mainland, earning numerous awards from the mainland government in recognition of its achievements and contributions. Successful models in disaster-related responses and training programmes were developed for other cities to follow, ultimately benefitting a greater population in need.

Hong Kong is fortunate enough not to be affected by natural disasters as much as our neighbouring cities and countries. Nonetheless, the city was hard hit by severe acute respiratory syndrome (SARS) back in 2003, and has been affected by coronavirus disease 2019 (COVID-19) in recent years together with the other parts of the world now living under a number of "new normals". Still battling with the current pandemic, this new book comes at the right time to provide anyone interested in the topic with insights from academics and professionals with first-hand experience.

I have known Professor Kenneth Fong since 2008. We worked together on the disaster programme and student involvement in the Sichuan earthquake projects at The Hong Kong Polytechnic University. Kenneth is a warm-hearted person. He was the programme leader then and travelled frequently between

Hong Kong and Chengdu. His professionalism in academics as well as in disaster relief projects impressed me greatly. I find it particularly moving that he and Professor Ben Fong have published this meaningful book by summarising the cases and observations from Sichuan that remain very timely.

Dr Laura LO

Associate Vice-President (Mainland Affairs & Entrepreneurship)

City University of Hong Kong

Foreword

I would like to offer my enthusiastic congratulations to Prof Kenneth Fong and Prof Ben Fong for constructing this accomplished handbook and, above all, thank them for the gift of their time in prepping and completing it.

I believe there is no place on Earth that is spared from disaster, be it natural or man-made. Hong Kong has, over the years, experienced differing disasters; to name but a few, ravaging typhoons, major fires, civil disasters, and pandemic outbreaks. Our past experiences have left us with many woeful griefs, but more importantly, they are just lessons to learn from. Unpreparedness spells disaster!

Dr Jimmy Chan and I founded the Hong Kong Association for Conflict and Catastrophe Medicine in 2008. For 15 years we have involved ourselves in educating and training related to disaster medical response, disaster preparedness and recovery, and conflict medicine in Hong Kong, Macao, and mainland China. Even since the 2008 Sichuan earthquake, we have seen a major revamp of disaster preparedness plans from many agencies and governments, particularly those in Asia. Political leaders are now blithely ready to allocate resources to cope with disasters, predictable or otherwise. That being said, there is always room for improvement by taking a step further to ensure abiding preparedness.

It is understandable to presume that after a major disaster many people should emerge wiser from the experience. However, many people may, over time, live down their disaster preparedness. This neglect of preparedness is worrisome, and every effort should therefore be taken to ensure abiding preparedness. As an old saying goes, failing to prepare is preparing to fail. Resources aside, I believe apropos and timely physical and mental disaster drills to inculcate the virtues of preparedness are of equal importance. The chapter on earthquake preparedness in this handbook is particularly spot on, hitting the nail on the head. This comprehensive handbook, I am sure, will systematically guide readers to navigate the necessary steps relevant to instrumental disaster preparedness.

Dr Yuk Yin CHOW
Part-time consultant, Department of Orthopaedics & Traumatology, Tuen Mun Hospital
Visiting Advisor, Advisory Committee on Disaster Preparedness,
Infection Emergency and Contingency, Hospital Authority
Honourary Advisor, The Police College, Hong Kong Police Force
Honourary Advisor, The SDU Medical Support Unit, Hong Kong Police Force
Founding Vice-President,
The Hong Kong Association for Conflict and Catastrophe Medicine

In the past 20 years, human lives have been threatened by various disasters (natural and man-made) in many parts of the world because of geographic features, climatic conditions, man-made structures and facilities, warfare, biohazards, pandemics, and so on. A disaster is defined as "a serious disruption of the functioning of a society at any scale due to hazardous events interacting with conditions of exposure, vulnerability and capacity, leading to one or more of the following losses in human, material, economic and environmental" (United Nations General Assembly, 2016, p. 13).

To the best of our memory, the tsunami at the end of 2004 was perhaps one of the worst disasters in recent human history (World Vision, 2023). On the Sunday morning after Christmas Day, seawater smashed into different South Asian countries including Indonesia, Thailand, Malaysia, Myanmar, Bangladesh, Sri Lanka, and India, almost instantly killing around 230,000 people. There was sorrow worldwide over victims missing, injured, and homeless.

The 2008 magnitude 8.0 earthquake in Sichuan was likely China's worst natural disaster since the Tangshan earthquake in 1976 (Fong, 2008). At 2:28 p.m. on 12 May 2008 (only three months before the Olympic Games were to be staged in China for the first time), the earth shook and thousands of buildings collapsed. Rescue workers dug through the debris, bricks, and concrete looking for their relatives. Cities in Sichuan province like Wenchuan, Dujiangyan, Mianzhu, Deyang, and Shifang were the most affected. More than 69,226 people died, around 400,000 were injured, 4.8 million became homeless, and 15 million were displaced. A lot of children and adults were severely injured when buildings collapsed, their legs and arms quickly amputated by surgeons in order to save their lives if possible.

On 11 March 2011, an earthquake greater than magnitude 8.0 occurred in northeastern Japan near Sendai in Miyagi prefecture. Called the Great East Japan Earthquake, this event caused a large tsunami that devastated the northeastern coastal areas of Japan (National Geographic, 2023). More importantly, the tsunami damaged three reactors at the Fukushima Daiichi Nuclear Power Plant situated on the coast. All three reactors largely melted in the first three days, causing the first major accident at a nuclear plant since the 1986 Chernobyl disaster in Ukraine. The accident was rated a Level 7 on the International Nuclear and Radiological Event Scale, and over 100,000 people were evacuated from their homes in Japan. At the time of writing this preface, a 7.8 magnitude earthquake struck southeast Turkey near Syria on 6 February 2023; 57,759 people were killed and 121,704 injured (ReliefWeb, 2023).

Although the probability of Hong Kong being exposed to earthquakes and tsunamis is minimal, there is an increasing trend of being hit by the effects of climate change due to global warming such as super typhoons, heavy rainstorms, extreme hot (heatwave) and cold weather (cold spell), and so on over the past decade which has caused significant casualties locally (Cheung, 2022). On 5 September 2018, Super Typhoon Mangkhut, the strongest typhoon to affect Hong Kong since Typhoon Ellen in 1983, slammed into the city and caused a vast amount of structural damage to buildings, roads, and public vehicles. The Signal No. 10 typhoon (the highest tropical cyclone warning signal in Hong Kong) was in effect throughout the day, and most importantly led to the largest mass collapse of public transportation in Hong Kong in the past 20 years. It is rare that the public asks the Hong Kong government to have a more efficient and effective response towards unexpected natural disasters, but that is exactly what occurred in Mangkhut's aftermath. Apart from natural disasters, however, we cannot forget the painful experience of pandemics such as the 2003 severe acute respiratory syndrome (SARS) and coronavirus disease 2019 (COVID-19) outbreaks in Hong Kong, especially their impact to the healthcare system. During the first six months of 2003, 1,755 people were infected and 299 people died in three months, including eight medical staff. Most recently, in early 2020 the COVID-19 pandemic struck Hong Kong and still had not abated when the draft of this book was finished in July 2022. In the fifth wave of the COVID-19 pandemic in Hong Kong, mainly caused by the Omicron variant, 1,317,743 people were infected as of 22 July 2022, and 9,461 had already died—mainly older people aged 80 or above.

As learned from the COVID-19 pandemic, essential healthcare services may be unexpectedly and widely disrupted. Because of numerous lockdowns and social distancing restrictions, this pandemic has also had a big impact on society at large and led to a "new normal" for many people. There were grave consequences to the physical and psychosocial health of older people living in nursing homes and patients in hospitals during the COVID-19 pandemic because their families and friends were not allowed to visit them. Adults, students, and even patients are now familiar with online learning, working from home, and the use of telehealth.

Quite often, the worst disasters of the past encourage us to work harder and look for a better tomorrow. Although during the fifth wave of COVID-19, the Hong Kong government became more alert to the need for acute medical care and infection control, there has been strong criticism that the healthcare authorities lack systematic disaster response and management skills. It was reported that a majority of medical personnel and public officials felt that they were not adequately able to assist recovery and preparation for disasters (regardless of their own countries or organisations), which calls for a practical model guiding the establishment of sustained teamwork for effective post-disaster management (Fung et al., 2008; Mercer et al., 2014; Usher et al., 2015). We are glad to know that the government civil services conducted a drill named "Touch Down 1" on 16 February 2023, involving about 5% of the government's workforce from all 77 bureaus and departments. This was a good demonstration that the government is ramping up emergency response capabilities after widespread criticism over its handling of the fifth wave of the COVID-19 pandemic crisis (Wong, 2023).

In 2013, with the support of a sizable donation from The Hong Kong Jockey Club and approval from the Ministry of Education in China, The Hong Kong Polytechnic University and Sichuan University jointly set up China's first Institute for Disaster Management and Reconstruction (IDMR) at Sichuan University, aiming to serve as a base for disaster management research for the whole nation and foster closer collaboration between the country and the global community, particularly in the Asia-Pacific region, in related research areas. The Institute is first of its kind for disaster preparedness, disaster risk reduction, and disaster reconstruction in the Chinese mainland; not only focused on research, it also aims to provide training in healthcare, rehabilitation, and disaster management. Subsequently, The Hong Kong Polytechnic University

Sichuan University-The Hong Kong Polytechnic University Institute for Disaster Management and Reconstruction

launched four master's degree programmes at IDMR, including two full-time entry-level master's programmes—the Master in Occupational Therapy (China) and the Master in Physiotherapy (China)—for graduates who already possess a bachelor's degree in rehabilitation therapy to enter into the two professions as qualified occupational therapists and physical therapists and participate in rehabilitation services as a result of a crisis or disaster such as an earthquake, and two postgraduate master's degree programmes—the Master of Science in Disaster Nursing and the Master of Science in Prosthetics and Orthotics—in order to train healthcare professionals who are capable of working in a disaster-affected healthcare system to deal with the complexities of disasters. Some of the chapters in this book are written by graduates of these four master's programmes.

Disaster risk reduction aims "to prevent new and reduce existing disaster risk and managing residual risk by the society in a cost-effective manner, which can result in sustainable development, and thus strengthen the community to be more resilient" (United Nations Office for Disaster Risk Reduction, 2015, p.

The exterior of the institute building

10). Disaster management and emergency care are not widely taught in schools or professional programmes. Therefore, the purpose of this book is to present the experiences and knowledge of numerous experts in the fields of higher education and healthcare in Hong Kong and neighbouring regions in order to consolidate the work that has been done in the Asian and Hong Kong context. Some of the authors were involved in disaster relief work immediately after the Sichuan earthquake in 2008. There are also review chapters on disaster management, mitigation of disasters via adoption of policy frameworks of disaster risk reduction, and sustainability and systems thinking.

This book consists of three parts. The first five chapters in Part I describe disaster management and reconstruction: what we can learn from earthquakes, with reviews of the impacts of earthquakes on the physical and mental health of survivors, the progress and development of national disaster teams, and professional disaster training and education since the Sichuan earthquake in 2008. The quality of life of lower limb amputees is presented, as is a study on earthquake preparedness among people in China with and without experience of earthquakes and injuries. Rehabilitation in infectious disease epidemics and a service-learning project for victims in Yunnan with amputations illustrate reconstruction after a disaster. The application of emerging technology is demonstrated via its role in the smart transformation of disaster management. Part II is about the importance of healthcare and emergency medical treatment in disaster management, including preparedness and training for major incidents and the roles of primary care in times of major community events, as well as a case report on the management of the COVID-19 pandemic, perhaps the most serious public health disaster since SARS. The significance of the operation and practices of humanitarian and emergency logistics is also presented in a case study. Finally, Part III concludes the book by looking forward to the mitigation of disasters with chapters on the adoption of technology and policy frameworks for disaster risk reduction, sustainability, and systems thinking.

Community resilience is "the ability of the community exposed to disasters, crises and underlying vulnerabilities to anticipate, prepare for, reduce the impact of, cope with and recover from the effects of shocks and stresses without compromising their long-term prospects" (International Federation of the Red Cross and Red Crescent Societies, 2016, p. 11). This book is the first of its kind in Hong Kong, shedding light onto future work in disaster management and emergency medicine in Hong Kong and the East Asian context, and thus contributes to strengthening community resilience in these societies. This book is suitable for students of tertiary and postgraduate programmes, teachers and academics, practitioners, healthcare providers, policymakers, and community leaders.

Kenneth N. K. FONG, Ben Y. F. FONG
Editors

References

Cheung, E. (2022). "What's wrong with Hong Kong's weather? How climate change has caused recent erratic conditions." *South China Morning Post*. 31 May 2022. www.scmp.com/news/hong-kong/health-environment/article/3179722/whats-wrong-hong-kongs-weather-how-climate-change.

Fong, K. (2008). Rehabilitation after the Sichuan earthquake: Can we follow the way? *Hong Kong Journal of Occupational Therapy, 18*(2), v–vi.

Fung, O. W. M., Loke, A. Y., and Lai, C. K. Y. (2008). Disaster preparedness among Hong Kong nurses. *Journal of Advanced Nursing, 62*(6), 698–703.

International Federation of the Red Cross and Red Crescent Societies (2016). *Road map to community resilience: Operationalizing the framework for community resilience*. www.ifrc.org/sites/default/files/1310403-Road-Map-to-Community-Resilience-Final-Version_EN-08.pdf.

Mercer, M. P., Ancock, B., Levis, J. T., and Reyes, V. (2014). Ready or not: Does household preparedness prevent absenteeism among emergency department staff during a disaster? *American Journal of Disaster Medicine, 9*(3), 221–232.

National Geographic. (2023). *Mar 11, 2011 CE: Tohoku earthquake and tsunami*. Retrieved on 21 April 2023 from education.nationalgeographic.org/resource/tohoku-earthquake-and-tsunami/.

ReliefWeb. (2023). *Türkiye and Syria earthquakes response: Situation report #8, February 17, 2023*. Retrieved on 21 April 2023 from reliefweb.int/report/turkiye/2023-turkiye-syria-earthquakes-response-situation-report-8-february-17-2023.

United Nations General Assembly. (2016). *Report of the open-ended intergovernmental expert working group on indicators and terminology relating to disaster risk reduction*. Document no. A/71/644. New York: United Nations.

United Nations Office for Disaster Risk Reduction. (2015). *Sendai Framework for Disaster Risk Reduction 2015–2030*. www.preventionweb.net/files/43291_sendaiframeworkfordrren.pdf.

Usher, K., Mills, J., West, C., Casella, E., Dorji, P., Guo., A., Koy, V., Pego, G., Phanpaseuth, S., Phouthavong, O., Sayami, J., Lak, M. S., Sio, A., Ullah, M. M., Sheng, Y., Zang, Y., Buettner, P., and Woods, C. (2015). Cross-sectional survey of the disaster preparedness of nurses across the Asia-Pacific region. *Nursing & Health Sciences, 17*(4), 434–443.

Wong, N. (2023). "10,000 civil servants join tsunami drill as Hong Kong ramps up emergency response capabilities after flood of Covid-19 criticism." *South China Morning Post*. 16 February 2023. www.scmp.com/news/hong-kong/society/article/3210478/10000-civil-servants-join-tsunami-drill-hong-kong-ramps-emergency-response-capabilities-after-flood.

World Vision. (2023). *2004 Indian Ocean earthquake and tsunami: Facts, FAQs, and how to help*. Retrieved on 21 April 2023 from www.worldvision.org/disaster-relief-news-stories/2004-indian-ocean-earthquake-tsunami-facts.

Part I

Disaster Risk Management and Reconstruction: What We Can Learn from Earthquakes

1

Emergency Medicine and Disaster Management
Concepts and Models

Wei Kwang LUK
Hong Kong Disaster Medicine Association

Wang-kin CHIU
College of Professional and Continuing Education, The Hong Kong Polytechnic University

Alan K. T. LEUNG
College of Professional and Continuing Education, The Hong Kong Polytechnic University

Alfred P. H. YIP
College of Professional and Continuing Education, The Hong Kong Polytechnic University

Derrick K. W. LAW
College of Professional and Continuing Education, The Hong Kong Polytechnic University

Ben Y. F. FONG
College of Professional and Continuing Education, The Hong Kong Polytechnic University

Both emergency medicine and disaster management play a critical role in all types of disasters. Good planning, effective implementation, and timely adjustments can reduce the catastrophic impacts of disasters, and enhance processes such as emergency preparedness, relief, and rehabilitation. In this chapter, important aspects of emergency medicine and disaster management are discussed. The role of emergency medicine is illustrated with different models of pre-hospital emergency medicine and triage systems, and examples of disaster management systems are described. Over the past decades, the disaster management cycle has been a widely recognised framework and comprehensive approach adopted in disaster management. This chapter discusses the important components of a disaster management cycle. Perspectives on the adoption of the management framework are summarised based on some illustrative examples and experience derived from international collaboration in humanitarian responses to disastrous events. Furthermore, research and education in emergency medicine and disaster management are presented. The cases described in this chapter provide insights into emergency medicine and disaster management, which are paramount for the effective preparation for and management of future disastrous events.

Disasters, Emergency Medicine, and Disaster Management

Every year, over 190 million people are affected by disasters around the world, which has huge impacts on the health of people in general. There are serious national, regional, and global events, such as earthquakes, cyclones, disease outbreaks, bushfires, floods, and droughts. There are also localised incidents, such as fires, traffic accidents, and the collapse of structures such as buildings and bridges. A large number of these events are devastating, involving a massive cost of human life and property (World Health Organisation, 2019).

A disaster is a major event in which the normal livelihoods of people and the operations of society are seriously affected. Disasters cause huge human and material loss, which exceeds the capacity of the affected society to cope using its own resources. The basic structures and essential functions of the society, particularly the government and the community, are slowed down or halted. Disasters are usually the consequences of unexpected—but occasionally anticipated or predicted—events or large-scale incidents that result in the destruction of property and damage to social, economic, and political infrastructures, with potentially fatal or long-term health and economic effects. There are two types of disasters: natural and human-caused. Natural disasters arise from extreme climate-related causes or are due to the geographical ecology of the Earth. Examples include floods, droughts, hurricanes, storms, snow-related disasters such as avalanches, tornadoes, earthquakes, volcanic eruptions, and tsunamis. Human-caused disasters can be either intentional or unintentional. Examples of unintentional human-caused disasters include traffic accidents, fires, gas poisoning, chemical spills, collapsed buildings, and nuclear disasters. Examples of intentional human-caused disasters are often forms of attacks or terrorism, including cyber attacks, shootings, biological and chemical sabotage, riots, and damage to public property (Klein and Irizarry, 2021). They can also be overt or covert, which make prevention and response challenging.

The Roles of Emergency Medicine in Major Events

Emergency medicine is a medical specialty concerned with the care of illnesses or injuries requiring immediate medical attention. Emergency medicine consists of four main components: assessment, management, treatment, and prevention. It requires constant readiness, as it focuses on the assessment and care of patients in unpredictable medical and social emergencies, whenever and wherever they occur. Emergency medicine has to come to the rescue of the injured in a limited timeframe, making it stressful for caregivers (Bouillon-Minois et al., 2021). Some victims may die because of late responses or treatment. Thus, detailed planning and immediate response procedures are essential in emergency medicine, as well as in disaster management. There are guidelines for directing medical and health professionals in terms of taking care of the affected individuals in an emergency.

Emergency medicine plays an important professional role in all disasters. It entails spotting the issue faster and speedier clinical diagnoses than in normal medical practice, and is the most appropriate and urgent form of interim management during disasters, as it increases the chances of survival. There is a practice called the triage system, which categorises disaster victims into different levels of injuries, and they are treated according to the seriousness of their injuries and the urgency of medical care needed. This system plays a critical role in allowing patients most in need to be treated first in the aftermath of a major disaster, though it has been noted that there may be needy patients not designated as high acuity at triage (Hinson et al., 2019). Without the support and development of emergency medicine in disaster management, the number of deaths from injuries and illnesses will increase. Hence, emergency medicine and disaster management are closely linked.

Models of Pre-hospital Emergency Medicine and Triage Systems

Pre-hospital emergency medicine specialists treat patients who need rapid and supporting treatment through quick assessment, prompt diagnosis, appropriate treatment, and the coordination of procedures and care. In contrast to general medicine, the provision of emergency medicine is not confined to a single or fixed location and can occur in a variety of settings—not only in medical institutions but also inside ambulances, at the scene of disaster, and in site hospitals (American College of Emergency Physicians, 2021).

To make emergency medicine a more representative and concrete discipline, the United States government has established the Model of the

Clinical Practice of Emergency Medicine (EM Model). Its creation involved six collaborating organisations: the American Board of Emergency Medicine, the American College of Emergency Physicians, the Council of Emergency Medicine Residency Directors, the Emergency Medicine Residents' Association, the Residency Review Committee for Emergency Medicine, and the Society for Academic Emergency Medicine (Council of Residency Directors in Emergency Medicine, 2019). The EM Model has three main components. The first component is an assessment of the acuity of the victim. This assessment is carried out by medical staff, and not by the affected person, because the latter can seldom identify the underlying issue; they can only present their symptoms. The second component is a description of the provision of appropriate emergency medical care. A full description of the medical care allows the disaster victim to understand the process of care and to follow the instructions from practitioners more easily. Finally, the third component consists of medical knowledge, patient care, and procedural skills. Through this, the victim is made aware of their own physical condition (Council of Residency Directors in Emergency Medicine, 2019).

Emergency medicine is inseparable from disaster management, in that it is used to help and treat injured patients in the immediate hours following a disaster. In the aftermath of a disaster, there is usually a large number of casualties, each with very different kinds of injuries, such as radiation poisoning, blood loss, hypothermia, and infectious diseases. Emergency medicine encompasses a wide range of expertise in order to deal with such a wide range of patients and injuries (Drzezo, 2019). In addition, there is a special classification system—the triage system—in emergency medicine, which helps medical and nursing staff to provide care according to the type and urgency of treatment. The emergency medicine teams are led by emergency physicians, who help to allocate resources and direct the management of casualties in order to save lives (Drzezo, 2019).

Emergency medicine is not just about helping patients to heal. It can also mitigate the effects of a disaster before it happens (Catlett et al., 2011; Liu et al., 2021). It comprises preparedness, disaster relief, and community recovery. Emergency medicine involves a well-defined system of emergency response, which prepares resources and equipment for the aftermath of a disaster and sets up emergency centres and field hospitals. In terms of communication, emergency medicine integrates the communication systems of various departments to enhance the flow of information. It is crucial that team members undertaking emergency medicine regularly undergo training and drills. Their knowledge and skills must be continually evaluated and improved with reference to clinical and scientific findings (Catlett et al., 2011; Liu et al., 2021). Protocols for the even transfer of disaster victims to a group of hospitals are also developed in order to avoid overloading one hospital.

In the event of a disaster, practitioners of emergency medicine work across four areas: (i) participating as leaders of a unified command, (ii) carrying out triage, (iii) acting as an authority in the establishment of protocols, and (iv) taking up a community and national role in the provision of emergency medical services.

Participation in a unified command enables the development of appropriate strategies and the establishment of a clear leadership role. Emergency medical care providers have a high level of authority to make important decisions (Catlett et al., 2011; Liu et al., 2021). Then, there are appropriate triage systems to prioritise the care of victims in terms of seriousness and acuity, and to decide on either the provision of immediate treatment or transfer.

Each country uses a different triage system. The most common classification systems are the Australasian Triage Scale (ATS), the South African Triage Scale (SATS), the Canadian Triage and Acute Scale (CTAS), the Manchester Triage Scale (MTS), and the Emergency Severity Index (ESI). They all involve five levels of severity that can be used to prioritise patients. Each classification system is different. The ESI is concerned with the patient's vital signs and relies on the intuition of healthcare workers. In contrast, the CTAS and MTS have strict rules, and both systems rely on data to determine the category to which a patient belongs. The ATS, CTAS, MTS, and ESI require more resources, while the SATS works in a limited resource environment and is more effective in developing countries and in places where resources are scarce (Hinson et al., 2019).

Emergency medical services (EMS) play important roles in disaster response. It has been acknowledged that standard protocols, such as the National EMS Scope of Practice Model in the US, may need to be modified in emergency events (Catlett et al., 2011). EMS providers should be flexible in their use of medication and procedures in cases that require decisions beyond the typical protocols. Such conditions may arise from the lack of availability of ordinary interventions due to disrupted transport and limited access to healthcare facilities. During pandemics, expanded scopes of practice are critical for exploring the administration of vaccines and new medications.

In the aftermath of a disaster, emergency medical care also plays an important role in community recovery. Most hospitals and emergency centres are often severely understaffed after a disaster, and they need to replenish a large number of staff and refill patient care supplies and equipment. Emergency healthcare workers are normally expected to work until the affected hospital is back to its normal operating level. In addition, different caregivers and staff are prone to experiencing significant psychological stress, and emergency medical staff will help to alleviate the stress and develop plans to improve the psychological impact of the disaster (Catlett et al., 2011; Liu et al., 2021).

Goals of Disaster Management

Disaster management is the process of anticipating the type of disaster, preparing for action, estimating the chances of a disaster occurring, and initiating appropriate responses. The goals of disaster management are to prevent a disaster from occurring and to minimise the impact if it does occur. This includes the recognition of disastrous events as early as possible, so that rescue teams and the public are alerted; immediate and holistic management of disasters in order to minimise the damage to human life, infrastructure, and property; and the mitigation of the impacts on the community with the preventive measures already developed. There are five areas that need to be taken into account when preparing and developing disaster prevention measures: staff psychology, tools and equipment, sources of supplies, the training of staff and drills for the disaster, and a thorough understanding of disaster prevention and management plans. It is important to note that reducing the loss of human lives and resources is an important part of disaster management, as there is always a shortage of human resources arising from injury, loss of life, or difficulty accessing the scene during a disaster. After a disaster, the community needs to return to normalcy quickly and smoothly, so disaster management must also include relief work to help the community to recover. All the processes of disaster management are therefore grouped together to form a disaster management cycle.

Disaster Management Cycle

There are a number of models, procedures, and frameworks that can be used to help the government, agencies, and rescuers handle a disastrous event. The disaster management cycle is the most preferred framework and has been recognised as a successful and well-known approach to disaster management. It involves preparation, assistance, and rebuilding the community when a human-caused or natural disaster occurs (Al-Jazairi, 2017). The cycle also helps to assure the safety and security of the community and the workplace. Conventionally, the disaster management cycle is composed of four stages—preparedness, response, recovery (rehabilitation, reconstruction), and mitigation (prevention) (Bhattacharya, 2012; Sawalha, 2020). Unfortunately, many governments and institutions only focus on the steps to be taken when a disaster strikes. There have been suggestions to include strategic thinking, future-open thinking, and systems thinking in the cycle so that it will operate more effectively and reduce avoidable impacts (Sawalha, 2020). In 2019, the World Health Organisation (WHO) released the Health Emergency and Disaster Risk Management Framework (WHO, 2019).

1. Preparedness

The first stage of the disaster management cycle is preparedness, which is an ongoing process in disaster management. Individuals, communities, businesses, governments, and non-governmental organisations (NGOs) plan, train, and prepare for what everyone should do during emergencies and disasters. Preparedness is defined as a continuous cycle of planning, organising, training, and exercising actions, which ensure the highest level of readiness and improve the capacities of the government, the community, and civil society to manage natural and human-caused catastrophes (Bhattacharya, 2012). Fire drills, major event exercises, aircraft crash simulations, sea rescue exercises, and evacuation rehearsals are regularly organised by the government as preparation for prompt and effective responses to disasters. Examples of preparedness measures are (i) the development and maintenance of updated and valid disaster strategies that can be activated at any moment; (ii) preparation for emergencies by evacuating and temporarily moving people to safe havens; (iii) the installation of early warning systems; (iv) the building of a robust communication network with wide geographic coverage; (v) the implementation of smart logistical and transportation plans; and (vi) the enhancement of public awareness and continual public education, plus drills and exercises related to emergency plans. Such measures should be reviewed and improved with time, new technology, and evaluation. Preparedness is discussed further in both a later part of this chapter and several other chapters.

2. Response

The response stage consists of an intervention that fulfils the immediate needs of the impacted population during or immediately after a disaster (Ha et al., 2019). The government should have designated officials as disaster management leaders who will be in command and will coordinate the response process in the appropriate and timely use of materials and human and financial resources, including rescuers, supplies, and equipment, to help restore and maintain the safety of the people and environment affected, as well as to minimise or avoid the risk of further damage to life and property. This stage should be as brisk and brief as possible but, depending on the nature of the disaster, it may last for a long time. Appropriate disaster response depends on well-informed choices made by senior officials as the result of an assessment of the impacts and support at hand, in combination with the management of both public and private institutions. The response stage is also guided by the needs of the affected communities, based on reliable information and data from the scene, not on assumptions made from afar or through "word of mouth". For instance, Blumont, the United Nations (UN), and the media have made use of appropriate data to evaluate the number of people likely to be exposed to major disasters, such as Cyclone Nargis in Myanmar and earthquakes in the Sichuan province of China. The US National Aeronautics and Space Administration's (NASA's) Socioeconomic Data and Application Centre also provides data that estimate the number of people who are exposed to specific disasters around the world.

The response stage also involves meeting the interests and urgent needs of victims during or immediately after the occurrence of a disaster (Sandler and Schwab, 2021). It involves the location, organisation, and mobilisation of emergency equipment and human resources, particularly time-sensitive actions, such as search and rescue operations; evacuations; the provision of emergency medicine, food, water, and shelters; and the planned recovery of impaired services and systems. During the response stage, existing and potential hazards must be removed from the affected area to allow for recovery, rehabilitation, and reconstruction to rebuild the community.

The 2008 Sichuan Earthquake: A strong earthquake struck the Sichuan province of China on 12 May 2008. It caused 87,500 deaths and led to 45.5 million wounded and 14.4 million displaced. The economic damage to 21 million buildings was estimated to be worth US$86 billion (Hoyer, 2009). After the disaster, the direct provision of aid by the Chinese military was a significant component in the emergency response phase. The People's Liberation Army was dispatched to the affected districts within 14 minutes of the earthquake. According to official records (Mulvenon, 2008), about 150,000 military and police officers were sent across the country to assist with rescues, and they saved about 700,000 casualties from danger. A total of 100,000 medical experts were deployed across the country to assist with operations. The national government enlisted the help of 18 provinces and localities to rehabilitate the most affected areas. This response demonstrated that, in addition to having a contingency plan, dedicated and decisive central command and coordination are important for a timely response to a disaster.

The Hong Kong Red Cross dispatched its first responder personnel to Sichuan province on 13 May 2008 to examine the effects of the disaster and to prepare rescue operations (Li-Tsang and Lam, 2015). On 14 May, it sent its first medical rescue team to the county of Beichuan, the hardest hit area. It also dispatched two medical teams to the town of Yanmen and the city of Mianyang in June to assist the local health centres in providing medical assistance to those affected. A total of HK$350 million from a Disaster Relief Fund (Chu, 2019) was injected by the Legislative Council of the Hong Kong Special Administrative Region (SAR) Government into emergency relief operations on 14 May 2008, two days after the earthquake. As the needs of the disaster victims exceeded the capacity of existing resources, any unsolicited support was helpful in meeting the immediate demand.

New lessons are always learned from each disaster, especially in terms of how to minimise damage to property and the impacts on people. Hopefully, in future, disasters can be prevented and, when they do occur, damage can be confined.

3. Recovery

The recovery phase may take a long time—perhaps years or even decades. It involves the stabilisation of the affected areas and the restoration of all essential community functions and activities. Rehabilitation and reconstruction are also part of this stage, although the recovery of services and social provisions have to be prioritised. For instance, essential services such as the provision of food and clean water, sewage treatment, public utilities, transportation, and healthcare should be restored or reconstructed with the utmost urgency. Then, other services can follow in an orderly manner.

Rehabilitation

Rehabilitation focuses on helping individuals, communities, businesses, and organisations to return to normal operations or to a "new normal", depending on the impacts of the disaster. There are medium- to long-term actions that can be undertaken to help people affected by disasters to resume their normal activities (Ha et al., 2019). This work is extremely demanding and difficult for the government and professional bodies involved, so they have to plan ahead. Ideally, a disaster risk reduction component should be included in their rehabilitation strategy. Knowledge, skills, and experience are key factors that can help the victims get back to their normal lives, regardless of whether they have to adjust to new ways their body functions or new ways of living. Financial resources are needed for staffing, equipment, and supplies, such as prostheses and technology-assisted devices. More details of this process are available in the first few chapters of this book.

The 1999 Odisha Super Cyclone: In October 1999, a super cyclone wreaked havoc on the Orissa coast, on the east coast of India, killing 9,885 people (Gramin, 2006). The super cyclone not only resulted in a huge amount of damage, but also decimated millions of people's lives. Almost 15 million people were affected. Houses were demolished, infrastructure wrecked, the environment damaged, livelihoods destroyed, and the economy shattered. To repair tube wells and sterilise drinking water sources in remote areas, 287 repair teams and 149 mobile vans were dispatched. A total of 39,985 tube wells were repaired and disinfected. In addition, 105 new shallow tube wells were built and 19 water tankers were sent to saline inundation zones to provide drinking water in the cyclone- or flood-affected areas. Half, or 61 of the 121 Rural Water Supply Schemes that had been disrupted were restored to normalcy.

Support after the 2008 Sichuan Earthquake: With the support of the Red Cross Society of China and the society's Sichuan branch, the Hong Kong Red Cross, the Deyang Disabled Persons' Federation, and the Deyang Red Cross Society jointly set up the Deyang Disabled Persons' Federation: Hong Kong Red Cross Rehabilitation, Prosthetic and Orthotic Centre in July 2008 to provide one-stop inter-professional rehabilitation services for earthquake victims, after more than a month of evaluation and coordination work.

Reconstruction

Reconstruction is usually a medium-term project. At this stage, devastated physical infrastructure is repaired, which allows disaster victims and the community to return to their normal lives. Roads, schools, hospitals, power and telephone lines, houses, and sources of drinking water are fixed or rebuilt (Ha et al., 2019). The need and urgency for reconstruction is assessed and an effective recovery strategy should be the top priority. As a precaution, means to reduce vulnerability to future damage to the affected community should also be developed. Adequate funding and a practical timeframe should be put into place to reinstate the normal order of things.

The 1980 Orissa Flood: In September 1980, a devastating flood swept over the tribal people of Gudari Block in the modern Rayagada district of Orissa in India (Bhattacharya, 2012). The recovery initiative was overseen by the Orissa State Special Relief Commissioner and a member of the Board of Revenue on behalf of the state. Within two months, all 352 tribal households were each granted 242 square yards of land, with strong support from the local subdivisional magistrate. The indigenous people shared meals and their living quarters with the relief team during the reconstruction.

Hong Kong's Support after the 2008 Sichuan Earthquake: The Sichuan Provincial People's Government and its departments worked closely with the various policy bureaus and departments of the Hong Kong government and established a three-tier coordination and liaison mechanism made up of personnel from different backgrounds to supervise and monitor the reconstruction work following the 2008 Sichuan earthquake (Constitutional and Mainland Affairs Bureau (CMAB), 2019). The Hong Kong construction industry and the Hong Kong government collaborated quickly and set up the Hong Kong Construction Sector 5.12 Reconstruction Project Joint Conference along with the Development Bureau, workers from the construction industry, professional groups, and chambers of commerce to mobilise professionals in Hong Kong to take up the volunteer redevelopment and reconstruction work. A total of 16 NGOs acquired funding to carry out 32 reconstruction projects with partner institutions in Sichuan. Regular joint meetings and inspections at the government and project levels were conducted to guarantee the smooth operation of the redevelopment projects.

The Legislative Council also set aside HK$9 billion in three instalments in 2008 and 2009 to establish a trust fund that could support the reconstruction project work in the earthquake-stricken areas (CMAB, 2019). In addition, the Hong Kong Jockey Club (HKJC) provided emergency aid of HK$30 million in order to support immediate relief work shortly after the earthquake, and then guaranteed a donation of HK$1 billion for a number of restoration projects (CMAB, 2019), including the following:

- The Mianyang 3rd City Hospital HKJC Medical Complex
- Mianyang Youxian Zhongxing HKJC Junior Middle School
- Deyang HKJC No. 5 Middle School
- Ya'an HKJC Vocational College
- Sichuan HKJC Olympic School
- The Institute for Disaster Management and Reconstruction, Sichuan University–
  The Hong Kong Polytechnic University
- Sichuan Provincial 8–1 Rehabilitation Centre

4. Mitigation

The fourth stage of the disaster management cycle is mitigation, which aims to minimise the loss of human life and negative consequences of disasters through long-term efforts that consist of both structural and non-structural measures (Carter, 2008; Singh et al., 2018). Structural measures include changes made to the physical characteristics of buildings, or those of the whole environment, to reduce the effects of future disasters. Non-structural measures entail the amendment and adoption of appropriate and prophylactic building codes to optimise safety for the environment and to ensure all future constructions will have earthquake-resistant structures. The Disaster Management Act in India and its grassroots implementation, as well as the National Building Code of 2005, are examples of mitigation strategies (National Disaster Management Authority, 2010). Their National Cyclone Risk Mitigation Project and other climate change adaptation programmes are mitigation projects that address the risks of cyclones in the country, alongside the challenges of climate change. Their actions take the form of specialised initiatives aiming to reduce threats to the community and country arising from technology and environmental degradation (Singh et al., 2018).

Mitigation includes the following actions or programmes: (i) establishing building codes, land-use rules, high-rise building safety standards, and hazardous material management restrictions; (ii) setting safety regulations in all modes of transportation, including land, sea, and air; (iii) carrying out agricultural projects that reduce the impact of crop hazards; and (iv) making infrastructure improvements, such as rerouting new highways away from disaster-prone areas and putting in place procedures to protect critical infrastructure such as power stations and communication hubs.

Prevention

One form of mitigation is prevention, which includes proactive activities and permanent measures that aim to minimise risks associated with disasters and reduce the negative impact of disasters on life, property, infrastructure, health, and the environment (Bhattacharya, 2012). Preventive measures include building flood and cyclone shelters; setting up early warning systems for droughts, cyclones, floods, tsunamis, tornados, and other natural catastrophes;

and providing disaster management training to key players and rescuers (Carter, 2008). Examples of common preventive strategies are (i) carrying out construction work, such as dams or levees, to control floodwaters in order to protect people, buildings and other infrastructure, livestock, and means of production and subsistence; (ii) removing potential risks, such as controlled burn-offs in bushfire-prone areas prior to the peak fire-risk season, in order to stop any fire from burning out of control; and (iii) enacting legislation such as land-use laws to forbid communities from being built on flood plains. Other strategies, including education and training for the public, the development and promulgation of warning systems, the surveillance and monitoring of parameters, and regular inspections, all contribute in one way or another to the prevention or reduction of the chance of disasters, or a decrease of their impacts.

Many countries now develop and implement new and improved construction procedures and programmes. Experience from disasters is often used in research and development projects, such as innovative technologies in disaster prevention (Chen and Xia, 2017). Even in peaceful times with no sign of disasters, there should still be regular routine reviews and inspections of infrastructure and utilities to discover potential problems that can be rectified to ensure safety.

Views on the Disaster Management Cycle

Some inadequacies and omissions are observed in the disaster management cycle. In the consideration of disaster preparedness, according to the cycle, one would think that countries with abundant resources are able to implement adequate mitigation strategies to deal with disasters and developing countries may not have sufficient means for such pre-disaster measures. Developed countries should therefore perform better during and after a disaster. However, during the coronavirus disease 2019 (COVID-19) pandemic, it was observed that some developing countries were more successful in containing outbreaks than developed countries were (Al-Tammemi, 2020). One explanation for this finding may be that, during the response phase of the disaster management cycle, the early or first implementers often do not know where to start. They experience excessive pressure, and, as a result, there are many inadequacies in their responses, which lead to less effective disaster management. Moreover, there may be different organisational responses and behavioural patterns during an unprecedented disaster. Various models of behavioural responses have been proposed to explain how people respond to emergencies (Sawalha, 2018).

Disaster management is characterised by its multi-stage nature. Considering the increasing hazards and frequency of both natural and human-caused disasters, there is an urgent need to establish adequate levels of national resilience, in which enterprise resilience is one of the key fundamental elements. Entrepreneurship emphasises capitalising on opportunities and taking risks, as well as creativity and innovation. Therefore, it is suggested that entrepreneurial insight is an important element in the effective management of disasters when they occur (Branicki et al., 2018). When training disaster relief workers, it is important to start by educating them to become entrepreneurs with insight and enhancing their understanding of the environment. With skills for innovation, disaster relief workers are able to fully understand the context of their work, and ways to develop innovative and appropriate solutions (Sawalha, 2020).

In addition, effective approaches such as systems thinking should be advocated in the disaster management cycle. Systems thinking is a useful approach to addressing the complexity of disaster management, which covers various aspects of urban emergency responses, disaster resilience, and future sustainability (Uddin et al., 2019). A key aspect of the disaster management cycle is the recovery phase, which should also include resilience in order to ensure individuals can bounce back following the unexpected (Ma et al., 2018). It is therefore important that, after a disaster, all relevant information and findings from evaluations are documented and stored. This includes documentation on what has not been done properly, lessons learned, and so on, so as to prepare for future disasters and make changes to present practices (Alexander, 2012).

Examples of Disaster Management Systems

Disaster management, often referred to as the management of the risks and consequences of a disaster, is an established procedure for protecting the infrastructure of the affected community and reducing casualties. Some countries have established a system to alert and warn the public of the occurrence of disasters. In the United States, the Integrated Public Alert and Warning System (IPAWS) under the US Department of Homeland Security was established to inform the entire nation about emergencies and what residents can do to prevent disasters. First and foremost, the IPAWS is able to transmit authenticated emergency and life-saving information through mobile phones. The messages are also distributed through the IPAWS public web platform. The information is disseminated to as many people as possible in order to protect the lives and property of the public (Federal Emergency Management Agency, 2022).

Different areas in the world practise different disaster management models. Some places, such as Queensland, Australia, have established disaster management arrangements. Queensland's mechanism involves a four-level disaster management system. The level or status of a disaster is determined and upgraded according to the increasing level of risk (Queensland Government, 2018). There are different disaster management teams and organisations involved in the system. Disaster management groups, for example, are responsible for planning, coordinating, and implementing effective measures to mitigate damage and restore communities to normal operations. In addition, the Queensland central government has established procedures for implementing disaster management plans. First and foremost, local governments are given the primary responsibility of developing and implementing local disaster management plans. When a local government does not have sufficient resources to manage post-disaster issues, they can seek assistance from the District Disaster Coordination Centre. If the situation becomes serious, the local government can seek support from the Australian Government through the State Disaster Coordination Centre, which can provide emergency assistance to the affected area (Queensland Government, 2018).

In addition to the promulgation of disaster management systems, some countries use a disaster management information system (DMIS) to determine and analyse the extent of the impacts of disasters (Ayyangar, 2010). The DMIS assists in identifying the extent of the impact, developing preventive measures, and planning mitigation measures. It makes use of satellite remote sensing and the technology of the geographic information system (GIS) to analyse and monitor the extent of the impact of a disaster. It can stage simulations that provide a clearer picture of the disaster even when rescuers are not in the affected area (Ayyangar, 2010). The GIS not only simulates the local terrain, but also provides a detailed view of the drainage system, soil conditions, and other information that will help rescue workers to provide support and relief work as quickly as possible and to prevent the next disaster. In addition, the GIS has a large database that can be used to design mitigation and prevention measures, as well as to help governments formulate policies and allocate resources based on scientific data (Ayyangar, 2010). There are two types of DMIS: (i) the disaster inventory system (DIS) and (ii) the information management system (IMS) (Rafi et al., 2018). The DIS primarily stores data such as disaster history, missing persons, participating relief agencies, and facilities available for use. The IMS is divided into four main categories: mitigation, administrative control, response and recovery, and communications infrastructure. Mitigation involves hazard scenario analysis and how disaster risk reduction strategies are carried out. Monitoring systems, emergency declarations, and information windows are used to facilitate administrative control, as well as communication and liaison. The response and recovery category uses a systematic approach and includes missing persons management, resource management, and an early warning system. The communication infrastructure enables communication with the outside world at all times and enhances the flow of information. This component includes equipment that provides wireless local area network (LAN)/wide area network (WAN), general packet radio service (GPRS), and internet access (Rafi et al., 2018).

It is not advisable to manage disasters by just relying on a disaster management system, because systems such as these have limitations. They do not include executive leadership, risk assessment, and planning for drills. Furthermore, in view of today's advanced information technology, contemporary social media may be more effective in coordination and communication work, especially during a disaster, than dated communication technologies (Beydoun et al., 2018).

International Collaboration in Humanitarian Responses to Disasters

When a disaster occurs, many international organisations will provide different types of humanitarian relief. The local government can consider the quantity and type of resources it has, and decide if assistance from other countries or regions is needed. External assistance is required when the scale of the disaster is greater than the emergency management capacity of the local government and local organisations. International organisations involved in relief services are mainly NGOs, although some are multinational enterprises. Their main tasks are to provide relief and assistance at the time of the disaster and in the subsequent recovery period. One example is the organisation International Disaster Volunteers, which works with local communities to help the injured and other people rebuild their homes after a disaster. It helps maintain social cohesion and facilitate communication within the community, and hence enables the community to recover more efficiently (VolunteerMatch, n.d.). Meanwhile, the proper control and coordination of external assistance is essential because there may be an overwhelming response to assist, thus creating chaos in the rescue or relief work. In addition, a great deal of relief work, such as the provision of food, water, and shelter requires effective coordination.

Immediately after a disaster has occurred, the local government should respond as quickly as possible to mitigate the damage. For example, in the Netherlands, the overall coordination of the response to a disaster is managed by the Regional Operational Team, while administration work is conducted by the Municipal Policy Team or the Regional Policy Team (Beerens et al., 2013). During a major disaster, in addition to the country's internal human resources, the local government may request personnel assistance in disaster relief operations from various international organisations, such as the UN, the North Atlantic Treaty Organisation (NATO), and NGOs such as Oxfam, Médecins Sans Frontières, and the Red Cross (Beerens et al., 2013). This is because the government wishes to start post-disaster work as soon as possible, and sometimes it lacks the available liquidity and actual administrative staff to provide sufficient relief to the victims and to handle urgent relief services. Without international assistance, the disaster will result in more casualties and significant financial losses (Waugh, 2017). On the whole, international organisations are more flexible than local

NGOs, in the sense that they are less restricted by the authority of the host country, thus reducing the need for complicated administrative procedures during potentially very complicated and swift operations (Sapat et al., 2019).

In the event of a disaster, the UN Office for the Coordination of Humanitarian Affairs (OCHA) prepares for the relief efforts and coordinates the assistance of different UN departments. The main role of the OCHA is to work with the affected country to rescue victims, coordinate the activities of different organisations, including regional governments and NGOs, and to allocate the flow of funds. In addition, they have a specific coordination mechanism system known as the UN Disaster Assessment and Coordination (UNDAC) process, which is divided into four main areas: staff, methods, procedures, and equipment. People who work in the UNDAC are all professionally trained and equipped to respond to disasters. In terms of methodology, the UNDAC has an established coordination method that allows its staff to quickly assess the severity of a disaster and obtain the most current information. According to the UNDAC procedures, UNDAC workers can be deployed at short notice to the scene of a disaster, usually within 48 hours. Their equipment and provision must be adequate for them to be self-sufficient in the disaster area (OCHA, n.d.). Other UN departments also assist in specific situations. The World Food Programme is one of the UN departments that donates food and brings it to the affected areas to eliminate hunger and poverty when there is a temporary shortage of food and the victims do not have enough money to buy food because of the effects of the disaster (World Food Programme, n.d.).

NATO is also one of the key players in disaster relief. The major difference between NATO and the UN is that NATO uses both military and civilian tools to support the affected areas. However, some countries will not accept NATO's assistance due to political concerns. For this reason, NATO has set up a separate department that focuses on coordination in the event of a disaster: the NATO Euro-Atlantic Disaster Response Coordination Centre (EADRCC) (Beerens et al., 2013). The EADRCC is seen as less politically oriented. In the event of a disaster, the EADRCC will decide whether to provide assistance in response to the requests received. It has a close relationship with the OCHA and they often work together to resolve coordination issues in the event of a disaster (EADRCC, 2021). The EADRCC is a smaller organisation than the

OCHA and so, during smaller disasters, the OCHA may not be able to assist in the response; in such cases, the EADRCC will assist instead (Beerens et al., 2013).

In times of disaster, as noted above, NGOs can help more effectively than local authorities because they are independent of government agencies and are not constrained by political situations or complex documentation procedures. Some better-known NGOs are Oxfam, Médecins Sans Frontières, and Red Cross. The most notable of these are the International Federation of Red Cross and Red Crescent Societies (IFRC) and the International Committee of the Red Cross (ICRC) (Beerens et al., 2013). Following a disaster, the IFRC considers the long-term impact of the humanitarian response it provides and focuses its operations on saving lives and improving the livelihoods of refugees in its relief efforts. The IFRC ensures that the assistance it provides will not have a negative impact on the future development of the affected area, either politically or economically. It makes no change to the current situation and the future of the affected area, such as diplomatic relations with other countries or regions. The IFRC is also concerned about the well-being of its staff; it has put in place mitigation measures to prevent stress or physical damage to staff working as part of a relief project. After the emergency support it provides, the IFRC continues its work until the lives and health of the affected people begin to improve or when the local government is able to resolve the disaster themselves. This process gives the affected country a suitable transition period to return to normal; the organisation will not immediately leave the affected area once the disaster is over (IFRC, 2020).

The ICRC focuses on helping people affected by wars and providing rapid support to disaster areas in emergency situations. When ICRC staff arrive in a disaster area, they first work to understand the current situation, such as the most pressing needs of the victims and the local management capacity. They keep an appropriate distance from those affected due to restricted access or resources and find ways to communicate with them. Using appropriate communication methods, ICRC members interview the affected population, and learn more about them. At the same time, they attempt to represent themselves positively, which will help their later work. ICRC members then make recommendations for their relief work based on the information they have gathered and their own knowledge and expertise. Their recommendations are usually based on seven principles: appropriateness, necessity, effectiveness, timeliness, inclusiveness and accessibility, the absence of negative consequences, and local capacity (ICRC, 2021). The aim of their work is to protect and assist war-affected populations in different countries, and to promote respect for international humanitarian law, which is enshrined in the UN Charter (ICRC, 2004).

Some international companies are also involved in assisting affected areas. They do so across five categories or by taking up five roles. These include charitable, contractual, collaborative, advisory, and unilateral aspects. Different companies work in one or a combination of categories, but the majority take up the charitable role in helping the affected areas. Such companies provide financial and material donations and grants to organisations and groups that work on disaster relief. Often, these multinational companies just make short-lived or one-time contributions, and few help disaster-affected areas on a long-term basis (Twigg, 2001). In the contractual category, multinational companies sign contracts with other relief organisations or groups to provide relief efforts. In these cases, the multinational company controls the entire process and manages all resources. They develop their own approach to rescuing people affected by the disaster under a contract, which is usually short-term or one-off. They also work in a one-to-one relationship with relief organisations, but not with other companies or businesses (Twigg, 2001). The advantage of this process is that most of these multinational companies treat people as a priority.

Companies taking a collaborative role emphasise mutual communication and respect, and are willing to work in collaboration with other companies or stakeholders. They give greater control over resources to certain key players and are more willing to spend long hours helping the affected areas (Twigg, 2001). They are willing to assist mostly because of the impact on the public and the environment. Some small businesses may take an advisory role and are willing to take part in large-scale relief activities by basically providing a workforce to help the affected people, in order to create a positive image in the minds of the public. In such cases, all itineraries and details are planned by the relief organisations. Some companies take a unilateral or stand-alone approach in their rescue operations. They act in response to the urgent needs of the public and with compassion. They do not do so for commercial or financial gain. Often, these are temporary operations, such as immediate emergency relief services and obstacle clearance (Twigg, 2001).

Research and Education on Emergency Medicine and Disaster Management

Disasters are bound to happen in many countries or regions. In Asia, the most densely populated continent in the world, where cities in the Asia-Pacific region are characterised by high concentrations of people in environments with complex infrastructure, disasters can cause serious economic loss and loss of lives (Pal and Bhatia, 2018). Before a disaster occurs, experts need to investigate and prevent the various outcomes that could be caused by the disaster. The joint Collaborating Centre for Oxford University and the CUHK for Disaster and Medical Humanitarian Response (CCOUC) was established by the University of Oxford and The Chinese University of Hong Kong to mitigate and prevent the negative effects of disasters.

The CCOUC's main responsibilities are to conduct research on humanitarian responses, train people interested in disaster management and humanitarian responses, and educate the public about disaster responses. Their research focus is on Asia. Data on disasters that have occurred in Asia are collected, analysed, and evaluated, and guidelines for disaster responses are developed. The Centre also trains frontline disaster responders and runs internship programmes, such as the CCOUC Fellowship Programme, to develop disaster response skills and capacities in Asia (CCOUC, n.d.). In addition, in order to disseminate knowledge about disasters to different countries, the CCOUC organises regular seminars to share experiences of disasters and medical knowledge with academics, students, and practitioners in the areas of disaster health risk management, climate change and health, humanitarian medicine, and disaster case studies. The CCOUC also publishes books and educational materials on disasters and healthcare to educate the public on the importance of medical assistance in the aftermath of a disaster (CCOUC, n.d.).

The Hong Kong Jockey Club Disaster Preparedness and Response Institute (HKJCDPRI) is an educational unit that aims to raise public awareness of disaster preparedness, and to teach response capabilities (HKJCDPRI, n.d.). The HKJCDPRI provides a number of training and knowledge exchange opportunities for various organisations to raise public awareness of disaster preparedness. One example is their project in collaboration with the Amity Mutual Support Society. They use appropriate teaching methods, such as case re-enactment, to help slow-learning ex-mentally ill patients to learn disaster prevention and response measures (HKJCDPRI, n.d.). They also provide training for professionals and relief workers, and organise seminars and research talks for university departments, to facilitate the cross-fertilisation of ideas and enhance disaster management knowledge. Additionally, each year, they organise an annual conference on disaster preparedness and invite people from all walks of life to share their experiences of disaster responses. The conference includes workshops and group discussions. These activities allow people to exchange ideas and bring participants from different departments of the university closer together so that they communicate more effectively when a disaster occurs. In addition, the HKJCDPRI promotes education on disaster preparedness. The Institute has set up an e-learning platform that promotes knowledge about disaster prevention and allows users to exchange ideas with each other. There is an online course on disaster prevention and people can register and enrol in the course for free. The course is quite rigorous and allows the public to learn basic disaster prevention measures. The course is offered online, so anyone can learn at any time, from any place, and at any pace. Upon successful completion of the course, participants will receive a certificate from the Institute (HKJCDPRI, n.d.).

There are many courses available in different countries for people to learn about disaster management and emergencies. The Disaster Training Curriculum is one of them. It covers all aspects of a disaster and ways to rebuild a community after a disaster hits. The provider uses a mixed mode of teaching and learning and offers a variety of master's degrees on disaster management, such as programmes in environmental and human threats, social engineering, network and technical vulnerabilities, business impact analysis data collection, incident response budgeting, and managing evidentiary data in an electronic environment (Khorram-Manesh et al., 2016). Some critics are of the view that, although each programme specialises in one field of disaster management, the coverage is not comprehensive, and each is different in terms of uniformity and quality. As a result, different graduates may have different sets of competencies in disaster management, and they may face obstacles in their actual workplace. Khorram-Manesh et al. (2015) suggested the need to standardise these courses and to promote international cooperation to work on the curricula so that the content of each course is more uniform. The authors also suggested that a set of international standards be established to assess the competencies of students, so as to ensure a basic level of competence for each disaster relief worker. In addition, they advised that the curricula should be open to changes in the disaster field so that knowledge learned can be easily applied in practical ways in disaster management.

Education on emergency medicine is important to help prevent avoidable mortality in disasters. According to a recent report, one of the major reasons accounting for loss of life during a disaster is due to emergency medical conditions. This situation is much more alarming in low- and middle-income countries because of constraints in regard to infrastructure and the lack of trained practitioners available to provide quality emergency care (Razzak et al., 2019). In the context of educational research, a recent study by Ayoola et al. (2022) reported the perspectives of students on learning emergency medicine and the growing adoption of e-learning resources. In the future, more research should be conducted to develop effective resources for emergency medicine education, as well as to investigate the use of new technologies in the specialty of emergency medicine for training and the delivery of care.

Disaster Management in Hong Kong

The Hong Kong government is always vigilant about natural and human-caused accidents and disasters, because they are mindful that Hong Kong is an international city with a huge amount of international air, sea, and land traffic, and millions of visitors every year. The city itself is also densely populated and full of high-rise skyscrapers. The government is committed to providing an effective and efficient response to all emergency situations that threaten life, property, and public security (Hong Kong SAR Government, n.d.). Preparation for the prevention and mitigation of all possible disasters and major accidents is a top agenda item for the government and associate organisations.

Preparedness in Hong Kong

The government already has an emergency response management system in place, which establishes the principles and then sets up policies and emergency response actions for crises that emerge from natural disasters or terrorist attacks. The emergency response plan is a three-tier system, and it has provided timely and appropriate responses to disasters since 1996. At the Tier One response level, emergency services, such as the Hong Kong Police Force and the Fire Services Department, are involved. The departments advise, monitor, and assist in the emergency work with their own commands and resources. The Tier Two response level is triggered when the Secretariat is of the view that a more complex response is required for the incident, when a significant threat to life, property, and security is anticipated. A more significant governmental response, the Tier Three response level, is activated when an incident with critical, widespread, and extensive threat to life, human belongings, and safety occurs. The response involves the activation of the Emergency Monitoring and Support Centre (EMSC) under the command of the Secretary for Security or the designated Security Bureau official at a senior rank at the time of the incident (Hong Kong SAR Government, n.d.). There are six contingency plans currently in force in the emergency response system. They include plans for natural catastrophes, airline crashes, search and rescue in maritime and aeronautic incidents, emergencies at the Daya Bay Nuclear Power Station, and other emergency response actions in Hong Kong (Sim, Wang, and Han, 2018).

Let us examine the Contingency Plan for Dealing with an Aircraft Crash in Hong Kong. Different government and public departments, including the Hong Kong Police Force, the Fire Services Department, and the Hospital Authority, support the government in the planning, cooperation, and coordination of the policy related to disaster management, to ensure a rapid response to the incident. These departments are important in terms of main control at the scene of the disaster. Once an aircraft crash happens, the Duty Air Traffic Controller of the Civil Aviation Department will launch a system alert according to the contingency plan. The Officer-in-Charge of the Fire Services Department is the Crash Commander and he or she is in control of the crash scene and all associated firefighting and rescue services. A Forward Control Point will be established by the police to coordinate the actions of all agencies that respond to the crash, and to direct police action. The EMSC will be activated after an aircraft crash. The Centre facilitates the liaison between the Fire Services Communications Centre, the Police Headquarters Command and Control Centre, the Information Services Department and its Combined Information Centre, and other relevant parties (Hong Kong SAR Government, n.d.). The Director of Fire Services coordinates rescue institutions, while the cooperation of all institutions at the scene of a disaster is under the command of the Commissioner of Police. The Police Force has responsibility in terms of ensuring the protection and safety of the affected spot and occupants, traffic control in order to ensure emergency vehicles can move and the evacuation of the injured can take place unimpeded, and the collection and dissemination of casualty data. The Police Headquarters Command and Control Centre is activated to coordinate the disaster scene and facilitate the liaison with all other government departments involved in the disaster response, including the EMSC, the Fire Services Department, the Hospital Authority, the Home Affairs Department, the Government Flying Service, the Department of Health, the Auxiliary Medical Service (AMS), the Civil Aid Service, the Transport Department, the Housing Department, and the Hong Kong Observatory. The Fire Services Department responds to fire alarms, protects life and property, and carries out emergency rescue and pre-hospital emergency care immediately. The Hospital Authority is in charge of providing emergency medical services during an incident. It will dispatch a Medical Control Officer and a Medical Team to perform triage for casualties on the spot and subsequent emergency medical therapy and put forward a plan for casualty evacuation. Psychosocial services for the disaster are provided for injured and hospitalised victims when they are under the care of the Hospital Authority and after the incident (Hong Kong SAR Government, n.d.).

To ensure cooperation among government departments during an emergency incident, there are joint exercises to facilitate and enhance awareness, coordination, and capabilities. In 2015, a two-week government-wide anti-terrorism exercise codenamed "Windgate" was organised by the Security Bureau. The purpose of the exercise was to examine the effectiveness of anti-terrorism capabilities, as well as the improved consciousness, coordination, and response abilities of government departments (Hong Kong SAR Government, n.d.). The exercise focused on localised incidents and did not cover events with territory-wide involvement.

Voluntary Institutions

Over 7,400 volunteer members and a total of 14 ambulances are managed by Hong Kong St John Ambulance. Members of the organisation are trained volunteers and they provide first aid and assistance at a specific spot or at a public assembly (Hong Kong SAR Government, 2020). The Hong Kong Red Cross is another voluntary institution involved in disaster services. Trained psychological first aiders and psychologists are mobilised by the organisation to provide psychological support services to people in need (Hong Kong SAR Government, 2020). Short courses in the train-the-trainer programmes for disaster response are organised by the CCOUC and are supported by the HKJCDPRI. The Education Bureau also cooperates with the CCOUC to train secondary school teachers to solve disaster-related problems; they in turn educate students on the subject as a supplement to their secondary school studies (HKJCDPRI, 2020). In addition to helping teachers to integrate disaster preparedness into the school curriculum, the HKJCDPRI also designs educational programmes at kindergarten, primary, and secondary school levels, to achieve community resilience to disasters. In order to promote knowledge in regard to reducing disaster risks and raising disaster consciousness in primary school children, the HKJCDPRI has created a cartoon character called Mr Ready and a theme song entitled "Get Ready" (HKJCDPRI, 2019). These voluntary institutions provide training in first aid and short courses on disaster preparedness as part of the long-term development of disaster responses and preparedness that aim to allow the public to manage emergency situations. Their services are complementary to the government's efforts in their management of disasters.

The Private Sector

Many public services are provided by large corporations in the private sector in Hong Kong. They include public transportation and the supply of gas and electricity to households, and they are closely connected to the living environment and the quality of life of residents. These companies have large management systems and associated development plans. Within their plans, disaster response is always an essential component.

Taking public transport as an example, the MTR Corporation, a listed company, has a huge passenger capacity each day through its train system, with stations covering most areas in Hong Kong. The operational reliability of Mass Transit Railway (MTR) trains is insusceptible to traffic conditions, which are different from other types of public transport (MTR, n.d.). On average, MTR trains account for 43.4% of daily public transportation trips, and the MTR system is still expanding (Chan et al., 2021). The MTR network has 10 railway lines serving Hong Kong Island, Kowloon, and the New Territories, while its Light Rail network serves the local communities of Tuen Mun and Yuen Long in the New Territories. Passengers in Hong Kong can also take the intercity High Speed Rail service provided by MTR to travel to Guangdong province, Beijing, and Shanghai in mainland China (MTR, n.d.). In such a huge system, an unexpected incident or disaster in an MTR station area can affect a large number of people in a short amount of time. It is possible that the incident will worsen or become uncontrollable if there is no preparation for emergency situations. Hence, it is important to have in place a strategy involving preparation, monitoring, and rapid responses to emergency incidents and disasters, to ensure the safety of the system and the well-being of commuters. For example, the MTR Corporation receives notices of forthcoming storms from the Hong Kong Observatory in advance and arranges additional staff and buses for potential peaks in the traffic flow. These arrangements are supported by highly complex monitoring and reaction schemes (Newnham et al., 2015).

Another example is CLP Power, which has served Hong Kong for over 120 years. Nearly 80% of the Hong Kong population enjoy a steady electricity supply every day. CLP Power partly uses nuclear power and, in conjunction with Daya Bay Nuclear Power Operations and Management Company, Limited, jointly manages and operates the Guangdong Daya Bay Nuclear Power Station (CLP, n.d.). The nuclear power station is designed to resist natural hazards and is located in a seismically stable region, where the site is managed strictly according to international guidelines and stringent safety measures. The station has also been evaluated, analysed, and surveyed by the National Nuclear Safety

Administration. Contingency plans and communication mechanisms have been devised for the Daya Bay plant to facilitate communication with residents and between the government authorities in Guangdong and Hong Kong during a nuclear accident (CLP, n.d.).

Public Engagement

Training in Disaster Management and Preparedness

Hong Kong is fairly safe from major natural disasters, apart from occasional strong seasonal typhoons, which are often accompanied by extremely heavy rains. In the crowded metropolitan city, the harbour is surrounded by skyscrapers. There are also many high-rise commercial and residential buildings in nearby satellite towns, and all these have potential disaster risks involving environmental health and safety hazards, in terms of air quality, fire escapes, and mental stress. Fires can present a great challenge to the Fire Services Department because the height of buildings and the limited space inside buildings can jeopardise access to and the movement of victims. Fire prevention and emergency management education are two major responsibilities of the Fire Services Department. They also enforce statutory safety requirements in regard to structures and equipment, and educate the community in regard to emergency disaster and emergency preparedness, including basic skills in the use of automated external defibrillators (AEDs) (Fire Services Department, n.d.).

Disaster management training is mainly provided by public institutions. The aim of this training is to ensure that professionals and the general public acquire knowledge about disasters and are aware of the procedures to follow when a disaster occurs. Academic institutions also provide programmes, symposiums, and talks on disaster-related topics. These institutions include the CCOUC, the Hong Kong Disaster Medicine Association, The Hong Kong Polytechnic University, The University of Hong Kong, and the HKJCDPRI. NGOs also collaborate with the HKJCDPRI in terms of the implementation of disaster education activities. Graduate courses for disaster management, pre-hospital and emergency care, and disaster nursing are provided by The Hong Kong Polytechnic University and The Chinese University of Hong Kong (Sim, Wang, and Han, 2018). Besides symposiums and talks, the Hong Kong Disaster Medicine Association also organises visits, drills, and exercises with various parties.

In order to cope with injuries arising from various disasters, including small-scale events, different institutions offer different training programmes, encompassing physical skills and even psychological treatments. The Auxiliary Medical Service (AMS) of the Hong Kong SAR Government, for example, trains civilians in first aid skills and disaster medicine in a supporting role as volunteers in regular community activities and during major city events such as the Standard Chartered Hong Kong Marathon, as well as during disasters. New recruits of the AMS learn basic first aid skills and are then trained to become qualified disaster medical assistants. This training consists of handling casualties in a pre-hospital setting, nursing, lifesaving, and practical sessions in hospital wards and accident and emergency departments (AMS, n.d.). The tragic, sudden, and devastating nature of disasters can traumatise those affected, as well as rescuers, and they may suffer from negative psychological effects after a disaster (Mao et al., 2018). They may become depressed, or feel insecure or helpless. To address this psychological aftermath, the AMS began training its members in psychological first aid in 2003, and formed a psychological first aid response team to equip them with the knowledge and skills needed to help victims and to minimise the psychological impact on themselves as rescuers. The training is based on four principles of safety: calmness, a sense of efficacy for oneself and the community, connectedness, and hope (Hobfoll et al., 2007). If needed, those suffering from psychological distress after a disaster are referred to social workers or clinical psychologists for assistance. The Hong Kong Red Cross also provides emotional support services to help people affected by disasters or major accidents (Hong Kong Red Cross, n.d.).

However, Lam et al. (2017) found that the provision of training programmes on disaster preparedness was not as effective as expected. Only about 4% of interviewees indicated that they would attend disaster preparedness courses or take part in in-person training. Regarding knowledge of tropical cyclone warnings routinely issued by the Hong Kong Observatory, only one-tenth of the interviewees were able to give all correct answers and only about 30% to 50% of interviewees had an evacuation kit at home. Hence, the majority of

Hong Kong people still lack knowledge of how to prepare for and respond to a tropical cyclone. Community education in regard to disaster response and preparedness thus needs to be promoted and improved.

Information Flow and Smart Applications

Nowadays, most people use smartphones. It is convenient and efficient to deliver disaster-related information to the general public through electronic networks. Some NGOs have therefore created disaster warning applications. These apps are classified into formal and informal categories. Formal disaster warning apps alert the public of a disaster before it happens and provide advice on how to prepare for it and prevent injuries. They also have a wide range of features that help people affected by a disaster to survive. One example is the Hazard App created by the Global Disaster Preparedness Centre and the Global First Aid Reference Centre of the New Zealand Red Cross. The main function of the Hazard App is to send alerts before a disaster strikes. The app allows users to monitor the disaster in many locations, such as their home, business, or in terms of road traffic. It can also be used as a handy survival tool. There is a torch function, and an audible alarm is installed in the app. The frequency of the flashing light and the sound of the alarm can be adjusted, making it easier for searchers to locate the user during a disaster. Furthermore, the app has a messaging function to let friends and family know where the person is. It can also switch to a separate communication system when normal communication is disrupted during and after a disaster (New Zealand Red Cross, n.d.). In Hong Kong, there is a similar system to help the general public to receive emergency information. Local mobile network operators have established a joint emergency alert system, as required by the Hong Kong government. The emergency alert system is designed in such a way that time-critical public announcements and messages can be sent out via the mobile network to mobile service users during emergency circumstances (Office of the Communications Authority, 2021). They help the general public to take appropriate measures as soon as possible.

Informal applications have also been developed for use by the public to provide a simple, easy, and informal way to learn about disaster preparedness and raise awareness of the risks involved. Tanah (The Tsunami and Earthquake

Fighter) is a mobile game application, the main objective of which is for the public to easily learn about the occurrence of tsunamis and earthquakes in a short period of time, and about how to prepare for and survive them. The game consists of three parts—Preparation, Survival, and Recovery—which are based on actual disaster management procedures (Opendream, 2015). The app is particularly catered toward parents and children in a family. In general, there are more and more examples of apps related to emergency preparedness and disaster response, with a corresponding increase in popularity among emergency workers, healthcare providers, and the general public (Bachmann et al., 2015).

Public Education and Preparedness

Some short programmes, workshops, or seminars about disaster preparedness are made available as Massive Open Online Courses (MOOCs), in view of the fact that the general public lacks the knowledge to prepare for and respond to a disaster, and the way in which people need to enhance their sensitivity to the occurrence of a disaster and be fully prepared for evacuation in order to reduce the number of casualties in the community. Other examples of disaster education (i.e., joint emergency training programmes and community meetings after an emergency incident or a disaster) are also evident on social media (Dufty, 2020).

The Chinese government began the integration of disaster education in the education system after the 2008 Sichuan earthquake. The National Comprehensive Disaster Prevention and Reduction Plan 2011–2015 was published by the General Office of the State Council, and the 12th Five-Year Special Plan of Science and Technology Development for National Disaster Prevention and Reduction was created by the Ministry of Science and Technology (Kitagawa, 2021). The government has also established 12 May (the day of the 2008 Sichuan earthquake) as National Disaster Prevention and Reduction Day. Sri Lanka, one of the countries that was seriously affected by the 2004 tsunami, required a sustainable means to provide longer-term disaster education, to alleviate the use of disaster relief funds. A Tsunami Photo Museum was built in Telwatta, which exhibits children's paintings of and pictures taken during and after the tsunami (Kitagawa, 2021). In Japan, a voluntary training system for Disaster Prevention Officers is managed by the not-for-profit Japan Bousaisi Organization. There are more than 205,000 Disaster Prevention Officers in Japan at present and many of them actively contribute to the development of community-based disaster risk reduction (Kitagawa, 2021). There are plenty of opportunities and strategies for education in terms of disaster preparedness or response for the general public in Japan, allowing more residents to acquire knowledge of disasters and how to respond to and prepare for them.

Survival Supplies for the Community

In times of disaster, people need to be evacuated as quickly as possible. While waiting for help, they need survival kits and other supplies. In Japan, for example, every family is supposed to have an emergency evacuation backpack. This backpack contains food, water, clothing, space blankets, shelter, emergency toilet bags, and emergency equipment, such as torches, first aid kits, and multi-tools with knives and hammers. In the event of a disaster, people do not want to carry heavy and bulky backpacks with them. Therefore, the backpack must be designed with lightweight material and be waterproof so as to avoid damage and loss of items inside the pack due to flood waters. In addition, it is important to place heavy items close to the back of the pack to make it easier to carry, and it should include at least one set of clothes (Plaza Homes, 2023). In terms of food, perishable items should be avoided. Dehydrated, tinned food is less perishable and is thus preferred. However, such foods will add weight to the pack, especially for older people and children. An optional choice of food is an energy bar.

As space is limited in the backpack, it is important to have a few extra bags to store water. In case of the temporary loss of shelter and warmth due to the disaster, a tent, blanket, jacket, and some items such as a warm bag are handy (Plaza Homes, 2023). Some equipment is designed to deal with different situations in an emergency to avoid injury. Certain tools are essential for inclusion in the emergency evacuation backpack, such as a multi-tool pocketknife for cutting objects. In addition, a lighter, tape, and a torch are useful survival tools (Plaza Homes, 2023). One of the most important items is a whistle. In the event of a disaster, a whistle will enable rescuers to locate a victim more quickly, particularly when one is injured or immobilised (Plaza Homes, 2023). It is important to have a first aid kit in the backpack. The basic kit should include adhesive bandages, disinfectant, basic medications, and masks. It is also advisable to have sanitary supplies, such as disinfectant wipes, toilet paper, and rubbish bags (British Columbia, n.d.). Finally, one should carry copies of identity documents and enough money for emergencies, and keep these two items in a waterproof and airtight bag to protect them (British Columbia, n.d.).

Conclusion

Disasters are damaging and cannot be completely prevented. However, we can try to reduce the risk of disasters and their impact if they do occur. With good planning, we can minimise the damaging effects of disasters through preparedness, training, and rapid responses. The most important point is to always be prepared.

References

Alexander, D. (2012). Disasters: lessons learned? *Journal of Geography and Natural Disasters, 2*(1), 1–2.

Al-Jazairi, A. F. (2017). Disasters and disaster medicine. In: Alsheikhly, A. S. (Ed.), *Essentials of accident and emergency medicine* (pp. 93–118). London: IntechOpen.

Al-Tammemi, A. (2020). The battle against COVID-19 in Jordan: An early overview of the Jordanian experience. *Frontiers in Public Health, 8*(188).

American College of Emergency Physicians. (2021). *Definition of emergency medicine.* www.acep.org/globalassets/new-pdfs/policy-statements/definition-of-emergency-medicine.pdf.

Auxiliary Medical Service. (n.d.). *Roles & functions.* Retrieved on 11 February 2022 from www.ams.gov.hk/en/about-us/roles-functions.html.

Ayoola, A. S., Acker, P. C., Kalanzi, J., Strehlow, M. C., Becker, J. U., and Newberry, J. A. (2022). A qualitative study of an undergraduate online emergency medicine education program at a teaching hospital in Kampala, Uganda. *BMC Medical Education, 22*(1), 1–12.

Ayyangar, R. S. (2010). "Disaster management information system." *Geospatial Media and Communications.* 3 December 2010. www.geospatialworld.net/article/disaster-management-information-system-dmis/.

Bachmann, D. J., Jamison, N. K., Martin, A., Delgado, J., and Kman, N. E. (2015). Emergency preparedness and disaster response: There's an app for that. *Prehospital and Disaster Medicine, 30*(5), 486–490.

Beerens, R., Duyvis, M., and Tonnaer, C. (2013). *International disaster response.* Arnhem, The Netherlands: The Information Centre for Safety. www. preventionweb.net/files/ENG_KP_rampenbestrijding-nov-2013.pdf.

Beydoun, G., Dascalu, S., Dominey-Howes, D., and Sheehan, A. (2018). Disaster management and information systems: Insights to emerging challenges. *Information Systems Frontiers, 20*(4), 649–652.

Bhattacharya, T. (2012). *Disaster science and management.* New York: McGraw-Hill.

Bouillon-Minois, J. B., Schmidt, J., and Dutheil, F. (2021). SARS-CoV-2 pandemic and emergency medicine: The worst is yet to come. *The American Journal of Emergency Medicine, 42,* 246.

Branicki, L., Sullivan-Taylor, B., and Livschitz, S. (2018). How entrepreneurial resilience generates resilient SMEs. *International Journal of Entrepreneurial Behavior & Research, 24*(7), 1244–1263.

British Columbia. (n.d.). *Build an emergency kit and grab-and-go bag.* Retrieved on 11 February 2022 from www2.gov.bc.ca/gov/content/safety/emergency-management/preparedbc/build-an-emergency-kit-and-grab-and-go-bag.

Carter, W. N. (2008). *Disaster management: A disaster manager's handbook.* Manila: Asian Development Bank.

Catlett, C. L., Jenkins, J. L., and Millin, M. G. (2011). Role of emergency medical services in disaster response: Resource document for the National Association of EMS Physicians position statement. *Prehospital Emergency Care, 15*(3), 420–425.

Chan, H. Y., Chen, A., Li, G., Xu, X., and Lam, W. (2021). Evaluating the value of new metro lines using route diversity measures: The case of Hong Kong's Mass Transit Railway system. *Journal of Transport Geography, 91,* 102945.

Chen, B., and Xia, Y. (2017). Advanced technologies in disaster prevention and mitigation. *Advances in Structural Engineering, 20*(8), 1141–1142.

Chu, J. (2019). *Disaster relief fund: Independent auditor's report to the President of the Legislative Council.* www.try.gov.hk/internet/pde_cbac1819_drf19. pdf#:~:text=The%20Disaster%20Relief%20Fund%20provides%20a%20 ready%20mechanism,Finance%20Ordinance%20%28Cap.%202%29%20 on%20the%20same%20date.

CLP. (2021). *CLP information kit.* Retrieved on 25 October 2021 from www.clp. com.hk/en/media-resources/publications.

Collaborating Centre for Oxford University and CUHK for Disaster and Medical Humanitarian Response. (n.d.). *About CCOUC.* Retrieved on 11 February 2022 from ccouc.org/introduction.

Constitutional and Mainland Affairs Bureau. (2019). *Rebuilding Sichuan—A partnership of hope: When one suffers misfortune, aid comes from all sides.*

Retrieved on 11 February 2022 from www.cmab.gov.hk/en/archives/recon_sichuan_overview.htm.

Council of Residency Directors in Emergency Medicine. (2019). *2019 Model of the clinical practice of emergency medicine.* Retrieved on 11 February 2022 from www.cordem.org/resources/education--curricula/model-of-the-clinical-practice-of-emergency-medicine/.

Drzezo. (2019). "Role of Emergency Medicine in Disaster Management." *Anesthesia Key.* 25 August 2019. aneskey.com/role-of-emergency-medicine-in-disaster-management/.

Dufty, N. (2020). *Disaster education, communication and engagement.* Oxford: John Wiley & Sons.

Euro-Atlantic Disaster Response Coordination Centre. (2021). *Euro-Atlantic Disaster Response Coordination Centre.* Retrieved on 11 February 2022 from www.nato.int/cps/en/natohq/topics_52057.htm.

Federal Emergency Management Agency. (2022). *Integrated Public Alert & Warning System.* Retrieved on 29 March 2023 from www.fema.gov/emergency-managers/practitioners/integrated-public-alert-warning-system.

Fire Services Department. (n.d.). *Community emergency preparedness.* Retrieved on 11 February 2022 from www.hkfsd.gov.hk/eng/cep_edu/cep/.

Gramin, V. S. S. (2006). *Evaluation study of rehabilitation & reconstruction process in post-super cyclone Orissa.* Retrieved on 29 March 2023 from www.indiaenvironmentportal.org.in/content/382218/evaluation-study-of-rehabilitation-reconstruction-process-in-post-super-cyclone-orissa.

Ha, H., Fernando, R. L., and Mahajan, S. K. (2019). *Disaster risk management: Case studies in South Asian countries.* New York: Business Expert Press, LLC.

Hinson, J. S., Martinez, D. A., Cabral, S., George, K., Whalen, M., Hansoti, B., and Levin, S. (2019). Triage performance in emergency medicine: A systematic review. *Annals of Emergency Medicine, 74*(1), 140–152.

Hobfoll, S. E., Watson, P., Bell, C. C., Bryant, R. A., Brymer, M. J., Friedman, M. J., Friedman, M., Gersons, B. P., de Jong, J. T., Layne, C. M., Maguen, S., Neria, Y., Norwood, A. E., Pynoos, R. S., Reissman, D., Ruzek, J. I., Shalev, A. Y., Solomon, Z., Steinberg, A. M., and Ursano, R. J. (2007). Five essential elements of immediate and mid-term mass trauma intervention: Empirical evidence. *Psychiatry, 70*(4), 283–369.

Hong Kong Jockey Club Disaster Preparedness and Response Institute. (n.d.). *About us.* Retrieved on 29 March 2023 from www.hkjcdpri.org.hk/about-us-1.

Hong Kong Jockey Club Disaster Preparedness and Response Institute. (2019). *The "Disaster Preparedness cum Creative Workshop for Primary School Students" is on show!* 10 July 2019. www.hkjcdpri.org.hk/%E2%80%9Cdisaster-preparedness-cum-creative-workshop-primary-school-students%E2%80%9D-show.

Hong Kong Jockey Club Disaster Preparedness and Response Institute. (2020). *School programmes*. Retrieved on 11 February 2022 from www.hkjcdpri.org. hk/zh/node/71.

Hong Kong Red Cross. (n.d.). *Psychological support services*. Retrieved on 29 March 2023 from www.redcross.org.hk/en/services/psychological_support_service. html.

Hong Kong Special Administrative Region Government. (2020). *Hong Kong: The facts—Emergency services*. www.gov.hk/en/about/abouthk/factsheets/docs/ emergency_services.pdf.

Hong Kong Special Administrative Region Government. (n.d.). *Emergency response management*. Retrieved on 29 March 2023 from www.sb.gov.hk/eng/emergency/ index.html.

Hoyer, B. (2009). "Lessons from the Sichuan earthquake." *Humanitarian Practice Network*. 12 July 2009. odihpn.org/publication/lessons-from-the-sichuan-earthquake/.

International Committee of the Red Cross. (2004). *What is International Humanitarian Law?* www.icrc.org/en/doc/assets/files/other/what_is_ihl.pdf.

International Committee of the Red Cross. (2021). *Accountability to affected people*. Retrieved on 11 February 2022 from www.icrc.org/en/accountability-affected-people.

International Federation of Red Cross and Red Crescent Societies. (2020). *Disaster risk management policy from prevention to response and recovery*. www.ifrc. org/sites/default/files/2021-07/20210127_IFRC-DRM-EN%5B1%5D.pdf.

Khorram-Manesh, A., Ashkenazi, M., Djalali, A., Ingrassia, P. L., Friedl, T., von Armin, G., Lupesco, O., Kaptan, K., Arculeo, C., Hreckovski, B., Komadina, R., Fisher, P., Voigt, S., James, J., and Gursky, E. (2015). Education in disaster management and emergencies: Defining a new European course. *Disaster Medicine and Public Health Preparedness, 9*(3), 245–255.

Khorram-Manesh, A., Lupesco, O., Friedl, T., Arnim, G., Kaptan, K., Djalali, A. R., Foletti, M., Ingrasia, P. L., Ashkenazi, M., Arculeo, C., Fischer, P., Hreckovski, B., Komadina, R., Voigt, S., Carlström, E., and James, J. (2016). Education in disaster management: What do we offer and what do we need? Proposing a new global program. *Disaster Medicine and Public Health Preparedness, 10*(6), 854–873.

Kitagawa, K. (2021). Conceptualising 'disaster education'. *Education Sciences, 11*(5), 233.

Klein, T. A., and Irizarry, L. (2021). EMS disaster response. In: *StatPearls [Internet]*. Treasure Island (FL): StatPearls Publishing.

Lam, R. P. K., Leung, L. P., Balsari, S., Hsiao, K. H., Newnham, E., Patrick, K., Pham, P., and Leaning, J. (2017). Urban disaster preparedness of Hong Kong residents: A territory-wide survey. *International Journal of Disaster Risk Reduction, 23*, 62–69.

Li-Tsang, W. P., and Lam, C. P. (Eds.). (2015). *Post-disaster emergency rehabilitation service manual: An experience from 2008 Sichuan earthquake operation.* Hong Kong: The Hong Kong Red Cross and Department of Rehabilitation Sciences, The Hong Kong Polytechnic University.

Liu, J. M., Catlett, C. L., Jenkins, J. L., Lowe, R., and Millin, M. G. (2021). Role of emergency medical services in disaster response: National Association of EMS Physicians position statement. *Prehospital Emergency Care, 25*(4), 596.

Ma, Z., Xiao, L., and Yin, J. (2018). Toward a dynamic model of organizational resilience. *Nankai Business Review International, 9*(3), 246–263.

Mao, X., Fung, O. W. M., Hu, X., and Loke, A. Y. (2018). Psychological impacts of disaster on rescue workers: A review of the literature. *International Journal of Disaster Risk Reduction, 27,* 602–617.

MTR. (n.d.). *Operations details.* Retrieved on 29 March 2023 from www.mtr.com. hk/en/corporate/operations/detail_worldclass.html.

Mulvenon, J. (2008). The Chinese military's earthquake response leadership team. *China Leadership Monitor, 25.*

National Disaster Management Authority, Government of India. (2010). *National disaster management guidelines: Incident response system.* New Delhi: National Disaster Management Authority.

Newnham, E. A., Patrick, K. A., Balsari, S., and Leaning, J. (2015). *Community engagement in disaster planning and response.* Cambridge, Mass.: FXB Center for Health and Human Rights.

Office of the Communications Authority. (2021). *Emergency alert system.* Retrieved on 11 February 2022 from www.ofca.gov.hk/en/consumer_focus/guide/help_ for_consumers/emergency_alert_system/index.html.

Opendream. (2015). *Tanah: The tsunami & earthquake fighter.* Retrieved on 11 February 2022 from www.opendream.co.th/en/project/tanah-en.

Pal, I., and Bhatia, S. (2018). Disaster risk governance and city resilience in Asia-Pacific region. In: Shaw, R., Shiwaku, K., and Izumi, T. (Eds.), *Science and technology in disaster risk reduction in Asia.* Cambridge, Mass.: Academic Press.

Perera, S. M. V. C., Alinden, C. M., and Amaratunga, R. D. G. (2010). Investigating the status of disaster management within a world-wide context: A case study analysis. In: Barrett, P. S., Amaratunga, R. D. G., Haigh, R. P., Keraminiyage, K. P., and Pathirage, C. (Eds.), *CIB world congress 2020 proceedings.* Manchester: The University of Salford.

Plaza Homes. (2023). *Emergency evacuation backpack for natural disasters in Japan.* Retrieved on 29 March 2023 from www.realestate-tokyo.com/living-in-tokyo/ emergency-disaster/emergency-bag/.

Queensland Government. (2018). *Disaster management in Queensland.* Retrieved on 11 February 2022 from www.disaster.qld.gov.au/dmg/rr/Pages/default.aspx.

Rafi, M. M., Aziz, T., and Lodi, S. H. (2018). A comparative study of disaster management information systems. *Online Information Review, 42*(6), 971–988.

Razzak, J., Usmani, M. F., and Bhutta, Z. A. (2019). Global, regional and national burden of emergency medical diseases using specific emergency disease indicators: Analysis of the 2015 global burden of disease study. *BMJ Global Health, 4*(2), e000733.

Sandler, D., and Schwab, A. K. (2021). *Hazard mitigation and preparedness: An introductory text for emergency management and planning professionals* (3rd edition.). New York: Routledge.

Sapat, A., Esnard, A. M., and Kolpakov, A. (2019). Understanding collaboration in disaster assistance networks: Organizational homophily or resource dependency? *The American Review of Public Administration, 49*(8), 957–972.

Sawalha, I. H. (2018). Behavioural response patterns: An investigation of the early stages of major incidents. *Foresight, 20*(4), 337–352.

Sawalha, I. H. (2020). A contemporary perspective on the disaster management cycle. *Foresight, 22*(4), 469–482.

Sim, T., Wang, D., and Han, Z. (2018). Assessing the disaster resilience of megacities: The case of Hong Kong. *Sustainability, 10*(4), 1137.

Singh, A., Punia, M., Haran, N. P., and Singh, T. B. (2018). *Development and disaster management: A study of the northeastern states of India.* Singapore: Palgrave Macmillan.

New Zealand Red Cross. (n.d.). *Hazard app.* Retrieved on 29 March 2023 from www.redcross.org.nz/what-we-do/in-new-zealand/disaster-management/hazard-app/.

Twigg, J. (2001). *Corporate social responsibility and disaster reduction: A global overview.* London: Benfield Greig Hazard Research Centre.

Uddin, M. S., Routray, J. K., and Warnitchai, P. (2019). Systems thinking approach for resilient critical infrastructures in urban disaster management and sustainable development. In: Noroozinejad Farsangi, E., Takewaki, I., Yang, T., Astaneh-Asl, A., and Gardoni, P. (Eds.), *Resilient structures and infrastructure.* Singapore: Springer.

United Nations Office for the Coordination of Humanitarian Affairs. (n.d.). *UN disaster assessment and coordination (UNDAC).* Retrieved on 29 March 2023 from www.unocha.org/our-work/coordination/un-disaster-assessment-and-coordination-undac.

VolunteerMatch. (n.d.). *International disaster volunteers.* Retrieved on 29 March 2023 from www.volunteermatch.org/search/org680819.jsp.

Waugh, W. L. (2017). International humanitarian assistance and disaster recovery in Asia. In: Waugh, W. L., and Han, Z. (Eds.), *Recovering from catastrophic disaster in Asia (community, environment and disaster risk management vol. 18)* (pp. 177–194). Bingley: Emerald Publishing Limited.

World Food Programme. (n.d.). *Disaster risk reduction.* Retrieved on 11 February 2022 from www.wfp.org/disaster-risk-reduction.

World Health Organisation. (2019). *Health emergency and disaster risk management framework.* www.who.int/publications/i/item/9789241516181.

2

A Scoping Review of the Impacts of Earthquakes and Natural Disaster Management on Physical and Mental Difficulties of Earthquake Survivors

Kenneth N. K. FONG
Department of Rehabilitation Sciences, The Hong Kong Polytechnic University

This chapter is a scoping review of the impacts and the disaster risk management of earthquakes in different countries. The major earthquakes covered in this review are the Wenchuan (12 May 2008) and Ya'an (20 April 2013) earthquakes in Sichuan, China; the earthquake in Haiti (2010); the Kashmir earthquake in India (2005); the Manjil, Yazd City, and Azarbaijan earthquakes in Iran (1990, 2003, 2012); the earthquake in Nepal (2015); the earthquake in Pakistan (2013); and the Van earthquake in Turkey (2013). More recently, a 7.8 magnitude earthquake struck southeast Turkey near Syria on 6 February 2023; 57,759 people were killed and 121,704 injured. Based on the themes of the papers reviewed, they are grouped under the following headings: needs of children and adolescents, effectiveness of medical and rehabilitation services, prevalence of post-traumatic stress disorder (PTSD) after an earthquake, disaster management models focusing on the participation of the community in the recovery process, and in-person social networking and other social aspects of disaster management.

Natural Disasters and Management

Over the past 20 years, there have been numerous intense and fatal natural disasters in different countries of the world, which led to major challenges in healthcare services. According to statistics on global disasters from 1990 to 2010, 35.5% of major earthquakes occurred in 65 countries along the Belt and Road Initiative (Yang, Guo, and Xiao, 2016). Globally, there is an increasing trend of natural disasters every year (particularly prominent disasters such as earthquakes, storms, and floods), the majority of which have occurred in Asia. These have led to the devastation of human lives and huge economic losses that are often higher than the gross domestic product (GDP) of the country (Yang, Guo, and Xiao, 2016).

Disaster management encompasses many elements, including disaster prevention, reduction of disaster risk, and reconstruction of damage, as well as immediate responses to disasters in terms of healthcare services and rehabilitation (Deshpande, 2011). There are global agreements on its definition and guidelines for action, such as the Sendai Framework for Disaster Risk Reduction 2015–2030, which promotes various countries around the globe taking responsibility for disaster management and advocates cooperation among international communities to work towards the goal of strengthening their resilience for disaster responses (Bendito and Barrios, 2016). Among all natural disasters, the impacts of earthquakes are significant, causing injuries, deaths, and tremendous and instant destruction to communities.

Earthquake Disasters and their Impacts

The Sichuan earthquake in 2008 was one of the most devastating earthquakes in the history of modern China. According to the report of the United Nations Centre for Regional Development (UNCRD), in total, 69,226 people were killed, 17,923 were missing, and 374,643 were injured (UNCRD, 2009). The UNCRD report, however, only focused on damage to local facilities and houses, reconstruction work, and community-based recovery. It did not provide details on the social characteristics of the victims and how in their daily lives they coped with the injuries and social difficulties caused by the earthquake.

In the past 10 years, when studying the Sichuan earthquake, researchers have examined the characteristics of injuries among victims in different social groups. It was found that the types of injuries caused by the earthquake varied with different age groups. Zhang et al. (2014) reported that the most common injuries involved bone fractures (58.3%). Patients older than 80 years were more likely to suffer hip and thigh fractures, pelvis fractures, and chest injuries, while younger victims had fewer fractures and chest injuries but more skin and soft-tissue injuries.

The damage from the earthquake was not limited to physical injuries. A lot of adolescents recovered from their physical injuries over time, but some exhibited delayed onset of chronic post-traumatic stress disorder (PTSD) and depression. The latter usually occurred in those who had poor relationships with their parents or lived under precarious economic conditions (Tang et al., 2017). These mental issues could be related to the changes in the survivors' social networks. Fu et al. (2013) suggested that mental problems were more common in those who had lost close relatives in the earthquake, and that those who had been confronted with dead bodies were more likely to experience PTSD.

Scoping Review

In order to understand more about the collaboration in disaster management among different disciplines, the authors conducted a scoping review of literature to explore the subject in different countries. The scoping review method was used because of the emerging and diverse social research in disaster management (Arksey and O'Malley, 2005). A scoping review is used to identify types of available evidence, clarify key concepts and characteristics, and identify and analyse research gaps (Munn et al., 2018). First, using the electronic databases PubMed, SCOPUS, PsycINFO, Embase, CINAHL, and Web of Science, a search (confined to journal articles published in English from 2007 to 2017) was carried out on the topics of post-disaster medical services and rehabilitation. The search keywords were disaster management, disaster response, disaster preparedness, disaster recovery, multidisciplinary approach, transdisciplinary collaboration, natural disasters, medical services, and rehabilitation. Studies excluded from the search were those not directly related to disaster management and reconstruction (e.g., clinical studies on disability, traumatic brain injury, and policy and management of city services), studies related to human disasters but not related to earthquakes (e.g., burn care, fires, industrial accidents, mining disasters, nuclear explosions and radiation, terrorism, traffic accidents, water pollution, and war), studies related to natural disasters but not to earthquakes (e.g., floods, hurricanes, cyclones, and typhoons), studies not focusing on a specific type of disaster, and studies in disaster management but only related to architecture, religion, social economy, or tourism.

Table 2.1 Summary of 26 reviewed papers

Author (year of publication)	Title	Disaster site
Alipour et al. (2014)	Challenges for resuming normal life after earthquake: A qualitative study on rural areas of Iran	Azarbaijan, Iran
Busapathumrong (2013)	Disaster management: Vulnerability and resilience in disaster recovery in Thailand	Thailand
Chauhan and Chopra (2017)	Deployment of medical relief teams of the Indian army in the aftermath of the Nepal earthquake: Lessons learned	Nepal
Cheema et al. (2014)	Unnoticed but important: Revealing the hidden contribution of community-based religious institution of the mosque in disasters	Pakistan
Clover et al. (2011)	Experience of an orthoplastic limb salvage team after the Haiti earthquake: Analysis of caseload and early outcomes	Haiti
Erkan et al. (2019)	From emergency response to recovery: Multiple impacts and lessons learned from 2011 Van earthquakes	Van, Turkey
Ehring et al. (2011)	Prevalence and predictors of posttraumatic stress disorder, anxiety, depression, and burnout in Pakistani earthquake recovery workers	Pakistan
Fallah et al. (2015)	The social and physical vulnerability assessment of old texture against earthquake (case study: Fahadan district in Yazd City)	Yazd City, Iran
Fu et al. (2013)	Analysis of prevalence of PTSD and its influencing factors among college students after the Wenchuan earthquake	Wenchuan, Sichuan, China

Findings

At the end of the search, there were 26 papers extracted for discussion in this chapter. Table 2.1 provides a summary of the 26 papers reviewed, with each entry showing the author and year of publication, title, disaster site, study type, research method, and participants' information. The papers were then grouped under the following themes (see Table 2.2): (1) needs of children and adolescents; (2) effectiveness of medical and rehabilitation services (which was divided into (a) evaluation of services and (b) prevalence of PTSD and rehabilitation services); and (3) disaster management models (which were divided into (a) community participation in recovery, (b) importance of social networks, and (c) other social aspects of disaster management).

Study type	Research method	Subjects (n)	Age of subjects (mean or range)
Content analysis (Graneheim approach)	Semi-structured interviews and focus group discussions	27	Not mentioned
Qualitative study	Literature review	Not applicable	Not applicable
Case study	Paper-based system and case sheet-based method of case recording as used by field hospitals	Not applicable	Not applicable
Qualitative study	Interviews and focus groups	83 interviews and 9 focus groups	Not applicable
Retrospective study	Analysis of the operation data in the hospital	348	Not mentioned
Case study	Field observation, interviews, and literature review	Not applicable	Not applicable
Quantitative study	Questionnaires	267	Mean: 28.93
Case study	Architecture analysis of the field survey and on-site observation	Not applicable	Not applicable
Quantitative research	Questionnaires	2,987	Range: 16–26

Table 2.1: Continued

Author (year of publication)	Title	Disaster site
Keshkar et al. (2014)	Epidemiology and impact of early rehabilitation of spinal trauma after the 2005 earthquake in Kashmir, India	Kashmir, India
Li et al. (2012)	Evaluation of functional outcomes of physical rehabilitation and medical complications in spinal cord injury victims of the Sichuan earthquake	Wenchuan, Sichuan, China
Li et al. (2015)	Impacts of social network on therapeutic community participation: A follow-up survey of data gathered after Ya'an earthquake	Ya'an, Sichuan, China
Li et al. (2011)	Factors affecting functional outcome of Sichuan-earthquake survivors with tibial shaft fractures: A follow-up study	Wenchuan, Sichuan, China
Liu et al. (2017)	Comparison study on two post-earthquake rehabilitation and reconstruction modes in China	Wenchuan, Sichuan, China
Ni et al. (2013)	Dysfunction and post-traumatic stress disorder in fracture victims 50 months after the Sichuan earthquake	Wenchuan, Sichuan, China
Nikku (2012)	Children's rights in disasters: Concerns for social work—Insights from South Asia and possible lessons for Africa	Pakistan, India, Sri Lanka, and Nepal
Redmond et al. (2011)	A qualitative and quantitative study of the surgical and rehabilitation response to the earthquake in Haiti, January 2010	Haiti
Shamsalinia et al. (2017)	The life process of children who survived the Manjil earthquake: A decaying or renewing process	Manjil, Iran
Tang et al. (2017)	Mental health problems among children and adolescents experiencing two major earthquakes in remote mountainous regions: A longitudinal study	Ya'an, Sichuan, China
Thomas et al. (2011)	Coproduction, participation, and satisfaction with rehabilitation services following the 2001 earthquake in Gujarat, India	Gujarat, India
Tian et al. (2013)	Longitudinal study on health-related quality of life among child and adolescent survivors of the 2008 Sichuan earthquake	Wenchuan, Sichuan, China
Wang and Lum (2013)	Role of the professional helper in disaster intervention: Examples from the Wenchuan earthquake in China	Wenchuan, Sichuan, China
Zhang et al. (2014)	Epidemiological analysis of trauma patients following the Lushan earthquake	Ya'an, Sichuan, China
Zhang and Wang (2010)	Local political trust: The antecedents and effects on earthquake victims' choice of allocation of resources	Wenchuan, Sichuan, China
Zhao et al. (2013)	The association between post-traumatic stress disorder symptoms and the quality of life among Wenchuan earthquake survivors: The role of social support as a moderator	Wenchuan, Sichuan, China

Study type	Research method	Subjects (n)	Age of subjects (mean or range)
Hospital-based study (single-phase)	Medical examinations	2,621	Not mentioned
Prospective cohort study	Medical examinations	54	Range: 6–65+
Field study	Questionnaires	183	Mean: 48.12
Quantitative research	Questionnaires	174	Range: under 10 to 80+
Field study	Questionnaires and semi-structured interviews	300	Mean: 33.2
Retrospective cohort study	Physical examinations and questionnaires	459	Mean: 54.25 (rehabilitation group), 53.71 (control group)
Qualitative review	Literature	Not applicable	Not applicable
Mixed research	Interviews and surgical data from surgical providers	Not mentioned	Not mentioned
Qualitative research	Face-to-face in-depth interviews and telephone interviews	12	Not mentioned
Longitudinal study	Questionnaires	435	Mean: 14
Mixed research	Structured interviews and questionnaires	200	Not mentioned
Longitudinal study	Questionnaires	596	Range: 8–16
Qualitative review	Literature review	Not applicable	Not applicable
Epidemiological survey	Questionnaires	2,010	Range: under 10 to 94
Mixed research	Questionnaire and literature	424	Range: under 25 to 65+
Cross-sectional survey	Questionnaires	2,080	Mean: 38.24

Table 2.2 Papers categorised by themes

Rehabilitation and disaster management? Post-disaster medical services and rehabilitation?	References
1. Needs of children and adolescents	Zhang et al. (2014) Tian et al. (2013) Tang et al. (2017) Fu et al. (2013) Shamsalinia et al. (2017) Nikku (2012)
2. Effectiveness of medical and rehabilitation services (a) Evaluation of medical and rehabilitation services	Redmond et al. (2011) Chauhan and Chopra (2017) Clover et al. (2011) Keshkar et al. (2014)
(b) Prevalence of PTSD and rehabilitation services	Zhao et al. (2013) Li et al. (2012) Ni et al. (2013) Fu et al. (2013) Li et al. (2011) Ehring et al. (2011)
3. Disaster management models (a) Community participation in recovery	Zhang and Wang (2010) Liu et al. (2017) Thomas et al. (2011) Erkan et al. (2014)
(b) Importance of social networks	Zhao et al. (2013) Li et al. (2015) Cheema et al. (2014)
(c) Other social aspects of disaster management	Wang and Lum (2013) Alipour et al. (2014) Fallah et al. (2015) Busapathumrong (2013)

Needs of Children and Adolescents

After an earthquake, children younger than 10 years of age suffered fewer fractures and chest injuries than other ages but they had more skin and soft-tissue injuries (Zhang et al., 2014). Adolescents who were injured in an earthquake or lost their first-degree relatives and those adolescents who saw dead bodies were more likely to show signs of PTSD (Fu et al., 2013). The death of a family member is a significant predictor of PTSD and depression in children and adolescents in an earthquake area (Tang et al., 2017). The impacts of earthquake disasters can take some time to appear, so attention should also be paid to children without obvious traumatic experiences (Tian et al., 2013). Tian et al. (2013) found that mental health symptoms were identified as the biggest contributors to quality of life in children. In this regard, girls and older children reported lower quality of life scores than their counterparts. In their interview study, Shamsalinia et al. (2017) noted that the child survivors of earthquakes were confronted with "unexpected encounter", "transient relief activities", and "long-lasting consequences" in their life processes. The earthquake left this group of children with painful memories and the painfulness varied in different conditions (Shamsalinia et al., 2017). It was found that mental health services for child survivors of earthquakes could help address their potential psychological problems. Hence, policy makers should ensure children receive attention in rescue, relief, and rehabilitation efforts (Nikku, 2012).

Effectiveness of Medical and Rehabilitation Services

Evaluation of Medical and Rehabilitation Services

Redmond et al. (2011) reported challenges to the emergency medical response during the Haiti earthquake including issues of accountability, professional ethics, standards of care, unmet needs, involvement of patient agency, and expected outcomes for patients in such settings. It was found that the setup of a minimal victims' database was vital in the provision of medical and rehabilitation services. Rehabilitation responses required medical records, quality assurance, coordination, and resource allocation (Redmond et al., 2011). Keshkar et al. (2014) reported that in a massive natural calamity such as the Indian Kashmir earthquake, a rehabilitation team providing all-inclusive services of supportive care, assistive devices, and rehabilitation therapy significantly helped the recovery of the functional and psychological status of victims with spinal cord injuries. They concluded that while the lifesaving operations and definitive surgeries were undoubtedly important for combatting major injuries in such disasters, early medical rehabilitation was equally important in reducing injury-related disabilities. Patients were able to receive immediate surgical treatment but found it difficult to obtain adequate post-operation care and rehabilitation

(Chauhan and Chopra, 2017). Quantitative and qualitative data collected from patients were found useful for further evaluation of rehabilitation services.

It has been well-recognised that rehabilitation services have a positive effect on survivors who were injured in earthquake. Clover et al. (2011) reported on the work of a limbs-salvage team in an acute response after the Haiti earthquake. The team had a high success rate, and their work demonstrated the potential benefit of establishing such teams. After the earthquake, it was found that 73% of the injury cases were soft-tissue cases and 25% were bony or combined soft-tissue and bony cases (Clover et al., 2011). Li et al. (2011) showed that functional recovery of survivors with tibial shaft fractures was positively associated with rehabilitation intervention. Earthquake victims with spinal cord injuries had significantly improved functional outcomes after they went through a formal physical rehabilitation programme (Li et al., 2012). In addition, a rehabilitation team that provided physiotherapy and psychotherapy significantly aided recovery of the functional and psychological status in victims with spinal cord injuries (Keshlar et al., 2014).

Prevalence of PTSD and Rehabilitation Services

In both victims and recovery teams, PTSD is commonly found following earthquakes. The occurrence ranges from 14% to 44% of victims and recovery teams, and the disorder can last for a period of four to five years. Ehring et al. (2011) found a high prevalence of emotional problems in earthquake rehabilitation and recovery workers: 42.6% suffered from PTSD, and approximately 20% suffered from depression and anxiety disorders. Workers who were female, had high levels of earthquake exposure, high work stress, and low social support were associated with higher levels of PTSD symptoms (Ehring et al., 2011). In a 12-month longitudinal study, Tang et al. (2017) found that of children and adolescents, 43.9% had PTSD, 20.9% had depression, and 18.2% had both PTSD and depression. In their 30-month assessment study, the results showed that the PTSD rate was 15.7% and the depression rate was 21.6%. Ni et al. (2013), in an assessment administered 50 months after the earthquake, also found that being female, having an average or above average family income, and having witnessed death and fearfulness were risk factors for PTSD symptoms. Fu et al. (2013), on the other hand, found that 14.1% of college students in a severely earthquake-affected area were diagnosed with PTSD one year after the quake. Students who were injured in the earthquake, who had lost a first-degree relative, or who had been confronted with dead bodies were more likely to experience PTSD (Fu et al., 2013).

Two papers discussed the influence of social support and rehabilitation intervention on earthquake victims' development of PTSD. Zhao et al. (2013) identified, in their cross-sectional survey of survivors one year after the Sichuan earthquake, that being a woman, having a lower level of education, a lower level of income, a worse housing status, or a higher level of exposure were risk factors for poorer quality of life after the earthquake. They also found that interactions between social support groups and those suffering from PTSD lessened the negative effect of PTSD on victims' quality of life (Zhao et al., 2013). The incidence of PTSD was also significantly reduced in fracture victims who underwent rehabilitation (Ni et al., 2013). The above findings are very consistent with a recent cross-sectional survey of Sichuan earthquake victims with physical disabilities 10 years later (Fong et al., 2022). In this study, a total of 308 earthquake victims who suffered from physical disabilities resulting from the Sichuan earthquake were recruited from three hospitals in the province to participate in a 10-year cross-sectional survey (Fong et al., 2022). The prevalence of PTSD for earthquake victims with physical disabilities 10 years later was 42.21%; female gender, loss of relatives and friends, and a diagnosis of amputation or fracture were significant predictive factors for PTSD, however, participation and engagement in daily life and community activities was negatively correlated with PTSD (Fong et al., 2022). It is quite alarming that earthquake victims still presented with PTSD 10 years after the disaster, particularly among victims who had suffered permanent loss of body parts or other physical disabilities. This study suggested that risk factors in victims should be identified earlier in order to provide them with the best support for their mental well-being (Fong et al., 2022).

Disaster Management Models

Community Participation in Recovery

Community participation played a role in the success of earthquake reconstruction. In a field study by Liu et al. (2017), results indicated that the reallocated reconstruction mode, i.e., the new houses were constructed in another site/area, brought about a higher total degree of satisfaction with post-earthquake reconstruction when compared to the in-situ reconstruction mode, i.e., the houses were rebuilt in the same earthquake site. The latter only generated relatively better results in terms of neighbour relationships, communication with relatives, family harmony, and health of families. It is important to maintain sustainable recovery in post-disaster rehabilitation projects (Erkan et al., 2014). Local political trust was found to be positively correlated with perceived support and resource allocation for public infrastructure (Zhang and Wang, 2010). Community participation was the most important variable for non-governmental organisations (NGOs) in providing rehabilitation activities (Thomas et al., 2011). In the same paper, the authors examined participation in and satisfaction with the rehabilitation services that were offered by NGOs in Gujarat, India, following the earthquake (Thomas et al., 2011). They found that people in villages that used the non-coproduction approach to rehabilitation services were more satisfied with post-reconstruction services than people in villages that opted for the co-production approach—service users including victims and caregivers, and service providers, working together for decision-making.

Importance of Social Networks

In facilitating post-disaster recovery, social support has direct and indirect positive influences on the quality of life of earthquake victims (Alipour et al., 2014). In their qualitative study, Alipour et al. (2014) concluded that social uncertainty and confusion occurred because some important social aspects in the process of victims returning to normal life were neglected, and that understanding the challenges of life recovery for victims would help policymakers consider social rehabilitation as a key factor in facilitating the victims' return to normalcy. Li et al. (2015) pointed out that in the process of post-disaster recovery, relevant government departments need to focus more on the reconstruction and cultivation of victims' social networks and social capital, particularly those living in the remote districts or villages. They also claimed that their findings would contribute to a better understanding of how social networks influenced therapeutic community participation, and the role that local government could play in post-disaster recovery and public health improvement after natural disasters.

In general, social networks are important in helping earthquake survivors overcome difficulties in their daily lives. Day (2014) showed that personal networks were much more useful than government efforts in helping victims to return to normal life, although natural hazards often diminished the functioning of the local government in disaster areas. Informal relationships successfully provided relief to the victims (White et al., 2012). Hence, to help with post-disaster recovery, some local governments even mobilised villagers in rebuilding victims' social networks (Li , Chen, and Suo, 2015).

Other Social Aspects in Disaster Management

Cheema et al. (2014) found that the multifaceted and distinct contribution of religious beliefs (i.e., involvement with a mosque) played an important role in the cultural, economic, social, and political aspects of the lives of the earthquake-affected communities during the response, relief, recovery, reconstruction, and rehabilitation phases of the Pakistani earthquake in 2013.

Conclusion

This chapter highlights the importance of integrating rehabilitation as a component of disaster management, including medical rehabilitation, mental health support, community participation in recovery, and consideration of social networks. In particular, this chapter reviews the psychosocial characteristics of earthquake victims, with a focus on children, adolescents and those suffering from physical injuries. Although local governments have an important role in the provision of medical services/rehabilitation and housing reconstruction, this review also discusses how survivors made use of social networks to cope with daily difficulties, for example, local governments should mobilise NGOs to facilitate informal social networks for the victims and provide rehabilitation activities to promote community participation and mental health recovery. Through this scoping review, research evidence has been identified to help scientists and professionals of different disciplines (as well as governments around the world) to collaborate in establishing effective disaster management systems. The papers reviewed highlight the importance of multidisciplinary collaboration in disaster management. According to the experience of countries that have suffered from disasters, lack of proper inter-operation and collaboration will likely lead to under-performance in disaster responses. It is expected that more studies will be needed to provide analysis of the cost-effectiveness and outcome measurement of the disaster management models identified in this chapter.

References

Alipour, F., Khankeh, H. R., Fekrazad, H., Kamali, M., Raflry, H., Sarrami, P., Rowell, K., and Ahmadi, S. (2014). Challenges for resuming normal life after earthquake: A qualitative study on rural areas of Iran. *PLoS Currents, 6.*

Arksey, H., and O'Malley, L. (2005). Scoping studies: Towards a methodological framework. *International Journal of Social Research Methodology, 8*(1), 19–32.

Bendito, A., and Barrios, E. (2016). Convergent agency: Encouraging transdisciplinary approaches for effective climate change adaptation and disaster risk reduction. *International Journal of Disaster Risk Science, 7*(4), 430–435.

Busapathumrong, P. (2013). Disaster management: Vulnerability and resilience in disaster recovery in Thailand. *Journal of Social Work in Disability & Rehabilitation, 12*(1–2), 67–83.

Chauhan, A., and Chopra, B. K. (2017). Deployment of medical relief teams of the Indian army in the aftermath of the Nepal earthquake: Lessons learned. *Disaster Medicine and Public Health Preparedness, 11*(3), 394–398.

Cheema, A. R., Scheyvens, R., Glavovic, B., and Imran, M. (2014). Unnoticed but important: Revealing the hidden contribution of community-based religious institution of the mosque in disasters. *Natural Hazards, 71*(3), 2207–2229.

Clover, A. J. P., Rannan-Eliya, S., Saeed, W., Buxton, R., Majumder, S., Hettiaratchy, S. P., and Jemec, B. (2011). Experience of an orthoplastic limb salvage team after the Haiti earthquake: Analysis of caseload and early outcomes. *Plastic and Reconstructive Surgery, 17*(6), 2373–2380.

Day, J. M. (2014). Fostering emergent resilience: The complex adaptive supply network of disaster relief. *International Journal of Production Research, 52*(7), 1970–1988.

Deshpande, V. (2011). Disaster management as part of curriculum for undergraduate and postgraduate courses: The symbiosis model. *Indian Journal of Occupational and Environmental Medicine, 15*(3), 97–99.

Ehring, T., Razik, S., and Emmelkamp, P. M. G. (2011). Prevalence and predictors of posttraumatic stress disorder, anxiety, depression, and burnout in Pakistani earthquake recovery workers. *Psychiatry Research, 185*(1–2), 161–166.

Erkan, B. B., Karanci, A. N., Kalaycıoğlu, S., Özden, A. T., Çalışkan, I., and Özakşehir, G. (2015). From emergency response to recovery: Multiple impacts and lessons learned from the 2011 Van earthquakes. *Earthquake Spectra, 31*(1), 527–540.

Fallah, A. S., Sarsangi, A., and Modiri, E. (2015). The social and physical vulnerability assessment of old texture against earthquake (case study: Fahadan district in Yazd City). *Arabian Journal of Geosciences, 8*(12), 1077510787.

Fong, K. N. K., Law, Y. M., Lou, L., Zhao, Z. E., Chen, H., Ganesan, B., Lai, A. W. Y., Lee, B. H. C., Leung, A. N. T., Liu, K. Y. S., Wong, C. S. M., Li, C. W. P., Wong, M. S., and Shum, D. H. K. (2022). Post-traumatic stress disorder (PTSD) after an earthquake experience: A cross-sectional survey of Wenchuan earthquake victims with physical disabilities 10 years later. *International Journal of Disaster Risk Reduction, 80*(3), 103225.

Fu, Y., Chen, Y., Wang, J., Tang, X., He, J., Jiao, M., Yu, C., You, G., and Li, J. (2013). Analysis of prevalence of PTSD and its influencing factors among college students after the Wenchuan earthquake. *Child & Adolescent Psychiatry & Mental Health, 7*(1).

Keshkar, S., Kumar, R., and Bharti, B. B. (2014). Epidemiology and impact of early rehabilitation of spinal trauma after the 2005 earthquake in Kashmir, India. *International Orthopaedics, 38*(10), 2143–2147.

Li, J., Xiao, M., Zhang, X., and Zhao, Z. (2011). Factors affecting functional outcome of Sichuan-earthquake survivors with tibial shaft fractures: A follow-up study. *Journal of Rehabilitation Medicine, 43*(6), 515–520.

Li, Y., Reinhardt, J., Gosney, J. E., Zhang, X., Hu, X., Chen, S., Ding, M., and Li, J. (2012). Evaluation of functional outcomes of physical rehabilitation and medical complications in spinal cord injury victims of the Sichuan earthquake. *Journal of Rehabilitation Medicine, 44*(7), 534–540.

Li, Z., Chen, Y., and Suo, L. (2015). Impacts of social network on therapeutic community participation: A follow-up survey of data gathered after Ya'an earthquake. *Iranian Journal of Public Health, 44*(1), 68–78.

Liu, H., Zhang, D., Wei, Q., and Guo, Z. (2017). Comparison study on two post-earthquake rehabilitation and reconstruction modes in China. *International Journal of Disaster Risk Reduction, 23*, 109–118.

Munn, Z., Peters, M. D., Stern, C., Tufanaru, C., McArthur, A., and Aromataris, E. (2018). Systematic review or scoping review? Guidance for authors when choosing between a systematic or scoping review approach. *BMC Medical Research Methodology, 18*(1), 143.

Ni, J., Reinhardt, J. D., Zhang, X., Xiao, M., Li, L., Jin, H., Zeng, X., and Li, J. (2013). Dysfunction and post-traumatic stress disorder in fracture victims 50 months after the Sichuan earthquake. *PLoS One, 8*(10), e77535.

Nikku, B. R. (2013). Children's rights in disasters: Concerns for social work—Insights from South Asia and possible lessons for Africa. *International Social Work, 56*(1), 51–66.

Redmond, A. D., Mardel, S., Taithe, B., Calvot, T., Gosney, J., Duttine, A., and Girois, S. (2011). A qualitative and quantitative study of the surgical and rehabilitation response to the earthquake in Haiti, January 2010. *Prehospital and Disaster Medicine, 26*(6), 449–456.

Shamsalinia, A., Ghaffari, F., Dehghan-Nayeri, N., and Poortaghi, S. (2017). The life process of children who survived the Manjil earthquake: A decaying or renewing process. *PLoS Currents, 9.*

Tang, W., Zhao, J., Lu, Y., Yan, T., Wang, L., Zhang, J., and Xu, J. (2017). Mental health problems among children and adolescents experiencing two major earthquakes in remote mountainous regions: A longitudinal study. *Comprehensive Psychiatry, 72,* 66–73.

Thomas, T., Ott, J. S., and Liese, H. (2011). Coproduction, participation, and satisfaction with rehabilitation services following the 2001 earthquake in Gujarat, India. *International Social Work, 54*(6), 751–766.

Tian, W., Jia, Z., Duan, G., Liu, W., Pan, X., Guo, Q., Chen, R., and Zhang, X. (2013). Longitudinal study on health-related quality of life among child and adolescent survivors of the 2008 Sichuan earthquake. *Quality of Life Research, 22*(4), 745–752.

United Nations Centre for Regional Development. (2009). *Report on the 2008 Great Sichuan earthquake.* Retrieved on 6 May 2023 from www.recoveryplatform.org/resources/publications/199/report_on_the_2008_great_sichuan_earthquake.

Wang, X., and Lum, T. Y. (2013). Role of the professional helper in disaster intervention: Examples from the Wenchuan earthquake in China. *Journal of the Social Work in Disability & Rehabilitation, 12*(1–2), 116–129.

White, J. H., Miller, B., Magin, P., Attia, J., Strum, J., and Pollack, M. (2012). Access and participation in the community: A prospective qualitative study of driving post-stroke. *Disability and Rehabilitation, 34*(10), 831–838.

Yang, T., Guo, Q., and Xiao, T. (2016). Research on distribution characteristics of natural disasters along the "Belt and Road". *Journal of Safety Science and Technology, 12*(10), 108237.

Zhang, L., Zhao, M., Fu, W., Gao, X., Shen, J., Zhang, Z., Xian, M., Jiao, Y., Jiang, J., Wang, J., Gao, G., Tang, B., Chen, L., Li, W., Zhou, C., Deng, S., Gu, J., Zhang, D., Zheng, Y., and Chen, X. (2014). Epidemiological analysis of trauma patients following the Lushan earthquake. *PLoS One, 9*(5).

Zhang, Q., and Wang, E. (2010). Local political trust: The antecedents and effects on earthquake victims' choice for allocation of resources. *Social Behavior and Personality: An International Journal, 38*(7), 929–939.

Zhao, C., Wu, Z., and Xu, J. (2013). The association between post-traumatic stress disorder symptoms and the quality of life among Wenchuan earthquake survivors: The role of social support as a moderator. *Quality of Life Research, 22*(4), 733–743.

Medical and Public Health Disaster Competencies in Education and Training Curricula in China after the 2008 Sichuan Earthquake

Sijian LI
School of Nursing, The Hong Kong Polytechnic University

Lu CHEN
School of Nursing, Beijing Capital Medical University

Nana WU
Chengdu Women's and Children's Central Hospital,
School of Medicine, University of Electronic Science and Technology of China

Hao DAI
Emergency Department, Chengdu No. 2 People's Hospital

Shaohua CHEN
School of Nursing, Fujian Medical University

Rui XIA
Emergency Department, Chengdu No. 2 People's Hospital

Sunshine CHAN
School of Nursing, The Hong Kong Polytechnic University

This chapter reviews and identifies existing competency domains in disaster management education and training curricula for medical and public health professionals in China from the 2008 Sichuan earthquake until the present. The 2008 Sichuan earthquake was a turning point in developing disaster medicine and nursing education in China. Little is known about the medical and public health disaster competencies that should be included to prepare qualified healthcare responders. A review of Chinese-language articles from May 2008 to December 2021 was conducted using the China National Knowledge Infrastructure (CNKI) and Wanfang databases. A total of 11 articles were reviewed and analysed.

Four common themes emerged from this review: physical and psychosocial care; public health emergency preparedness, response, and recovery; communication and coordination; and ethical issues. The findings can serve as important guidance for developing an effective disaster training and education programme. Recommendations in this respect are suggested.

Introduction

Disasters strike daily in different parts of the world, with huge impacts on individuals, families, and communities. The 2008 Sichuan earthquake in China was one of the deadliest disasters in the world; it killed 87,476 people (Centre for Research on the Epidemiology of Disaster and United Nations Office for Disaster Risk Reduction, 2020). It has been considered as the most destructive event in human history, as it triggered thousands of co-seismic hazards, such as landslides, rainfall, and debris flows (Fan et al., 2018). These multiple hazards disrupted community infrastructure for transportation, communication, hospital facilities, and electricity; additionally, many medical workers were killed or injured, which caused the disruption of local hospital care and emergency services (Chen et al., 2010).

In response to the 2008 Sichuan earthquake and in accordance with the National Natural Disaster Relief Emergency Plan, China's National Disaster Reduction Committee and the Ministry of Civil Affairs urgently launched a second-level national emergency disaster relief response on 12 May 2008, and raised the level to a first-level response that night (ChinaNews, 2008). The State Council's disaster relief working group rushed to the earthquake-stricken area and helped lead the earthquake relief coordination and management (Shen et al., 2012).

Several authors have reviewed and reflected on the lessons learned from these rescue experiences (Chen et al., 2010; Zhang, 2009; Zhang, Liu, Liu, and Zhang, 2011; Zhang et al., 2012). Major obstacles and barriers were encountered, which largely affected the quality of medical relief efforts because of the delayed arrival of medical relief teams (Zhang et al., 2012); an absence of emergency generators, water purification equipment, satellite communication devices, and medications (Chen et al., 2010); insufficient information obtained from the affected areas (Zhang et al., 2011; Zhang et al., 2012); and, in particular, a lack of protocols and guidelines for disaster triage, care of the critically injured, and psychological support for the affected individuals and communities (Chen et al., 2010). Moreover, preparedness training for the medical relief workforce and the supply of materials were largely insufficient (Zhang, 2009).

The need for qualified medical and public healthcare responders has been widely investigated globally. In the past decades, universities and healthcare organisations have started to highlight the issue by developing competencies to describe the knowledge, skills, and attitudes of healthcare professionals who are adequately prepared for disaster, in order to improve the effectiveness of response and recovery. The competencies have served as a fundamental principle used to guide the process of designing, implementing, and evaluating the effectiveness of specialised and tailored training and education programmes for disaster health workforces (Walsh et al., 2012; Walsh, Altman, King, and Strauss-Riggs, 2014). Discipline-based competencies have been established for public health workers (Schor and Altman, 2013; Magnusson, 2017), healthcare workers (Hsu et al., 2006), hospital nurses (Noh et al., 2020), emergency nurses (Gebbie and Qureshi, 2002; Xu and Zeng, 2016), perinatal and neonatal nurses (Jorgensen, Mendoza, and Henderson, 2010), social workers (Sim and Dominelli, 2022), mental health workers (King, Burkle, Walsh, and North, 2015), and emergency managers (Feldmann-Jensen, Jensen, Smith, and Vigneaux, 2019). As nurses are the largest group of health professionals, they need to develop basic (for general practice) (International Council of Nurses (ICN), 2009) and advanced (for specialised practice) (ICN, 2019) competencies. Therefore, disaster education and training for all medical and public healthcare workers are becoming indispensable.

The 2008 Sichuan earthquake was a turning point in the development of disaster medicine and nursing education in China (Huang et al., 2011; Liu, 2009). The Ministry of Health first entrusted the Institute of Hospital Management with this education; the Institute then collaborated with the International Commission for Primary Trauma Treatment (PTC). A standardised, practically-oriented training programme for pre-hospital care was developed and completed within three years (2010–2013). The PTC training was guided by the World Health Organisation (Mock et al., 2004) and used as a teaching manual for emergency doctors, anaesthetists (Mai et al., 2013), and other health professionals, such as nurses (Cui et al., 2014). Each participant was able to obtain credits for an annual qualification.

However, the nature of this continuing programme was largely oriented around clinical medicine, and there were many issues to be solved (Hou et al., 2018). There were inconsistencies in the use of terminology related to disasters and emergencies. For example, the definition of terms such as emergency medicine and disaster medicine, as well as emergency nursing and disaster nursing, are blurred in regard to the scope and focus of the care, as emergency medicine and emergency nursing are clearly limited to acute care in hospital settings during an emergency.

Furthermore, disaster nursing education showed an increasing, rapid trend of development. Although disasters were not a compulsory part of undergraduate teaching plans in relevant fields of study, there were diversified teaching contents and methods. Some universities had a disaster preparedness subject available as a public elective course for all undergraduate students (Du and Shi, 2014) to increase public awareness. There were also short-term intensive training programmes for disaster nursing undergraduates, jointly organised by the Chinese Consortium for Higher Nursing Education in 2009. This was the first competency-based training programme using the ICN framework available following the 2008 Sichuan earthquake (Pang, Chan, and Cheng, 2009; Chan et al., 2010). A review of this programme found that a higher level of competence could be gained in regard to policy development, planning, education, and psychological care. A lower level of competence could be gained in ethical practice, legal practice and accountability, and the care of vulnerable groups. The target audience of the programme was limited to nursing students and the long-term effects in terms of post-course evaluation were unknown. The findings of this pioneering study were valuable, as they could provide the foundation for future development and act as a guide to construct a high-quality disaster education and training curriculum, so as to improve disaster preparedness, response, and recovery in future disasters.

There are several issues that are commonly addressed in undergraduate curricula on disaster preparedness and response in China. For the subject of Emergency Teaching, teaching time ranges from just two to four hours (Zhang,

Figure 3.1 Disaster rescue drill for postgraduate nursing students

Photo taken by the first author in Sichuan on 8 June 2014.

2009), and increases to six hours in Community Health Nursing (four hours of theory and two hours of practice) (Li and Courtland, 2009). Moreover, disaster-related subjects are often available only as an elective. For example, the School of Nursing at Yanbian University added Disaster and Emergency Nursing as an elective course in 2009 to enhance students' understanding of disaster nursing (Li and Courtland, 2009). Several military universities feature disaster- or emergency-related content in their nursing curricula, but it only serves the purpose of meeting military demands during a state of war. For example, Field Nursing (100 contact hours, mostly covering knowledge and skills related to caring for the injured and wounded, alongside the prevention and treatment of diseases) is delivered by the Second and Third Military Medical University of the Chinese People's Liberation Army, and first aid and war wound care are commonly taught in Emergency Nursing by the Fourth Military Medical University (Zhang, 2009; Wang et al., 2010) (Fig. 3.1).

More attention has been paid to these issues when designing and implementing disaster education and training programmes (Wang et al., 2008; Huang et al., 2011; Su et al., 2013; Hou et al., 2018). However, little is known about what disaster domains should be included in disaster education and training at present. The aim of this chapter is to identify existing competency domains for medical and public health professionals since the 2008 Sichuan earthquake. The findings can serve as guidance for developing disaster training and education curriculum and content.

A review of Chinese-language articles published from May 2008 to December 2021 was conducted using the China National Knowledge Infrastructure (CNKI) and Wanfang databases. The Chinese search key terms included were safety management, education, disaster response, emergency management, risk management, countermeasures, crisis management/ measures, disaster management, emergency plan, training planning; disaster, earthquake, disaster medicine, disaster nursing, natural disaster, geological disasters, public health emergencies, earthquake disasters, disaster prevention and mitigation, Wenchuan earthquake; and nurses, nursing staff, health staff, volunteers, community health workers, doctors, medical students, medical workers.

A total of 5,432 references were produced. After excluding duplicates, 225 titles were identified for further screening. Inclusion criteria were articles that reported competencies or competency domains/subdomains for professionals relevant to disaster relief support following the 2008 Sichuan earthquake. A total of 11 references with full texts were found. The retrieval process is shown in Figure 3.2.

As a result, 11 studies were included for analysis. Of these, three were peer-reviewed articles and eight were dissertations available on Chinese websites. The most common target audiences were nurses and nursing students and medical and public health professionals (Table 3.1).

All papers and dissertations provided a list of competences and sub-competencies (Table 3.2). Three papers listed competencies using two levels of indicators (Yang, 2009; Han et al., 2012; He, 2014) and the rest across three levels (n = 8, 73%). A total of eight studies featured literature reviews and Delphi methods to establish domain and subdomain indexes (Yang, 2009; Zhang,

Figure 3.2 Literature search flowchart

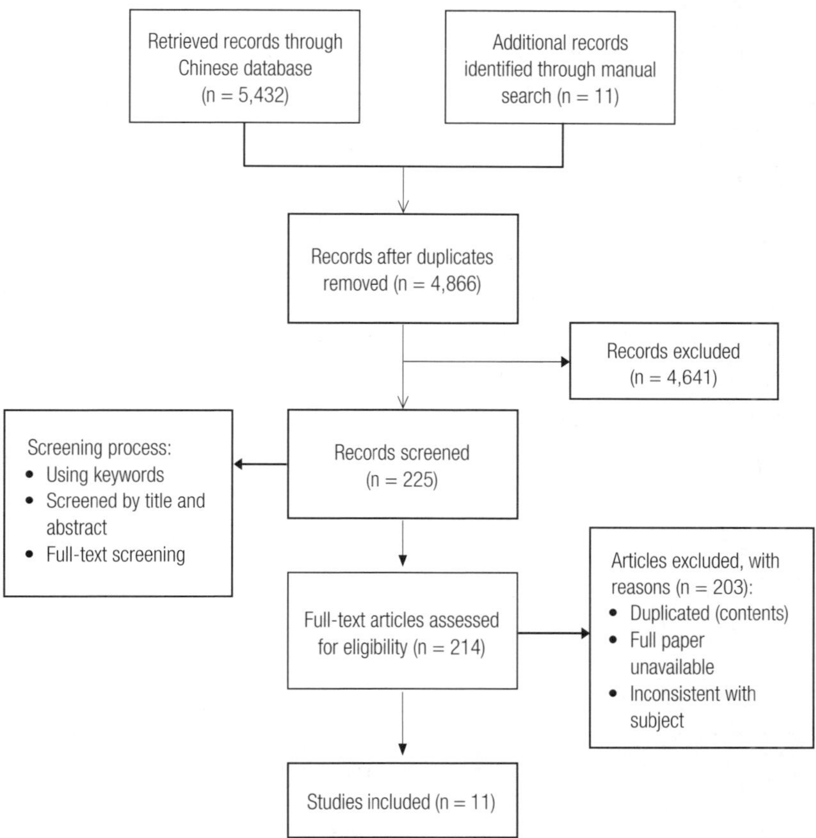

Table 3.1 References categorised by target audience (n = 11)

Audience	References
Public and medical health professionals	Yang (2009), Kan (2018)
Hospital nurses	Zhang (2011), Han et al. (2012), Hu (2019), Wu et al. (2021)
Emergency nurses	Hou and Gong (2017)
Undergraduate nursing students	Yang (2013), Gao (2016)
Military healthcare workers	He (2014)
Specialist clinical nurses	Sun (2014)

2011; Han et al., 2012; Yang, 2013; He, 2014; Sun, 2014; Hou, Gong, and Kong, 2017; Hu, 2019; Wu et al., 2021); two further implemented and evaluated the effects of the programme using the developed domains (Gao, 2016; Kan, 2018). One provided operational definitions of the competencies, knowledge, and skills, as well as procedures regarding how the learning objectives could be achieved (Kan, 2018).

The current findings show that many domains were developed and explored based on educational and training purposes. The most common domains related to core competencies were identified as necessary knowledge, skills, and abilities, including competencies related to physical and psychosocial care; public health emergency preparedness, response, and recovery; communication and coordination; and ethical issues.

Table 3.2 Domains and subdomains of core competencies

Author(s)	Year	Core competency domains (I)	Sub-core competency domains (II)	Sub-core competency domains (III)
Yang	2009	1. Overview	1.1 Age 1.2 Working years 1.3 Highest education diploma/ degree 1.4 Position 1.5 Health status 1.6 Academic position 1.7 Professional background	N.A.
		2. Knowledge	2.1 Basic understanding 2.2 Basic knowledge 2.3 Specialised knowledge 2.4 Management knowledge 2.5 Legal knowledge 2.6 Psychological knowledge 2.7 Other knowledge	N.A.

Author(s)	Year	Core competency domains (I)	Sub-core competency domains (II)	Sub-core competency domains (III)
		3. Practice and skills	3.1 Specialised skills 3.2 Training drills 3.3 Past experience 3.4 Communication and coordination 3.5 Risk accountability	N.A.
Zhang	2011	1. Pre-disaster competencies	1.1 Special competencies	1.1.1 Disaster information assessment 1.1.2 Developing disaster contingency plans 1.1.3 Outdoor survival
			1.2 Physical and psychological attributes	1.2.1 Psychological attributes 1.2.2 Physical attributes
		2. During-disaster competencies	2.1 First aid ability	2.1.1 Casualty assessment 2.1.2 First aid 2.1.3 Triage 2.1.4 Evacuation 2.1.5 Intensive care
			2.2 Patient management	2.2.1 Managing common diseases 2.2.2 Transferring the injured 2.2.3 Multidisciplinary teamwork 2.2.4 Materials management 2.2.5 Fundamental nursing
			2.3 Psychological care	2.3.1 Self-adjustment 2.3.2 Psychological assessment 2.3.3 Psychological intervention
			2.4 Safety and protection ability	2.4.1 Personal protection 2.4.2 Special infection identification 2.4.3 Environmental risk assessment 2.4.4 Epidemic prevention and control
		3. Post-disaster competencies	3.1 Post-disaster care ability	3.1.1 Psychological assessment 3.1.2 Psychological interventions 3.1.3 Infection prevention and control 3.1.4 Caring for the sick and wounded 3.1.5 Rebuilding or restoring normal operations 3.1.6 Health promotion and education

Table 3.2: Continued

Author(s)	Year	Core competency domains (I)	Sub-core competency domains (II)		Sub-core competency domains (III)
Han et al.	2012	1. First aid ability	1.1	Basic first aid knowledge and skills	N.A.
			1.2	Pre-hospital assessment and observation	
			1.3	Key observation during transfer and transportation	
			1.4	Outdoor knowledge and skills	
			1.5	Self- and mutual-help knowledge and skills	
			1.6	Triage and transfers	
			1.7	Knowledge of performing diversified health support tasks	
			1.8	Disaster rescue care knowledge	
			1.9	Collaboration ability	
			1.10	Planning, organisation, and coordination	
		2. Plateau nursing ability	2.1	Plateau characteristics and their impacts on the human body	N.A.
			2.2	Plateau nutritional requirements	
			2.3	Psychological response in plateau	
			2.4	Plateau disease knowledge	
			2.5	Plateau and its impacts on casualties	
			2.6	Trauma care in plateau	
			2.7	Adaptation knowledge in plateau	
			2.8	Plateau oxygen therapy	
			2.9	Plateau IV administration	
			2.10	Communication with ethnic minorities	
		3. Post-disaster ability	3.1	Psychological crisis and intervention	N.A.
			3.2	Self-adaptation for rescue workers	
			3.3	Infectious diseases	
			3.4	Disinfection and isolation	
			3.5	Environmental hygiene management	
			3.6	Drinking water management and disinfection	

Author(s)	Year	Core competency domains (I)	Sub-core competency domains (II)	Sub-core competency domains (III)
Yang	2013	1. Knowledge	1.1 Fundamental disaster knowledge	1.1.1 Disaster terminology 1.1.2 Disaster clarification 1.1.3 Consequences of disasters
			1.2 Specialised knowledge	1.2.1 Crisis assessments 1.2.2 Casualty assessments 1.2.3 Triage 1.2.4 Transportation 1.2.5 Critical care 1.2.6 Organisation and coordination 1.2.7 Health education
			1.3 Management knowledge	1.3.1 Medical supplies management and allocation 1.3.2 Staff management and coordination 1.3.3 Logistic management
			1.4 Legal knowledge	1.4.1 Disaster laws and rules 1.4.2 Infection prevention and control
			1.5 Psychological knowledge	1.5.1 Emergency rescue 1.5.2 Psychological recovery
			1.6 Health education	1.6.1 Food and water safety education after a disaster
		2. Practical skills	2.1 Pre-hospital first aid skills	2.1.1 Cardiopulmonary resuscitation (CPR) 2.1.2 Trauma care 2.1.3 Transportation of casualties
			2.2 Rescue management	2.2.1 Rapid response 2.2.2 Being alert and sensitive 2.2.3 Nursing assessment 2.2.4 Pre-hospital decision-making
			2.3 Communication and coordination	2.3.1 Team communication and role positioning 2.3.2 Collection and judgment of disaster information
			2.4 First aid supplies management	2.4.1 Use of devices to monitor vital signs (e.g., ECG monitoring) 2.4.2 Use of haemostatic materials (e.g., sterile dressings, tourniquets) 2.4.3 Use of fracture fixation materials (e.g., cervical collars) 2.4.4 Use of emergency medications

Table 3.2: Continued

Author(s)	Year	Core competency domains (I)	Sub-core competency domains (II)	Sub-core competency domains (III)
		3. Physical and psychological attributes	3.1 Psychological attributes	3.1.1 Psychological coping 3.1.2 Psychological crisis interventions 3.1.3 Personal self-protection
			3.2 Ethics	3.2.1 Professional ethics 3.2.2 Upholding humanitarianism
			3.3 Physical attributes	3.3.1 Physical fitness and adaptation
He	2014	1. Emergency response attributes	1.1 Health regulations 1.2 Fitness and training 1.3 Military skills 1.4 Weaponry introduction 1.5 Ability to work in special environments	N.A.
		2. Emergency and rescue	2.1 Introduction to emergency and rescue care 2.2 Natural disaster and rescue care 2.3 Public health emergency and rescue care	N.A.
		3. Pre-hospital care	3.1 Pre-hospital first aid skills 3.2 Pre-hospital first aid monitoring 3.3 Shock and infection first aid 3.4 Common injuries and pre-hospital rescue 3.5 Pre-hospital care in special contexts	N.A.
		4. Psychological care	4.1 Public health emergency and infection control care 4.2 Common psychological crises in public health emergencies 4.3 Common psychological disorders and care 4.4 Common psychological interventions 4.5 Pre-hospital care in special contexts	N.A.

Author(s)	Year	Core competency domains (I)	Sub-core competency domains (II)	Sub-core competency domains (III)
Sun	2014	1. Disaster nursing theory and training	1.1 Introduction to disaster nursing	1.1.1 Concepts (disaster fundamentals and theories) 1.1.2 Current status and development of disaster nursing 1.1.3 Interpersonal relationships and coordination
			1.2 Core knowledge in disaster nursing	1.2.1 Disaster care for common medical diseases 1.2.2 Disaster care for common surgical diseases 1.2.3 Care for special populations 1.2.4 Rescue care for common injuries 1.2.5 Care for environmental, physical, and chemical factors related to diseases 1.2.6 Rescue knowledge for toxic, chemical, nuclear, and biological events 1.2.7 Management principles for common acute poisoning care 1.2.8 Basic theory of public and preventive medicine 1.2.9 Disaster preparedness and response
			1.3 Disaster psychological interventions	1.3.1 Psychosocial support for disaster victims 1.3.2 Psychological protection knowledge for rescue workers 1.3.3 Post-traumatic stress disorder (PTSD) and psychological health knowledge 1.3.4 Communication skills
			1.4 Occupational protection knowledge for rescue workers	1.4.1 Humanitarian rescue knowledge 1.4.2 Search and rescue knowledge 1.4.3 Outdoor survival knowledge

Table 3.2: Continued

Author(s)	Year	Core competency domains (I)	Sub-core competency domains (II)	Sub-core competency domains (III)
			1.5 Disaster nursing management	1.5.1 Nursing management approaches in stressful situations
				1.5.2 Command and Control, Safety, Communication, and Assessment management principles for disaster emergency responses
				1.5.3 Features of disaster rescue and organisation systems
				1.5.4 Hospital rescue management and infection control
				1.5.5 Nursing information management and utilisation
				1.5.6 Disaster rescue coordination and organisation management
				1.5.7 Public health emergency incident surveillance systems
		2. Disaster nursing skills training	2.1 Specialised skills	2.1.1 Triage and category skills for injuries
				2.1.2 Injury assessments
				2.1.3 Transportation of the injured
				2.1.4 Establishment of rescue stations
				2.1.5 On-site disinfection equipment utilisation
				2.1.6 Sample collection and rapid detection methods for public health emergencies
				2.1.7 Recognition of communication systems and equipment utilisation
				2.1.8 Special medical problems and techniques
				2.1.9 Personal protective equipment for medical workers
				2.1.10 Unintentional injury management skills

Author(s)	Year	Core competency domains (I)	Sub-core competency domains (II)	Sub-core competency domains (III)
			2.2 First aid skills	2.2.1 Basic first aid skills (pre-hospital rescue and basic and advanced life support) 2.2.2 First aid medication usage 2.2.3 Use of rescue equipment and survival skills 2.2.4 Rescue skills 2.2.5 Hospital emergency care 2.2.6 Emergency care for unconscious patients 2.2.7 Incident organisation and command 2.2.8 Use of emergency equipment
		3. Disaster rescue contingency plans and drills	3.1 Disaster early warning systems and contingency plans 3.2 Casualty rescue and contingency plans 3.3 Pre-hospital contingency plans 3.4 Mass casualty public health emergency incidents and contingency plans 3.5 Natural disaster contingency plans 3.6 Disaster accidents contingency plans	N.A.
Gao	2016	1. Theoretical knowledge	1.1 Overview of disaster nursing and pre-hospital rescue knowledge for trauma care in an earthquake	1.1.1 Basic concepts for disasters and disaster nursing 1.1.2 Overview of disaster nursing developments 1.1.3 Features of earthquakes and their impacts on humans 1.1.4 Characteristics of earthquake trauma, pre-hospital care, and basic skills 1.1.5 Ethical issues in pre-hospital trauma care
			1.2 Earthquake field rescue and nursing care	1.2.1 Earthquake relief team recruitment and classification 1.2.2 Roles and responsibilities of rescue nurses 1.2.3 CPR

Table 3.2: Continued

Author(s)	Year	Core competency domains (I)	Sub-core competency domains (II)	Sub-core competency domains (III)
			1.3 Pre-hospital rescue and trauma care in an earthquake	1.3.1 Categories and triage 1.3.2 Pre-hospital trauma care during an earthquake 1.3.3 Transportation and monitoring of earthquake casualties
			1.4 Psychological intervention in pre-hospital trauma care after an earthquake	1.4.1 Psychological stress response and interventions in pre-hospital care after earthquakes
		2. Skill knowledge		2.1.1 Infusion during rescues and transfers in pre-hospital trauma care during earthquakes 2.1.2 Pre-hospital first aid care after earthquakes: maintaining airways, haemostasis, bandaging, handling, and transferring 2.1.3 CPR 2.1.4 On-site trauma care during earthquakes 2.1.5 Psychological care for earthquake casualties 2.1.6 Trauma care and rescues in simulated earthquake settings
Hou and Gong	2017	1. Specialised skills	1.1 Theoretical knowledge	1.1.1 Basic first aid knowledge 1.1.2 Rescue procedures and methods 1.1.3 Contingency plans 1.1.4 First aid-related laws 1.1.5 Psychosocial-related knowledge
			1.2 Practical skills	1.2.1 Equipment use 1.2.2 Triage 1.2.3 Transportation 1.2.4 Field first aid 1.2.5 Self-help and mutual rescue 1.2.6 Monitoring ability 1.2.7 Special patient care 1.2.8 Documentation in an emergency 1.2.9 Psychological interventions

Author(s)	Year	Core competency domains (I)	Sub-core competency domains (II)	Sub-core competency domains (III)
		2. Response ability	2.1 Disaster awareness	2.1.1 Disaster knowledge 2.1.2 Disaster awareness
			2.2 Risk assessment	2.2.1 Risk recognition 2.2.2 Environmental assessment
			2.3 Response ability	2.3.1 Rapid response ability 2.3.2 Decision-making ability 2.3.3 Analytical ability 2.3.4 Outdoor survival knowledge and skills
			2.4 Psychological response	2.4.1 Self-adaptation 2.4.2 Seeking social support
			2.5 Physical response	2.5.1 Physical fitness 2.5.2 Environmental adaptation ability
		3. Coordination and management ability	3.1 Teamwork and collaboration	3.1.1 Role awareness 3.1.2 Coordination 3.1.3 Obeying commands 3.1.4 Communication
			3.2 Management ability	3.2.1 Rescue coordination: planning, organising, and monitoring 3.2.2 Relief material supplies 3.2.3 Patient management 3.2.4 Information management 3.2.5 Documentation management
		4. Disease prevention and control ability		4.1.1 Health promotion and education 4.1.2 Disease prevention 4.1.3 Vaccinations 4.1.4 Infection control 4.1.5 Protection 4.1.6 Dead body management 4.1.7 PPE utilisation
		5. Professional development		5.1.1 Knowledge acquisition 5.1.2 Knowledge utilisation 5.1.3 Knowledge synthesis 5.1.4 Teaching materials collection 5.1.5 Communication 5.1.6 Presentation ability

Table 3.2: Continued

Author(s)	Year	Core competency domains (I)	Sub-core competency domains (II)	Sub-core competency domains (III)
Kan	2018	1. Prevention of infectious disease emergencies	1.1 Fundamentals of infectious disease prevention and control	1.1.1 Describing the spectrum of infectious diseases 1.1.2 Describing the transmission process of infectious diseases
			1.2 Immunisations and vaccinations	1.2.1 Memorising the immunisation schedule for common infectious diseases that cause emergencies
		2. Preparedness for infectious disease emergencies	2.1 Contingency plans	2.1.1 Understanding the National Emergency Response Plan for public health emergencies 2.1.2 Understanding the National Emergency Rescue Plan for public health emergencies
			2.2 Laws and legal policies and regulations	2.2.1 Understanding the Emergency Regulations for Public Health Emergencies 2.2.2 Understanding the Law of the People's Republic of China on the Prevention and Treatment of Infectious Diseases
			2.3 Reporting	2.3.1 Remembering the time limit for reporting notifiable infectious diseases 2.3.2 Correctly filling in the Report Card of Infectious Diseases of the People's Republic of China 2.3.3 Memorising the scope of reporting information related to common infectious disease emergencies 2.3.4 Correctly filling in the Report Card for Information Related to Public Health Emergencies

Author(s)	Year	Core competency domains (I)	Sub-core competency domains (II)	Sub-core competency domains (III)
		3. Response to infectious disease emergencies	3.1 Surveillance and monitoring	3.1.1 Symptom monitoring: Understanding the significance of symptom monitoring 3.1.2 Symptom monitoring: Memorising the definition of syndromes and target diseases 3.1.3 Case monitoring: Categorising patients according to established case definitions
			3.2 Medical responses	3.2.1 Describing common infectious diseases that cause emergencies 3.2.2 Properly performing patient specimen collections 3.2.3 Understanding the precautions for specimen preservation and transportation 3.2.4 Determining clear and reliable sources of information 3.2.5 Obtaining key information from selected information sources 3.2.6 Memorising the concept of overload 3.2.7 Understanding the deployment of limited resources such as ventilators 3.2.8 Understanding ethical considerations when dealing with overload 3.2.9 Describing self-adjustment methods 3.2.10 Understanding psychological counseling methods for patients and their families with infectious diseases

Table 3.2: Continued

Author(s)	Year	Core competency domains (I)	Sub-core competency domains (II)	Sub-core competency domains (III)
			3.3 Public health responses	3.3.1 Memorising the protection requirements for various infectious diseases
				3.3.2 Correctly putting on and taking off PPE
				3.3.3 Properly implementing hand hygiene
				3.3.4 Listing exposure prevention measures
				3.3.5 Properly dealing with medical waste
				3.3.6 Properly managing patients with infectious diseases or dead bodies
				3.3.7 Describing environmental disinfection methods
				3.3.8 Understanding the concept of standard prevention
				3.3.9 Describing isolation methods
				3.3.10 Properly implementing isolation methods for various infectious diseases
				3.3.11 Memorising the concept of quarantine
				3.3.12 Describing various quarantine methods
				3.3.13 Correctly implementing quarantine for close contacts of individuals with various infectious diseases
			3.4 Risk communication	3.4.1 Developing health education programmes to control the spread of infectious diseases
			3.5 Emergency responses to infectious diseases related to chemical, biological, radiation, and nuclear exposure	3.5.1 Understanding responses to bioterrorism attacks
				3.5.2 Understanding infectious disease emergency responses after natural disasters
				3.5.3 Understanding the dos and don'ts of participating in international relief

Author(s)	Year	Core competency domains (I)	Sub-core competency domains (II)	Sub-core competency domains (III)
Hu	2019	1. Knowledge	1.1 Fundamentals of disaster nursing	1.1.1 Concepts and theory related to disaster and disaster medicine and nursing 1.1.2 Disaster classification and common hazards 1.1.3 Ethical and legal knowledge in disaster nursing
			1.2 Specialised disaster nursing knowledge	1.2.1 Prevention, preparedness, mitigation, and recovery 1.2.2 Contingency plans 1.2.3 Rescue knowledge in various disasters 1.2.4 Rescue care for common injuries 1.2.5 Infection prevention and control
		2. Skills	2.1 Assessment and observation	2.1.1 The nature and scope of disaster assessment for affected populations 2.1.2 Safety assessment for disaster relief teams and the injured 2.1.3 Injury assessments 2.1.4 Disaster vulnerability and analysis 2.1.5 Psychological assessments 2.1.6 Disease monitoring
			2.2 Routine care in an emergency	2.2.1 Outdoor survival and personal protection 2.2.2 Emergency evacuations for affected populations 2.2.3 Triage 2.2.4 Transportation 2.2.5 Rescuing the injured in temporary shelter
			2.3 First aid in pre-hospital care	2.3.1 Basic life support 2.3.2 Advanced life support 2.3.3 Trauma care skills 2.3.4 Emergency materials and supplies 2.3.5 Critically ill patient monitoring

Table 3.2: Continued

Author(s)	Year	Core competency domains (I)	Sub-core competency domains (II)	Sub-core competency domains (III)
			2.4 Disaster nursing management	2.4.1 Disaster rescue and contingency plans 2.4.2 Disaster rescue organisation and coordination 2.4.3 Disaster relief staff and supply organisation and allocation 2.4.4 Mass casualty incident management 2.4.5 Information management and utilisation 2.4.6 Disaster command and leadership 2.4.7 Handling conflict
			2.5 Psychological and crisis intervention	2.5.1 Seeking social support 2.5.2 Crisis management for survivors 2.5.3 Crisis interventions for rescue workers 2.5.4 Crisis management for vulnerable populations 2.5.5 PTSD crisis management 2.5.6 Palliative care
			2.6 Communication and cooperation	2.6.1 Communication 2.6.2 Cooperation 2.6.3 Multicultural care
		3. Holistic attributes	3.1 Physical attributes	3.1.1 Physical fitness
			3.2 Psychological attributes	3.2.1 Strengths 3.2.2 Insight 3.2.3 Critical judgments and decision-making 3.2.4 Stable emotional status 3.2.5 Awareness of and attitudes toward disasters 3.2.6 Self-adjustment and stress management
			3.3 Moral quality	3.3.1 Professional ethics 3.3.2 Professional literacy 3.3.3 Humanitarianism

Author(s)	Year	Core competency domains (I)	Sub-core competency domains (II)	Sub-core competency domains (III)
Wu et al.	2021	1. Prevention/ mitigation	1.1 Disaster nursing theory	1.1.1 Disaster concepts, categories, and information judgment (e.g., natural and social incidents and public health emergencies)
				1.1.2 Features of disaster events and contingency plans
				1.1.3 Isolation, quarantine, purification, and sewage principles for public health emergencies
			1.2 Emergency contingency plans and principles	1.2.1 Nurse tasks in a disaster continuum and roles in hospital incident commandant systems
				1.2.2 Disaster and emergency drills in hospitals
				1.2.3 Disaster emergency response principles, human resource allocation, and material allocation
		2. Preparedness	2.1 Basic disaster nursing skills	2.1.1 Personal preparedness in disaster responses
				2.1.2 Basic principles and procedures in pre-hospital emergency care
				2.1.3 Pre-hospital first aid (e.g., CPR, wound care, bandaging, and fixing)
				2.1.4 Assessment, triage, and transferring principles and methods
				2.1.5 Injury characteristics and pre-hospital rescue (fires, earthquakes, electric shocks, lightning strikes, mining accidents, chemical injuries, etc.)
				2.1.6 Use of PPE
				2.1.7 Prevention and control of infectious diseases

Table 3.2: Continued

Author(s)	Year	Core competency domains (I)	Sub-core competency domains (II)	Sub-core competency domains (III)
			2.2 Ethics and legal practice, and information communication and coordination	2.2.1 Disaster ethics and legal regulations 2.2.2 Disaster information transmission processes and the application of communication tools 2.2.3 Interpersonal and communication skills in a disaster
		3. Response	3.1 Hospital care and management in hospitals	3.1.1 Triage, assessment, rescue principles, and strategies in an emergency 3.1.2 Documentation principles in an emergency 3.1.3 Infection control principles and strategies for mass casualty injuries 3.1.4 Patient signs and symptoms in chemical, biological, radioactive, explosive, and nuclear incidents: Isolation, decontamination measures, and health education 3.1.5 Cleaning and disinfection procedures and rescue measures for special patients 3.1.6 Hospital transferring principles and methods 3.1.7 Dead body management principles (i.e., ethics and legal and cultural factors) 3.1.8 Deployment and management of human resources, materials, and equipment for on-site ambulances 3.1.9 Medication safety management 3.1.10 Incident organisation and management in disasters

Author(s)	Year	Core competency domains (I)	Sub-core competency domains (II)	Sub-core competency domains (III)
			3.2 Psychological care and intervention	3.2.1 Psychological assessments for injuries in an emergency
				3.2.2 PTSD and psychological care knowledge
				3.2.3 Crisis intervention
				3.2.4 Personal self-adjustment and health protection
			3.3 Care for vulnerable groups	3.3.1 Care for people with chronic illnesses, elders, children, pregnant people, disabled individuals, and their families
				3.3.2 Care for bereaved survivors and their families
				3.3.3 Recognition and care in vulnerable groups
				3.3.4 Multidisciplinary teamwork and continuing care plans
		4. Rehabilitation/ recovery	4.1 Continuing care for individuals, families, and communities	4.1.1 Rehabilitation care and health education for injuries after a disaster

Physical and Psychosocial Care Competencies

Competency domains related to physical and psychological care were found in all 11 studies. Most featured cross-sectional study designs and mainly focused on the disaster response phase, consistent with previous studies (Ranse, Hutton, Jeeawody, and Wilson, 2014; Chang and Dong, 2015).

The specific domains of physical care for injuries included field first aid (Zhang, 2011; Han et al., 2012; He and Song, 2014; Sun, 2014; Hou and Gong, 2017; Hu, 2019; Wu et al., 2021), such as basic and advanced life support, the assessment of injuries through triage, transferred or trauma care in emergency or high-altitude situations (Han et al., 2012), and psychological care (Yang, 2009; Zhang, 2011; Han et al., 2012; Yang, 2013; Sun, 2014; Gao, 2016; Hu, 2019; Wu et al., 2021) or crisis intervention (He and Song, 2014; Hu, 2019). In relation to requirements for responders, the domains also covered outdoor survival (Zhang, 2011; Sun, 2014; Hou and Gong, 2017; Hu, 2019) or fitness training (He and Song, 2014; Hu, 2019), personal protective equipment (PPE; Zhang, 2011; Hu, 2019; Wu et al., 2021), and stress management (Zhang, 2011) or self-adaptation (Han et al., 2012; Sun, 2014; Hou and Gong, 2017; Wu et al., 2011).

Competencies related to applying physical care are fundamental to managing the surge in demand (WHO, 2008) in pre-hospital settings. Important knowledge and skills related to physical care include (Fig. 3.3) the following: 1) first aid, basic life support, advanced life support, cardiopulmonary resuscitation (CPR); 2) trauma/wound assessment and care, basic surgical skills; 3) triaging and rapid assessment; and 4) pain management. These components are important and are addressed by the requirements for developing undergraduate nursing curricula (WHO, 2008) and trauma first aid training to improve medical responders' confidence in responding to disasters (Andrade, Hayes, and Punch, 2020).

Furthermore, individuals who experience a disaster may experience trauma as a result. Disaster healthcare responders should be able to address stress-related reactions among affected people immediately after a disaster (Birkhead and Vermeulen, 2018). Disaster mental health training, such as psychological first aid, is an important element of preparing to offer psychological support

**Figure 3.3 Trauma and life support workshop for postgraduate students at the
Institute on Disaster Management and Reconstruction at Sichuan University**

Photo taken by the third author on 7 October 2020.

immediately after a traumatic event (Jacobs et al., 2016). Birkhead and
Vermeulen further state that responders should be able to help the affected
individuals feel safe, reduce stress-related symptoms by meeting their basic
needs, and foster positive coping strategies by connecting the affected
individuals with social resources and support. The ICN (2009, 2019) emphasises
that disaster health workers, including nurses, must be competent in identifying
the physical and psychological needs of and providing holistic care support for
the affected individuals and community, in order to ensure the well-being of the
population following a disaster.

Public Health Emergency Preparedness, Response, and Recovery

In the current review, 10 papers clearly described the domains of public
health emergency preparedness, response, and recovery, such as infection

control measures (Han et al., 2012; Sun, 2014; Hou and Gong, 2017; Kan, 2019; Wu et al., 2021) and surveillance (Kan, 2019; Wu et al., 2021). Khan and colleagues (2018) have summarised 11 crucial elements of public health emergency preparedness (PHEP) aiming at promoting readiness for disasters and emergencies. These elements are governance and leadership, planning process, collaborative networks, community engagement, risk analysis, surveillance and monitoring, practice and experience, resources, workforce capacity, communication, and learning and evaluation. The elements are important as they help public health educators and frontline practitioners to define what are essential to be prepared (Fig. 3.4).

Post-disaster health management was examined in some, including in regard to sanitation, drinking water management and disinfection, and public health education (Han et al., 2012; Wu et al., 2021). Kan (2018) points out the importance of public health emergency response competencies. These should include elements such as implementing specimen collection correctly, safe transportation, collecting reliable and valid information, and allocating reasonable resources. For both public and medical health workers, effective

Figure 3.4 Public health emergency preparedness and response workshop for undergraduate nursing students at Ya'an Polytechnic College, Sichuan

Photo taken by the third author on 1 January 2020.

knowledge and skills should cover the proper wearing and removal of personal protective equipment, proper hand hygiene, post-exposure preventive disposal methods, the disposal of medical waste, the selection of disposal measures for patients with suspected infectious diseases, and dead body management.

Communication and Coordination

In the current research, eight studies scrutinised communication and coordination. Communication and collaboration concerns medical relief workers and the affected people, as well as various rescue teams (Yang, 2009; Han et al., 2012; Yang, 2013; Sun, 2014; Hou and Gong, 2017; Kan, 2018; Hu, 2019; Wu et al., 2021). The specific domains examined involved the ability to communicate with ethnic minorities (Han et al., 2012), effective communication skills in health education (Hou and Gong, 2017; Kan, 2018; Hu, 2019; Wu et al., 2021), and risk communication (Hou and Gong, 2017) in terms of delivering information about risks to the public during an emergency (see Fig. 3.5).

Figure 3.5 Hospital command incident simulation workshop on communication and coordination for hospital staff in Sichuan

Photo taken by the first author on 20 September 2018.

Communication and coordination are an integral part of preparedness and responses to disasters and epidemics (Hyvärinen and Vos, 2016; Khan et al., 2018) which cover ways to convey information, to provide guidance, and share information internally and externally. At present, risk communication has been used widely in disaster education and training before a disaster strikes because it helps people to understand and adopt protective behaviours in disaster preparedness and response (WHO, 2017). It has been well defined by the WHO (2017, vii) as "the real-time exchange of information, advice and opinions between experts, community leaders, officials and the people who are at risk and is an integral part of any emergency response". Shaw and colleagues (2013) have addressed the key roles that risk communication can play in holistic learning, the facilitation of information sharing, and the development of trust. A study conducted by Hongda and colleagues (2022) reported the effects of a risk communication competencies training programme for public health nurses in Japan. Their findings showed that there was an improved ability to respond to residents' concerns, relieve residents' distress, build trust, and support health-related self-efficacy. The purpose of crisis communication is to support the public in understanding risks and to exchange information with the public, as well as to gain the cooperation and participation of those affected. Therefore, elements such as the role of communication, information needs, diversity, communication technology, and trust (Hyvärinen and Vos, 2016) must be considered when designing teaching and learning activities.

Ethical Issues in Coping with Mass Casualty Incidents

A total of six papers examined ethical competence (Yang, 2013; He, 2014; Gao, 2016; Kan, 2018; Hu, 2019; Wu et al., 2021). For example, Yang (2013) proposed that principles of professional ethics and humanitarianism practice should be followed in order to improve the quality of care. Ethical issues are often faced in medical and public relief responses, such as in the management of dead bodies during disasters (Gao, 2016; Hu, 2019; Wu, 2021). In this situation, ethical considerations should be carefully examined when medical and public health responses fail to meet the demands of the survivors or victims during outbreaks and epidemics, and if healthcare systems are overloaded

(Kan, 2018). As a result, healthcare providers may be unable to cope with medical and public healthcare effectively due to issues of resource allocation, triage, and shortage of manpower or conflicting dual loyalty (Strous and Gold, 2019).

The WHO (2015) has stated that, due to time and resource constraints, healthcare providers are often unable to treat all of the injured and dead in a timely manner. A recent study has reviewed the practical issues involved in dealing with managing dead bodies (Suwalowska, Amara, Roberts, and Kingori, 2021). Suwalowska and colleagues have stated that, when millions of lives are affected during epidemics and natural disasters, issues such as dignity for the dead, delay in disposal, disposal when there are high mortality rates and a fear of infection, the use of mass burials and cremations, the lack of identification, and inequality in caring for the dead have been overlooked globally. These issues will have a significant long-term impact on the affected individuals, families, and communities.

Khan and colleagues (2018) have stated that ethics and values are becoming core principles to guide public health emergency preparedness (PHEP) and response policy. These principles cover equity, trust, public protection, reciprocity, duty to care, stewardship, and solidarity. According to these principles, decision-making actions for PHEP should include inclusiveness, accountability, transparency, responsiveness, and reasonableness.

In short, all of these issues should be addressed and informed by ethical best practice and education, and core principles should guide all healthcare behaviour under challenging medical and public health emergencies and disasters.

Limitations

The review presented in this chapter is limited to Chinese-language published articles and theses, all of which were conducted in mainland China. However, it is a comprehensive review of these studies and covers most competency-based disaster education and training elements in the papers reviewed. This study includes all articles published in the past 13 years (June 2008 to December 2021), which cover the process of the conceptual development of core competencies through various methodologies, such as reviewing previous published articles, conducting Delphi expert consultations, describing competencies and sub-competencies covering requisite knowledge and skills, and validating questionnaires.

Recommendations for the Future Development of Disaster Education and Training in China

This chapter reviews the competency domains for medical and public healthcare professionals in disaster responses in China since 2008. However, this review indicates there is a lack of consensus with regard to how to define competencies or competency statements, which are hard to measure. The term "competence" is used to "describe the knowledge that enables a practitioner to perform activities consistently in a safe manner" (ICN, 2009, p. 34). Performance is key to "competence", which reflects how knowledge, skills, and judgment can be applied effectively (ICN, 2009). Competency statements should describe specific observable and measurable activities that people are competent in performing (Gallardo et al., 2015). For example, they should include an action verb (e.g., apply/compare, identify/value, and align/grasp) to describe the level of performance across three domains of learning (cognitive, affective, and psychomotor). Furthermore, the subject matter, type of performance, outcome, or specific operational task, such as disaster response or recovery or public health emergency, as well as the context to which the competency statement is referring, should be included. An example from ICN (2009) in Table 3.3 demonstrates the domains of competencies, disaster management, and outcome performance.

Furthermore, various disaster education and training programmes have been developed over the past few decades worldwide, but the development of optimal goals for the programmes, which are actionable and feasible, remains inconsistent (Swann et al., 2022). Lawlor and Hornyak (2012) have suggested that the "SMART plan" can be effective in helping to set a clear focus and goal for programmes. For example, goal-setting and action-planning constructs are used by senior nursing students to improve their mass casualty incident (MCI) triage competencies in pre-hospital situations (Xia et al., 2020).

**Table 3.3 Examples of competency domains,
disaster management stages, and outcomes**

Disaster nursing competency domains	Disaster management stages/context	Outcomes or specific operational tasks/ domains of learning
Risk reduction, disease prevention, and health promotion	Prevention/mitigation competencies	• Evaluates the risks and effects of specific disasters on the community and the population and determines the implications for nursing using epidemiological data (cognitive) • Collaborates with other healthcare professions to develop risk reduction measures to reduce the vulnerability of the population (cognitive)
Communication and information sharing	Preparedness competencies	• Accepts accountability and responsibility for one's actions (affective) • Delegates to others in accordance with professional practice, applicable laws and regulations, and the specific disaster at hand (psychomotor)
Care of individuals and families	Response competencies	• Performs a rapid assessment of the disaster and nursing care needs (affective) • Recognises symptoms of communicable diseases and takes measures to reduce exposure to survivors (cognitive)
Long-term individual, family, and community recovery	Recovery/rehabilitation competencies	• Develops plans to meet the short- and long-term physical and psychological nursing needs of survivors (cognitive) • Teaches survivors strategies for the prevention of diseases and injuries (affective)

Source: International Council of Nurses (2009). ICN framework of disaster nursing competencies.

According to SMART constructs, the participants were able to define the triage categories (red, yellow, green, and black) and perform primary disaster triage. Specifically, they were able to categorise cases (e.g., earthquake survivors) who were injured, using the START (simple triage and rapid treatment) triage method in order to effectively sort them into four different colour-coded tags (e.g., 50 cases in five minutes) and efficiently provide sound rationale for the groups in two minutes. Thus, the five elements of SMART were used as a guide to provide care in ways that were specific (i.e., what exactly the learner will accomplish, for example, primary disaster triage in MCI situations with limited resources available), measurable (i.e., how the learner will know when he or she has reached the goal, for example, learners are able to identify four different colour-coded tags correctly), achievable (i.e., if achieving this goal is realistic with effort and commitment, for example, the learners are able to complete the allocated tasks in two or three minutes), relevant (i.e., significant for the learners, for example, it is believed that all nurses should be able to demonstrate triage knowledge and skills), and time-bound (i.e., when this goal will be achieved, for example, after completing the training programme, all participants are able to define and identify the four categories of triage and perform the procedure using the START triage method).

Finally, the competency domains, particularly contents related to education and training programmes, should be formed from evidence-based practice, which should be relevant to local situations. For example, three areas contributed to high mortality and mobility rates based on medical relief responses following the 2008 Sichuan earthquake (Chen et al., 2010; Zhang et al., 2011; 2012): injuries from being crushed and acute kidney failure, pain management issues either in acute or chronic stages, and psychological support and care issues either for the affected population or healthcare responders. None of these topics can be found in this review.

In short, there are many studies on the development of competencies and related frameworks, but empirical research is necessary and must focus on actual training and education needs. Healthcare providers must be competent in making rational decisions regarding care based on the medical resources available, in order to be able to do the most good for the benefit of the greatest number of people (WHO, 2015; Ghanbari et al., 2019) through adequate education and training. Efforts should be made to define domains of competences in order to achieve a consensus and strengthen the design of concrete competency domains and their implementation. The use of SMART goals in particular is important to help students to achieve the learning outcomes required by educators and facilitate educators in designing teaching and learning activities in an effective manner.

Conclusion

This chapter identifies the most common domains of core competencies in both medical and public healthcare responses, such as medical and public health workers and nurses working in hospital and community settings. In designing and implementing education and training for disaster healthcare workers, these domains, including medical and public healthcare responses, communication and coordination, and ethical dilemmas in coping with mass casualty incidents, will help strengthen and improve workers' readiness, ability, and willingness to respond to future disasters. All healthcare workers should be involved in continual training and education in order to improve their knowledge and skills in regard to disaster risk reduction and management. Finally, it is recommended that well-defined competence statements, the establishment of SMART goals in designing teaching and learning activities, and the relevance of the contents included in the competency domains are examined and implemented.

References

Andrade, E. G., Hayes, J. M., and Punch, L. J. (2020). Stop the bleed: The impact of trauma first aid kits on post-training confidence among community members and medical professionals. *The American Journal of Surgery, 220*(1), 245–248.

Birkhead, G. S., and Vermeulen, K. (2018). Sustainability of psychological first aid training for the disaster response workforce. *American Journal of Public Health, 108*(S5), S381–S382.

Centre for Research on the Epidemiology of Disaster and United Nations Office for Disaster Risk Reduction. (2020). *Human cost of disasters. An overview of the last 20 years 2000–2019.* Retrieved on 21 March 2023 from www.preventionweb. net/publication/human-cost-disasters-overview-last- 20-years-2000-2019.

Chan, S. S., Chan, W. S., Cheng, Y., Fung, O. W., Lai, T. K., Leung, A. W., Leung, K. L., Li, S., Yip, A. L., and Pang, S. M. (2010). Development and evaluation of an undergraduate training course for developing International Council of Nurses disaster nursing competencies in China. *Journal of Nursing Scholarship, 42*(4), 405–413.

Chang, X., and Dong, L. (2015). 災害護理能力及其評價工具研究進展 [Research progress on disaster nursing ability and evaluation tools]. 護理研究 [*Chinese Nursing Research], 29*(10), 3592–3595.

Chen, G., Lai, W., Liu, F., Mao, Q., Tu, F., Wen, J., Xiao, H., Zhang, J.-C., Zhu, T., Chen, B., Hu, Z.-Y., Li, R.-M., Liang, Z., Nie, H., Yan, H., Yang, B.-X., Du, Q., Huang, W.-X., Jiang, Y.-W., Kwan, A. S.-K., Song, L., Wu, C.-M.,

Xiang, T., Xu, H.-W., Lau, W. B., Song, H.-B., Wen, C.-B., Yao, Z.-H., Zhang, L., Zeng, J., Dai, Y.-E., Lopez, B. L., Zheng, J.-Q., Zhou, J., Christopher, T. A., Ma, X. L., Yu, H., Xu, L.-L., Guo, Q., Song, Z.-P., Volinn, E., Kryger, K., Cao, Y., Ge, H., Liu, H., Luo, C.-Z., Tao, W., Zuo, Y.-X., and Liu, J. (2010). The dragon strikes: Lessons from the Wenchuan earthquake. *Anesthesia & Analgesia, 110*(3), 908–915.

Chen, M., Tang, C., Xiong, J., Shi, Q. Y., Li, N., Gong, L. F., Wang, X. D., and Tie, Y. (2020). The long-term evolution of landslide activity near the epicentral area of the 2008 Wenchuan earthquake in China. *Geomorphology, 367,* 107317.

ChinaNews. (2008). "Sichuan Wenchuan earthquake continued: The National Disaster Reduction Commission launched the second-level disaster relief response." 12 May 2008. www.chinanews.com.cn/gn/news/2008/05-12/1246542.shtml.

Cui, Y. L., Li, Q. Y., He, S. Y., Luo, L. C., Gao, H. Y. (2014).初級創傷救治 (PTC) 培訓提高護士應對灾害救治護理能力淺析 [*Primary trauma treatment (PTC) training improves nurses' ability to deal with disaster treatment and nursing*]. Paper presented at the 3rd World Society of Disaster Nursing Conference, 21 June 2014, Beijing, China.

Du, Y. M., and Shi, N. (2014). *Comparative study on Japanese disaster nursing curriculum and its enlightenment to China.* Paper presented at the 3rd World Society of Disaster Nursing Conference, 21 June 2014, Beijing, China.

Fan, X., Juang, C. H., Wasowski, J., Huang, R., Xu, Q., Scaringi, G., van Westen, C. J., and Havenith, H. B. (2018). What we have learned from the 2008 Wenchuan earthquake and its aftermath: A decade of research and challenges. *Engineering Geology, 241,* 25–32.

Feldmann-Jensen, S., Jensen, S. J., Smith, S. M., and Vigneaux, G. (2019). The next generation core competencies for emergency management. *Journal of Emergency Management, 17*(1), 17–25.

Gallardo, A. R., Djalali, A., Foletti, M., Ragazzoni, L., Della Corte, F., Lupescu, O., Arculeo, C., von Arnim, G., Friedl, T., Ashkenazi, M., Fisher, P., Hreckovski, B., Khorram-Manesh, A., Komadina, R., Lechner, K., Stal, M., Patru, C., Burkle, F. M., and Ingrassia, P. L. (2015). Core competencies in disaster management and humanitarian assistance: A systematic review. *Disaster Medicine and Public Health Preparedness, 9*(4), 430–439.

Gao, R. (2016). 高職護生地震創傷院前救護能力培養模式研究 [Research on the training mode of pre-hospital rescue ability for high vocational nursing students following earthquake trauma] [Unpublished master's dissertation]. 成都中醫藥大學 [Chengdu University of Traditional Chinese Medicine].

Gebbie, K. M., and Qureshi, K. (2002). Emergency and disaster preparedness: Core competencies for nurses: What every nurse should but may not know. *The American Journal of Nursing, 102*(1), 46–51.

Ghanbari, V., Ardalan, A., Zareiyan, A., Nejati, A., Hanfling, D., and Bagheri, A. (2019). Ethical prioritization of patients during disaster triage: A systematic review of current evidence. *International Emergency Nursing, 43,* 126–132.

Han, R. J., Lu, H., Li, J., Zhang, H., Zhu, X. H., and Hu, J. (2012). 高原地區護理人員災害救護核心能力體系的構建 [The construction of nurses' core competency system for disastrous events in plateau regions]. 中華護理雜誌 [*Chinese Journal of Nursing*], *47*(7), 585–587.

He, S. (2014). 突發事件應急護理培訓課程設置研究 [Study on training courses for emergency using in nursing] [Unpublished master's dissertation]. 遼寧醫學院 [Liaoning Medical College].

Honda, K., Fujitani, Y., Nakajima, S., Goto, A., Kumagai, A., Komiya, H., Kobayashi, T., Takebayashi, Y., and Murakami, M. (2022). On-site training program for public health nurses in Fukushima Prefecture, Japan: Effects on risk communication competencies. *International Journal of Disaster Risk Reduction, 67*, 102694.

Hou, S. K., Lv, Q., Ding, H., Zhang, Y. Z., Yu, B. G., Liu, Z. Q., Su, B., Liu, J.-Y., Yu, M.-Y., Sun, Z.-G., and Fan, H. J. (2018). Disaster medicine in China: Present and future. *Disaster Medicine and Public Health Preparedness, 12*(2), 157–165.

Hou, X. L., Gong, Y. Q., and Kong, L. F. (2017). 護士災害應對能力評價指標體系的構建[Construction of an evaluation index system for nurses' disaster response ability]. 甘肅醫藥 [*Gansu Medical Journal*], *36*(5), 394–396.

Hsu, E. B., Thomas, T. L., Bass, E. B., Whyne, D., Kelen, G. D., and Green, G. B. (2006). Healthcare worker competencies for disaster training. *BMC Medical Education, 6*(1), 1–9.

Hu, X. (2019). 基于勝任力的災害護理培訓課程設置研究 [Research on establishing the curriculum of disaster nursing training based on competency] [Unpublished master's dissertation]. 華中科技大學 [Huazhong University of Science and Technology].

Huang, B., Li, J., Li, Y., Zhang, W., Pan, F., and Miao, S. (2011). Need for continual education about disaster medicine for health professionals in China: A pilot study. *BMC Public Health, 11*(1), 1–4.

Hyvärinen, J., and Vos, M. (2016). Communication concerning disasters and pandemics. In: Schwarz, A., Seeger, M. W., and Auer, C. (Eds.), *The handbook of international crisis communication research* (pp. 43–96). Oxford: John Wiley & Sons.

International Council of Nurses. (2009). *ICN framework of disaster nursing competencies.* Geneva: World Health Organisation. Retrieved on 1 June 2021 from www.apednn.org/doc/resourcespublications/ICN%20Framework%20of%20Disaster%20Nursing%20Competencies%20ICN%202009.pdf.

International Council of Nurses. (2019). *ICN framework of disaster nursing competencies version 2.0.* Retrieved on 1 June 2021 from www.icn.ch/sites/default/files/inline-files/ICN_Disaster-Comp-Report_WEB.pdf.

Jacobs, G. A., Gray, B. L., Erickson, S. E., Gonzalez, E. D., and Quevillon, R. P. (2016). Disaster mental health and community-based psychological first aid: Concepts and education/training. *Journal of Clinical Psychology, 72*(12), 1307–1317.

Jorgensen, A. M., Mendoza, G. J., and Henderson, J. L. (2010). Emergency preparedness and disaster response core competency set for perinatal and neonatal nurses. *Journal of Obstetric, Gynecologic & Neonatal Nursing, 39*(4), 450–467.

Kan T. (2018). 醫護人員傳染病突發事件應對能力培訓項目的開發與評價 [Development and evaluation of training program for infectious disease emergencies response competence of healthcare workers] [Unpublished doctoral dissertation]. 海軍軍醫大學 [Naval Medical University].

Khan, Y., O'Sullivan, T., Brown, A., Tracey, S., Gibson, J., Généreux, M., Henry, B., and Schwartz, B. (2018). Public health emergency preparedness: a framework to promote resilience. *BMC Public Health, 18*(1), 1–16.

King, R. V., Burkle, F. M., Walsh, L. E., and North, C. S. (2015). Competencies for disaster mental health. *Current Psychiatry Reports, 17*(3), 1–9.

Lawlor, K. B., and Hornyak M. J. (2012). Smart goals: How the application of smart goals can contribute to achievement of student learning outcomes. *Proceedings of the Annual ABSEL Conference, 39,* 259–267.

Li, C. Y., and Courtland, R. (2009). 構建災害應對護理人員培訓體系的研究與實踐. [Constructing a training system for disaster nurses research and practice]. 中國護理管理 [*Chinese Nurse Management*], *9*(5), 11–13.

Liu, J. T. (2009). 中國重大災害事故、突發事件醫療救援體系與精神衛生社會工作 [China's medical rescue system for major disasters, accidents and emergencies and mental health and social work]. 社會科學研究 [*Social Science Research*], *1,* 96–102.

Magnusson, R. (2017). *Public health emergencies in advancing the right to health: The vital role of law.* Geneva: World Health Organisation. apps.who.int/iris/bitstream/handle/10665/252815/9789241511384-eng.pdf;sequence=1.

Mai, Q. Y., Fu, Z. L., Zeng, Y., Yang, X. J., Ou, Y. H. H., and Liang, J. (2013). 初級創傷救治急救技能培訓實踐分析 [Practice analysis of first-aid skills training for primary trauma treatment]. 右江民族醫學院學報 [*Journal of Youjiang Medical University for Nationalities*], *35*(4), 583–584.

Mock, C., Lormand, J. D., Goosen, J., Joshipura, M., and Peden, M. (Eds.). (2004). *Guidelines for essential trauma care.* World Health Organisation. Retrieved on 1 June 2021 from www.who.int/publications/i/item/guidelines-for-essential-trauma-care.

Noh, J., Oh, E. G., Kim, S. S., Jang, Y. S., Chung, H. S., and Lee, O. (2020). Development and evaluation of a multimodality simulation disaster education and training program for hospital nurses. *International Journal of Nursing Practice, 26*(3), e12810.

Pang, S. M., Chan, S. S., and Cheng, Y. (2009). Pilot training program for developing disaster nursing competencies among undergraduate students in China. *Nursing & Health Sciences, 11*(4), 367–373.

Schor, K. W., and Altman, B. A. (2013). Proposals for aligning disaster health competency models. *Disaster Medicine and Public Health Preparedness, 7*(1), 8–12.

Shaw, R., Takeuchi, Y., Matsuura, S., and Saito, K. (2013). *Risk communication.* Washington, D.C.: World Bank.

Shen, J., Kang, J., Shi, Y., Li, Y., Li, Y., Su, L., Wu, J., Zheng, S., Jiang, J., Hu, W., Yang, Y., Tang, X., Wen, J., Li, L., Shen, J., and Zhong, D. (2012). Lessons learned from the Wenchuan earthquake. *Journal of Evidence-Based Medicine, 5*(2), 75–88.

Sim, T., He, M., and Dominelli, L. (2022). Social work core competencies in disaster management practice: An integrative review. *Research on Social Work Practice, 32*(3), 310–321.

Strous, R. D., and Gold, A. (2019). Ethical lessons learned and to be learned from mass casualty events by terrorism. *Current Opinion in Anesthesiology, 32*(2), 174–178.

Su, T., Han, X., Chen, F., Du, Y., Zhang, H., Yin, J., Tan, X., Chang, W., Ding, Y., Han, Y., and Cao, G. (2013). Knowledge levels and training needs of disaster medicine among health professionals, medical students, and local residents in Shanghai, China. *PloS One, 8*(6), e67041.

Sun J. (2014). 災害護理專科護士培訓課程核心知識體系的構建 [Construction of disaster nursing specialist training courses core knowledge system] [Unpublished master's dissertation]. 山東大學 [Shandong University].

Suwalowska, H., Amara, F., Roberts, N., and Kingori, P. (2021). Ethical and sociocultural challenges in managing dead bodies during epidemics and natural disasters. *BMJ Global Health, 6*(11), e006345.

Swann, C., Jackman, P. C., Lawrence, A., Hawkins, R. M., Goddard, S. G., Williamson, O., Schweickle, M. J., Vella, S. A., Rosenbaum, S., and Ekkekakis, P. (2022). The (over) use of SMART goals for physical activity promotion: A narrative review and critique. *Health Psychology Review.* Published online 31 January 2022.

Walsh, L., Altman, B. A., King, R. V., and Strauss-Riggs, K. (2014). Enhancing the translation of disaster health competencies into practice. *Disaster Medicine and Public Health Preparedness, 8*(1), 70–78.

Walsh, L., Subbarao, I., Gebbie, K., Schor, K. W., Lyznicki, J., Strauss-Riggs, K., Cooper, A., Hsu, E. B., King, R. V., Mitas 2nd, J. A., Hick, J., Zukowski, R., Altman, B. A., Steinbrecher, R. A., and James, J. J. (2012). Core competencies for disaster medicine and public health. *Disaster Medicine and Public Health Preparedness, 6*(1), 44–52.

Wang, C., Wei, S., Xiang, H., Xu, Y., Han, S., Mkangara, O. B., and Nie, S. (2008). Evaluating the effectiveness of an emergency preparedness training programme for public health staff in China. *Public Health, 122*(5), 471–477.

Wang, X. Y., Zhou, J., Li, W., Yin, H. H., Jiang, J., Zhou, M. F., Shu, Q., and Chen, B.Q. (2010). 〈野戰護理學〉課程建設與實踐 [Curriculum construction and practice of field nursing]. 護理研究 [*Nursing Research*], *24*(12), 3374–3376.

World Health Organisation. (2008). *Integrating emergency preparedness and response into undergraduate nursing curricula.* Retrieved on 6 May 2023 from www.who.int/hac/publications/Nursing_curricula_followup_Feb08.pdf.

World Health Organisation. (2015). *Ethics in epidemics, emergencies and disasters: Research, surveillance and patient care: Training manual.* apps.who.int/iris/bitstream/handle/10665/196326/9789241549349_eng.pdf?sequence=1.

World Health Organisation. (2017). *Communicating risk in public health emergencies: A WHO guideline for emergency risk communication (ERC) policy and practice.* apps.who.int/iris/handle/10665/259807.

Wu, L. L., Shen, Y., Gu, Y., Jin, L. H., and Shen, J. (2021). 基于德爾菲法的臨床護士災害護理能力培訓方案構建 [Construction of a disaster nursing competency training program for clinical nurses based on Delphi method]. 上海護理 [*Shanghai Nursing*], *21*(8), 6–9.

Xia, R., Li, S., Chen, B., Jin, Q., and Zhang, Z. (2020). Evaluating the effectiveness of a disaster preparedness nursing education program in Chengdu, China. *Public Health Nursing, 37*(2), 287–294.

Xu, Y., and Zeng, X. (2016). Necessity for disaster-related nursing competency training of emergency nurses in China. *International Journal of Nursing Sciences, 3*(2), 198–201.

Yang, F. (2009). 突發公共衛生事件醫務人員應對能力評價指標選擇和初步模型構建 [Establishment of a preliminary index model for evaluating medical personnel's abilities of responding to public health emergencies] [Unpublished master's dissertation]. 南方醫科大學 [Southern Medical University].

Yang, M. F. (2013). 本科護生災害護理能力評價指標構建及研究[The evaluation index building and research in disasters nursing ability of nursing undergraduates] [Unpublished master's dissertation]. 南昌大學 [Nanchang University].

Zhang, J. (2011). 基于勝任力的災難護理課程開發的理論研究 [A theoretical study to developing a competence-based disaster nursing curriculum] [Unpublished doctoral dissertation]. 第二軍醫大學 [The Second Military Medical University].

Zhang, L., Liu, Y., Liu, X., and Zhang, Y. (2011). Rescue efforts management and characteristics of casualties of the Wenchuan earthquake in China. *Emergency Medicine Journal, 28*(7), 618–622.

Zhang, L., Liu, X., Li, Y., Liu, Y., Liu, Z., Lin, J., Shen, J., Tang, X., Zhang, Y., and Liang, W. (2012). Emergency medical rescue efforts after a major earthquake: Lessons from the 2008 Wenchuan earthquake. *Lancet, 379*(9818), 853–861.

Zhang, Q. (2009). 我國災害護理學及灾害護理教育現狀分析與啟示 [Implication of the current situation of disaster nursing and disaster nursing education]. 護理研究 [*Nursing Research*], *23*(4A), 923–924.

Zhang, Y. L. (2009). 汶川特大地震醫學救援行動及戰略思考 [Wenchuan massive earthquake medical rescue action and strategic thinking]. 解放軍醫學雜誌 [*Medical Journal of Chinese People's Liberation Army*], *34*(1), 1–6.

4

Review of the Quality of Life of Lower Limb Amputees after the 2008 Sichuan Earthquake

M. S. WONG and Qian WANG
Department of Biomedical Engineering, The Hong Kong Polytechnic University

This chapter reviews the quality of life of lower limb amputees 10 years after the 2008 Sichuan earthquake in China. It concludes by suggesting some useful strategies for the preparation and delivery of effective prosthetic services.

Traumatic Amputations due to Earthquakes

Amputation is a permanent operational procedure that leads to significant functional, psychological, and social sequelae (Markatos et al., 2019). The most common aetiologies of amputation are attributed to vascular diseases and trauma (Castillo-Avila et al., 2021). In 2005, it was found that approximately 1.6 million American people had to undergo amputations due to diabetes and peripheral arterial diseases (Luetmer et al., 2019). The number of Americans living with limb loss is projected to double by 2050, partly due to the ageing population and an increase in the prevalence of those living with diabetes, which causes vascular problems (Luetmer et al., 2019). Individuals with amputations due to vascular diseases are often older and less ambulatory, and associated age-related comorbidities (e.g., cardiovascular problems) are likely to reduce their level of physical activity and increase disability. People with traumatic amputations, on the other hand, are generally younger and more active than those with vascular amputations (Devan et al., 2012). It was reported that the incidence of anxiety and depression were much higher in trauma-related amputees than in those whose amputations were vascular-related (Bartels and Van Rooyen, 2012).

Some severe earthquakes, such as those in Marmara, Turkey (1999), Kashmir (2005), Haiti (2010), and Sichuan, China (2008), have contributed to a large number of traumatic amputations, imposing a variety of physical and psychological challenges on earthquake survivors. Restricted daily activities, phantom limb sensations and pain, depression, changes to lifestyle, and unemployment have been reported by victims living with limb amputations after an earthquake (Awais et al., 2012; Chu and Wong, 2016; Li et al., 2015; Li et al., 2019). Moreover, it was found that, four years after the 2008 Sichuan earthquake, victims with amputations were still suffering from significantly lower quality of life (QoL) than the general population (Li et al., 2015). Since the demand from amputees for assistance was found to be high, it was proposed that optimal rehabilitation measures be developed to help post-earthquake victims restore normalcy in their lives.

Prosthetic Rehabilitation of Amputees

Prosthetic devices are necessary in order to assist amputees with performing activities of daily life and hence to help them maintain their QoL. For individuals with limb loss, current surgical strategies focus on keeping an optimal residual limb for prosthetic fittings. Following the amputation, the individual has to go through a prosthetic training phase of rehabilitation to improve their mobility and utilisation of their prosthesis while walking, in sit-stand transitions, and in turning. The real challenge to amputees is the optimal utility of the prosthesis—how to adapt to the prosthesis and start to reintegrate this new body part into their daily lives (O'Keeffe and Rout, 2019). To satisfy this requirement, the prosthetic service provider needs to work closely with the rehabilitation professional to resolve the amputee's challenges in the daily use of the prosthesis. Rehabilitation of the amputee starts only after the amputation, but the work of the prosthetic service provider is a continuous process from the design of the prosthesis to the training of the amputee, and to life-long prosthetic support.

Centre of Comprehensive Services for Disabled People

In 2008, a devastating earthquake in Sichuan resulted in many adolescent victims with amputations. To promote the prosthetic rehabilitation of amputees, the Deyang Disabled Persons' Federation: Hong Kong Red Cross Rehabilitation, Prosthetic and Orthotic Centre was established in Deyang city, which was one of the most severely affected regions in the earthquake. The centre was supported by the Hong Kong Red Cross to specifically provide prosthetic services, adaptive rehabilitative training, and regular follow-ups to amputees immediately after the Sichuan earthquake for 8 years. Chu and Wong conducted a study on the effects of prosthetic management to help adolescent amputees return to premorbid activity levels (Chu and Wong, 2016). They found that adolescents with a transfemoral amputation after the natural disaster were less active than those with transtibial amputations, and supported the view that adolescent amputees had a high level of potential to achieve a mobility level similar to the able-bodied population (Chu and Wong, 2016).

The StandTALL Rehabilitation Programme

Another rehabilitation programme, StandTALL, was initiated by a group of orthopaedic specialists in Hong Kong immediately after the 2008 Sichuan earthquake. The programme provided crucial prosthetic rehabilitation services to amputees, particularly young victims after the earthquake, to enable them to restore their daily functions and independent mobility (Li et al., 2019). A cross-sectional study on victims of the 2008 Sichuan earthquake found that the number of victims who had received bilateral lower limb amputations was 28,008, 0.06% of the earthquake victims (Li et al., 2009). The study also found that bilateral lower limb amputees tended to have lower levels of physical function and capacity than unilateral amputees. The success rate of rehabilitation among lower limb amputees varied greatly, ranging from 5% to 90% (Penn-Barwell, 2011). Hence, some effective measures were proposed in the StandTALL programme to augment rehabilitation success. These measures included revision surgeries to promote the fit of rapid bone growth to prosthetic changes, and therapeutic exercise programmes to facilitate the utility of prostheses. Subsequently, it was reported that 33.3% of the bilateral lower limb amputees in the StandTALL programme achieved rehabilitation success in terms of mobility, attaining the highest K-level in the amputee mobility predictor (AMP) used: 44% scored ≥ 9 on the Houghton Scale, and 12.5% attained "independent mobility" using a prosthesis in their household (Li et al., 2019).

Even though the bilateral lower limb amputees in the StandTALL programme were largely found to have lower levels of mobility, prosthesis usage, and QoL when compared with their unilateral lower limb counterparts, they obtained similar psychosocial adjustments and even better mental QoL (Li et al., 2019). The study also found that prosthesis usage was significantly higher in bilateral lower limb amputees with lower amputation sites. Those with knee joint salvage used their prostheses over 50% of their waking hours, with an average of 10 hours per day, while only 40% of those with no knee joint salvage used their prostheses over 50% of their waking hours. The prosthetic rehabilitation success was attributed to better general adjustment ($p = 0.021$), fewer activity restrictions ($p = 0.008$), and better physical QoL ($p = 0.083$) (Li et al., 2019).

Long-term Review of the Quality of Life and Pain Status of Amputees Since the Earthquake

To date, a great deal of research has focused on the daily functions and QoL of victims with spinal cord injuries and fractures, and very little information has been made available on amputation-related QoL and pain. According to the studies mentioned below, there is a huge demand for long-term rehabilitation to improve the daily functioning, QoL, and pain management of post-earthquake victims.

Quality of Life

Wang and colleagues conducted a cross-sectional study 10 years after the 2008 Sichuan earthquake to investigate and document the long-term outcomes of the prosthesis-related QoL of lower limb amputees (Wang et al., 2021b). The study was carried out at the Centre of Comprehensive Services for Disabled People in Deyang. The prosthesis-related QoL of the amputees was assessed using the Prosthesis Evaluation Questionnaire (PEQ), which includes scales relating to nine functional domains: utility, appearance, sounds, residual limb health, perceived response, frustration, social burden, ambulation, and well-being (Miller et al., 2018; Wurdeman et al., 2018). The PEQ has been validated as a self-report questionnaire for evaluating the prosthesis-related QoL of individuals with amputations (Parker et al., 2010). The PEQ scores of the scales for sounds, residual limb health, ambulation, and frustration of lower limb amputees in the study were still found to be low 10 years after the 2008 Sichuan earthquake. This study was carried out in comparison with findings in the literature (Chu and Wong, 2016; Harness and Pinzur, 2001; Legro et al., 1998; Pinzur et al., 2006). Since some of the participants in the study had extremely low PEQ values (less than 10 out of 100), the researchers recommended that more attention be paid to the areas of sounds, residual limb health, and frustration (Wang et al., 2021b). The researchers then analysed the whole profile of long-term outcomes regarding the QoL of the lower limb amputees, and found that the scales regarding sounds and residual limb health were related to the techniques used in prosthetic design, fabrication, and fitting. Wang et al. (2021b) were of the view that it was critical to optimise these prosthetic factors to suit lower limb amputees, so that their prostheses could offer improvements in energy expenditure, activity level, balance, and proprioception, as suggested by Friel (2005). The frustration scale also showed how frequently the participants felt frustrated with their prostheses (Wang et al., 2021b). Elsewhere, depressive symptoms were found to be prevalent among amputees (Darnall et al., 2005; Foote et al., 2015), and mental health outcomes were indicative of preparedness for full social reintegration (Ladlow et al., 2015). However, Chu and Wong (2016), also using PEQ, found that adolescent lower limb amputees resulting from the 2008 Sichuan earthquake had better QoL compared with the group in the study by Wang et al. (2021b).

The potential demographic factors associated with the PEQ scales were indirectly identified in lower limb amputees after the 2008 Sichuan earthquake (Wang et al., 2021b). The results showed that lower limb amputees aged 60 years or above reported lower scores in ambulation, suggesting that older amputees had lower levels of mobility than their younger counterparts when they used their prostheses. Moreover, lower limb amputees with no schooling or only primary school education scored lower in perceived responses, social burden, and ambulation compared with those who had completed high school or had a college education. Li et al. (2015) showed that education level was a significant predictor of the QoL, mental health, and satisfaction of amputees who had survived the Sichuan earthquake. Lower levels of education were reported to be linked to the post-traumatic depression and stress in lower limb amputees (Guo et al., 2017).

The study by Wang et al. (2021b) also revealed that lower limb amputees living dependently with their families scored lower in regard to the appearance scale than those living independently. Some amputees seemed to be unsatisfied with the appearance of their prostheses, particularly those living with their family members. In addition, divorced amputees had significantly lower scores on the frustration scale when compared with married or single amputees. Amputees with comorbidities obtained lower scores in regard to social burden than those without comorbidities, suggesting that pre-existing comorbidities caused more of a burden for their partners or family members.

Specific findings of the study are as follows: Amputees older than 60 years had significantly lower ambulation scores than younger amputees ($p = 0.047$).

Compared with married (p = 0.017) or single subjects (p = 0.033), the frustration scores were significantly lower in the divorced or widowed cohort. Those who lived dependently scored significantly less in regard to the appearance scale than those living alone (p = 0.032). Amputees with a high school or college education scored significantly higher on the perceived response (p = 0.049), social burden (p = 0.021), and ambulation (p = 0.006) scales, compared with those who were illiterate or who had received primary school education only. The social burden scores were lower among those who had one or more comorbidities than those without any comorbidities (p = 0.049). Taking all the above findings into consideration, it can be concluded that vulnerable amputees after an earthquake could be identified based on their demographic characteristics, such as age, marital status, way of living (living dependently or otherwise), level of education, and comorbidities (Wang et al., 2021b).

The level of amputation was found to be closely associated with the energy expended during ambulation (Yilmaz et al., 2016). However, there is no general consensus regarding the association between the level of amputation and QoL. In their study, Chu and Wong showed that there was no significant difference in any of the nine functional domains of PEQ scores between the transtibial and transfemoral adolescent amputees after the 2008 Sichuan earthquake (Chu and Wong, 2016). Similar findings were obtained 10 years after the Sichuan earthquake in victims with ages ranging from 17 to 86 years (Wang et al., 2021a). The above results indicate that the level of amputation did not appear to have an impact on the long-term QoL of the earthquake amputees.

After the 2008 Sichuan earthquake, Li and colleagues examined a group of bilateral lower limb amputees who were young and healthy before undergoing traumatic amputations (Li et al., 2019). The subjects' health-related QoL was evaluated through the Trinity Amputation and Prosthesis Experience Scale and the 12-Item Short Form Health Survey. The results indicated that bilateral amputees had lower physical QoL when compared with unilateral lower limb amputees, but there was no difference in mental QoL. Furthermore, the study showed that amputation level, knee joint salvage, prosthesis use, exercise, and education were associated with higher QoL scores. A prospective study with 72 amputees surviving the Sichuan earthquake showed that illiterate survivors with lower limb amputations had poorer QoL and life satisfaction (Li et al., 2015).

Similar results in other studies have also revealed that the education level of the survivors who underwent amputations after the Sichuan earthquake was a significant predictor of QoL, mental health, and life satisfaction.

Amputation-related Pain

It is noteworthy that amputation-related pain is frequently associated with functional impairment and psychological depression among amputees (Christensen et al., 2016; Trevelyan et al., 2016). The QoL of amputees was found to be adversely affected by phantom limb pain, which causes a significant decline in the domains of SF-36 (a general health questionnaire) in amputees when compared with the general population (Sinha and Van Den Heuvel, 2011). Moreover, chronic pain after amputation was found to have a negative impact on the amputees' employment and social activities (Richardson et al., 2015). Thus, the issue of amputation-related pain should be a therapeutic priority for the improvement of amputees' QoL. The identification of risk factors that contribute to amputation-related pain can assist with amputees' pain management.

A prospective cohort study was conducted by Li and colleagues to investigate the pain intensity of 46 victims residing in Mianzhu county who had undergone amputations following the 2008 Sichuan earthquake (Li et al., 2015). The victims' amputation-related pain was assessed by the visual analogue scale (VAS). The results showed a significant decline in pain level from a median of 4 (interquartile range 2–6) in 2009 to 3 (interquartile range 0–5) in 2010 and 2 (interquartile range 0–3) in 2012. Ten years after the Sichuan earthquake, Wang and colleagues reported that 90.9% of victims with lower limb amputations said they experienced one or more types of amputation-related pain (Wang et al., 2020). The most common types of pain experienced were phantom limb sensation (79.0%), phantom limb pain (77.3%), and residual limb pain (72.7%). The majority of the amputees reported that they had experienced amputation-related pain only once or twice in the four weeks before the investigation, but a few said the pain occurred almost all the time or several times a day. Demographic risk factors associated with the prevalence and intensity of amputation-related pain were identified: divorce, illiteracy, unemployment, poor general health, comorbidities, and wearing prostheses for fewer than five hours per day. Although the majority of the amputees reported that the intensity of the amputation-related pain and the extent to which it bothered them were moderate, 40% of amputees still experienced severe pain during the post-earthquake period. These results highlight the importance of the scientific assessment and rehabilitation management of pain as part of long-term post-disaster strategies for victims, especially those with lower limb amputations.

Phantom Limb Pain

Reports on pain experienced by amputees in different age groups showed that there was no statistically significant association between age and the prevalence of phantom limb pain (Smith et al., 1999). Smith noted that living conditions and source of income correlated with the prevalence of phantom limb pain (i.e., amputees who lived independently or who earned their own income were more likely to feel pain). Furthermore, 22% of amputees were found to have phantom limb sensations, and 31% of those with phantom limb pain characterised their pain as severe in the study by Smith et al. (1999). Similar to previous studies, the mean intensity ratings were 48.9 ± 23.1 and 44.9 ± 22.8 for phantom limb sensation and phantom limb pain, respectively. The following demographic characteristics were found to be associated with "moderate to severe intensity" phantom limb sensation or pain: aged between 50 and 69 years, divorced, illiterate, poor health, comorbidities, and wearing prostheses for fewer than five hours a day. These results are comparable to previous studies, which have identified age, comorbidities, and education level to be factors correlating with the intensity of phantom limb pain (Larbig et al., 2019; Morgan et al., 2017). Wang et al. (2020) found that 38% of amputees experienced phantom limb sensation and 40% of those with phantom limb pain characterised their pain as "severely bothersome". The potential demographic risk factors, including gender, age, marital status, education level, health condition, comorbidity, and hours of prosthetic wear per day, were found to correlate with the rating of how much the phantom limb sensation or phantom limb pain bothered respondents (Wang, 2020).

Residual Limb Pain

Residual limb pain usually occurs immediately after amputation; its prevalence was reported to range from 55% to 76% in studies among long-standing amputees (Ephraim et al., 2005; Smith et al., 1999). Wang and colleagues (2020) reported that 73% of amputees had experienced residual limb pain in the four weeks before the investigation. The prevalence of residual limb pain in amputees was found to be associated with ages between 30 and 49 years, being widowed, lower education levels, unemployment, poor health, comorbidities, and wearing prostheses for fewer than five hours a day. This is similar to a previous study, which suggested that the likelihood of experiencing residual limb pain was increased by traumatic disease, lower limb amputation, and comorbidities (Ephraim et al., 2005). In Wang et al.'s study (2020), one-third of the amputees who had residual limb pain characterised their pain as of "severe intensity", which is comparable to other studies among amputees with traumatic and vascular diseases or veteran amputees. In addition, 40% of the amputees with residual limb pain said they found the pain to be "severely bothersome". This is the same percentage as those with phantom limb pain (also 40%), suggesting that these two types of amputation-related pain are likely to have a similar impact on amputees 10 years after the earthquake. Amputees with ages ranging from 50 to 69 years, who were illiterate, had poor health, had comorbidities, and wore prostheses for fewer than five hours a day were more likely to characterise their residual limb pain as of "severe intensity" and "severely bothersome".

Non-amputated Limb Pain

It has been pointed out that the source of amputation-related pain is not necessarily limited to the amputated limb. In Wang et al.'s study (2020), the prevalence of pain in the non-amputated limb (leg or foot) appeared in 48% of the amputees. This figure is comparable to the 50% reported in a previous study (Ephraim et al., 2005). A possible link between the specific domain of age and non-amputated limb pain was noted in Wang et al.'s study; amputees aged between 30 and 69 years had a significantly higher prevalence (59.1–60%) than those aged under 30 (33.3%) or over 70 (37.5%). Moreover, amputees living independently were 15% more likely to report non-amputated limb pain than those living dependently. These results broke some new ground when compared with previous studies; previously, the prevalence of non-amputated limb pain had only been found to correlate with the time since amputation, gender, comorbidities, and the level of amputation, not with age or aetiology. More studies are needed to elucidate the relationship between non-amputated limb pain and demographic variables, such as the age and living conditions of amputees. In Wang et al.'s study, 22% of the amputees with non-amputated limb pain rated the intensity of pain as "severe", and the mean intensity was lower than that of phantom limb pain and residual limb pain. Similar to the findings of Ehde et al. (2000), this pain was described as being "severely bothersome" in Wang et al.'s study by 34% of the amputees with non-amputated limb pain, indicating the need for physicians to investigate if there is actually pain in the non-amputated limb as well as due to the phantom limb and the residual limb, and to further identify the impact if the pain does exist. It is also worth noting that the intensity of non-amputated limb pain was associated with the age of the amputee; those aged between 10 and 29 years reported significantly less pain intensity than those within the 30–69 range. Among all demographic characteristics, only poor general health was linked to a greater chance of amputees characterising their pain as being "severely bothersome".

Back Pain

Back pain is regarded as a secondary disability, affecting 52% to 89% of patients who have undergone lower limb amputations (Devan et al., 2017; Highsmith et al., 2019). This figure is much higher than the estimated mean global prevalence of 31% (Hoy et al., 2012). Back pain was reported by 67% of amputees 10 years after the Sichuan earthquake (Wang et al., 2020). It was found that the prevalence of back pain increased in amputees who were unemployed, had poor general health, and had comorbidities. In addition, two demographic variables—female amputees aged between 50 and 69 years and illiteracy—were found to be associated with "severely bothersome" back pain following amputations.

Summary

This chapter reviews the quality of life of lower limb amputees 10 years after the 2008 Sichuan earthquake in China. It concludes by suggesting some useful strategies for the preparation and delivery of effective prosthetic services.

The long-term impacts of the 2008 Sichuan earthquake on the prosthesis-related QoL of the victims have been investigated in several studies, as reviewed above. The findings enhance our understanding of prosthesis-related QoL and provide useful references for the future development of post-disaster rehabilitation strategies to improve the QoL of victims after amputations. Furthermore, potential demographic risk factors—namely, age, marital status, education level, living conditions, and comorbidities—were found to be associate with prosthesis-related QoL (Chu and Wong, 2016; Li et al., 2015; Li et al., 2019; Wang et al., 2021b). It is crucial for governments and healthcare professionals to take note of these findings, deliver appropriate support to vulnerable victims, and facilitate post-earthquake amputees in returning to their normal lives.

Phantom limb sensation, phantom limb pain, residual limb pain, non-amputated limb pain, and back pain were found to be highly prevalent in victims after amputations. Most of the amputation-related pain occurred just once or twice during a four-week period. Although the intensity of amputation-related pain was reported as moderate, up to 40% of amputees still experienced severe pain. These results highlight the importance of the scientific assessment and rehabilitation management of pain as part of long-term post-disaster strategies, especially for victims with amputations (Wang et al., 2020).

When researchers study the prescription and use of prosthetics interventions for individuals with limb loss, they find a significant lack of epidemiological information about the victims. Therefore, for amputees after a disaster, it is of utmost importance that a limb loss and disaster management registry be established. The registry will collect information about limb loss prevention, amputation surgery, prosthetic services, rehabilitation, as well as data on the assessment of the QoL of victims living with limb loss. The goal of this registry is to improve and optimise prosthetic care and outcomes for post-disaster amputees.

Over the past 25 years, advancements in prosthetics technologies have contributed substantially to the improvement of the function, participation, and QoL of individuals living with limb loss (Wolf et al., 2020). State-of-the-art scientific development in the areas of intuitive control and sensation across prosthetic devices has brought new hope to amputees, especially post-disaster victims. Disaster-affected amputees are counting on contemporary research and innovative development efforts in external systems, implanted systems, surgical approaches, and regenerative approaches to enable full restoration to their lives in future. Although prosthetics care tends to dominate attention in the rehabilitation field, it is important to note that optimising surgical and rehabilitative care is an equally vital component of enhancing the functional recovery and QoL of victims with limb loss. Prospective longitudinal studies investigating the long-term effects of post-disaster rehabilitation programmes on the QoL of amputees are therefore also needed.

References

Awais, S. M., Dar, U. Z., and Saeed, A. (2012). Amputations of limbs during the 2005 earthquake in Pakistan: A firsthand experience of the author. *International Orthopaedics, 36*(11), 2323–2326.

Bartels, S. A., and Van Rooyen, M. J. (2012). Medical complications associated with earthquakes. *Lancet, 379*(9817), 748–757.

Castillo-Avila, R., Arias-Vázquez, P., González-Castro, T., Tovilla-Zárate, C., Juárez-Rojop, I., López-Narváez, M., and Fresán, A. (2021). Evaluation of the quality of life in individuals with amputations in relation to the etiology of their amputation: A case-control study. *Physiotherapy Theory and Practice, 37*(12), 1313–1320.

Christensen, J., Ipsen, T., Doherty, P., and Langberg, H. (2016). Physical and social factors determining quality of life for veterans with lower-limb amputation(s): A systematic review. *Disability and Rehabilitation, 38*(24), 2345–2353.

Chu, C. K., and Wong, M. S. (2016). Comparison of prosthetic outcomes between adolescent transtibial and transfemoral amputees after Sichuan earthquake using Step Activity Monitor and Prosthesis Evaluation Questionnaire. *Prosthetics and Orthotics International, 40*(1), 58–64.

Darnall, B. D., Ephraim, P., Wegener, S. T., Dillingham, T., Pezzin, L., Rossbach, P., and MacKenzie, E. J. (2005). Depressive symptoms and mental health service utilization among persons with limb loss: Results of a national survey. *Archives of Physical Medicine and Rehabilitation, 86*(4), 650–658.

Devan, H., Tumilty, S., and Smith, C. (2012). Physical activity and lower-back pain in persons with traumatic transfemoral amputation: A national cross-sectional survey. *Journal of Rehabilitation Research and Development, 49*(10), 1457–1466.

Devan, H., Hendrick, P., Hale, L., Carman, A., Dillon, M. P., and Ribeiro, D. C. (2017). Exploring factors influencing low back pain in people with nondysvascular lower limb amputation: A national survey. *Physical Medicine and Rehabilitation, 9*(10), 949–959.

Ehde, D. M., Czerniecki, J. M., Smith, D. G., Campbell, K. M., Edwards, W. T., Jensen, M. P., and Robinson, L. R. (2000). Chronic phantom sensations, phantom pain, residual limb pain, and other regional pain after lower limb amputation. *Archives of Physical Medicine and Rehabilitation, 81*(8), 1039–1044.

Ephraim, P. L., Wegener, S. T., MacKenzie, E. J., Dillingham, T. R., and Pezzin, L. E. (2005). Phantom pain, residual limb pain, and back pain in amputees: Results of a national survey. *Archives of Physical Medicine and Rehabilitation, 86*(10), 1910–1919.

Foote, C. E., Kinnon, J. M., Robbins, C., Pessagno, R., and Portner, M. D. (2015). Long-term health and quality of life experiences of Vietnam veterans with combat-related limb loss. *Quality of Life Research, 24*(12), 2853–2861.

Friel, K. (2005). Componentry for lower extremity prostheses. *Journal of the American Academy of Orthopaedic Surgeons, 13*(5), 326–335.

Guo, J., He, H., Qu, Z., Wang, X., and Liu, C. (2017). Post-traumatic stress disorder and depression among adult survivors 8 years after the 2008 Wenchuan earthquake in China. *Journal of Affective Disorders, 210,* 27–34.

Harness, N., and Pinzur, M. S. (2001). Health related quality of life in patients with dysvascular transtibial amputation. *Clinical Orthopaedics and Related Research, 383,* 204–207.

Highsmith, M. J., Goff, L. M., Lewandowski, A. L., Farrokhi, S., Hendershot, B. D., Hill, O. T., Rabago, C. A., Russell-Esposito, E., Orriola, J. J., and Mayer, J. M. (2019). Low back pain in persons with lower extremity amputation: A systematic review of the literature. *The Spine Journal, 19*(3), 552–563.

Hoy, D., Bain, C., Williams, G., March, L., Brooks, P., Blyth, F., Woolf, A., and Buchbinder, R. (2012). A systematic review of the global prevalence of low back pain. *Arthritis and Rheumatology, 64*(6), 2028–2037.

Ladlow, P., Phillip, R., Etherington, J., Coppack, R., Bilzon, J., McGuigan, M. P., and Bennett, A. N. (2015). Functional and mental health status of United Kingdom military amputees post-rehabilitation. *Archive of Physical Medicine and Rehabilitation, 96*(11), 2048–2054.

Larbig, W., Andoh, J., Huse, E., Stahl-Corino, D., Montoya, P., Seltzer, Z., and Flor, H. (2019). Pre- and postoperative predictors of phantom limb pain. *Neuroscience Letters, 702,* 44–50.

Legro, M. W., Reiber, G. D., Smith, D. G., del Aguila, M., Larsen, J., and Boone, D. (1998). Prosthesis evaluation questionnaire for persons with lower limb amputations: Assessing prosthesis-related quality of life. *Archives of Physical Medicine and Rehabilitation, 79*(8), 931–938.

Li, L., Reinhardt, J. D., Zhang, X., Pennycott, A., Zhao, Z., Zeng, X., and Li, J. (2015). Physical function, pain, quality of life and life satisfaction of amputees from the 2008 Sichuan earthquake: A prospective cohort study. *Journal of Rehabilitation Medicine, 47*(5), 466–471.

Li, W. S., Chan, S. Y., Chau, W. W., Law, S. W., and Chan, K. M. (2019). Mobility, prosthesis use and health-related quality of life of bilateral lower limb amputees from the 2008 Sichuan earthquake. *Prosthetics and Orthotics International, 43*(1), 104–111.

Li, Y., Pan, F., and Li, Y. (2009). Analysis of rehabilitation needs, measures taken, and their effectiveness for the wounded following the Wenchuan Earthquake. *Journal of Evidence-Based Medicine, 2*(4), 258–264.

Luetmer, M., Mundell, B., Kremers, H. M., Visscher, S., Hoppe, K. M., and Kaufman, K. R. (2019). Low back pain in adults with transfemoral amputation: A retrospective population-based study. *Physical Medicine and Rehabilitation, 11*(9), 926–933.

Markatos, K., Karamanou, M., Saranteas, T., and Mavrogenis, A. F. (2019). Hallmarks of amputation surgery. *International Orthopaedics, 43*(2), 493–499.

Miller, M. J., Magnusson, D. M., Lev, G., Fields, T. T., Cook, P. F., Stevens-Lapsley, J. E., and Christiansen, C. L. (2018). Relationships among perceived functional capacity, self-efficacy, and disability after dysvascular amputation. *Physical Medicine and Rehabilitation, 10*(10), 1056–1061.

Morgan, S. J., Friedly, J. L., Amtmann, D., Salem, R., and Hafner, B. J. (2017). Cross-sectional assessment of factors related to pain intensity and pain interference in lower limb prosthesis users. *Archives of Physical Medicine and Rehabilitation, 98*(1), 105–113.

O'Keeffe, B., and Rout, S. (2019). Prosthetic rehabilitation in the lower limb. *Indian Journal of Plastic Surgery, 52*(1), 134–143.

Parker, K., Kirby, R. L., Adderson, J., and Thompson, K. (2010). Ambulation of people with lower-limb amputations: Relationship between capacity and performance measures. *Archives of Physical Medicine and Rehabilitation, 91*(4), 543–549.

Penn-Barwell, J. G. (2011). Outcomes in lower limb amputation following trauma: A systematic review and meta-analysis. *Injury, 42*(12), 1474–1479.

Pinzur, M. S., Pinto, M. A., Saltzman, M., Batista, F., Gottschalk, F., and Juknelis, D. (2006). Health-related quality of life in patients with transtibial amputation and reconstruction with bone bridging of the distal tibia and fibula. *Foot and Ankle International, 27*(11), 907–912.

Richardson, C., Crawford, K., Milnes, K., Bouch, E., and Kulkarni, J. (2015). A clinical evaluation of postamputation phenomena including phantom limb pain after lower limb amputation in dysvascular patients. *Pain Management Nursing, 16*(4), 561–569.

Sinha, R., and Van Den Heuvel, W. J. (2011). A systematic literature review of quality of life in lower limb amputees. *Disability and Rehabilitation, 33*(11), 883–899.

Smith, D. G., Ehde, D. M., Legro, M. W., Reiber, G. E., del Aguila, M., and Boone, D. A. (1999). Phantom limb, residual limb, and back pain after lower extremity amputations. *Clinical Orthopaedics and Related Research, 361,* 29–38.

Trevelyan, E. G., Turner, W. A., and Robinson, N. (2016). Perceptions of phantom limb pain in lower limb amputees and its effect on quality of life: A qualitative study. *British Journal of Pain, 10*(2), 70–77.

Wang, Q., Chen, C., Zhang, S., Tang, Y., Wang, H., Zhou, X., and Wong, M. S. (2020). Pain issues in the victims with lower-limb amputation: 10 years after the 2008 Sichuan earthquake. *Disability and Rehabilitation, 44*(8), 1346–1353.

Wang, Q., Chen, C., Zhang, S., Tang, Y., Wang, H., Zhou, X., and Wong, M. S. (2021a). Comparison of pain and quality of life between the victims with transfemoral and transtibial amputation 10 years after the Wenchuan earthquake. *West China Medical Journal, 36*(12), 1686–1691.

Wang, Q., Chen, C., Zhang, S., Tang, Y., Wang, H., Zhou, X., and Wong, M. S. (2021b). Quality of life in lower-limb amputees 10 years after the 2008 Sichuan earthquake: A cross-sectional study. *Disaster Medicine and Public Health Preparedness, 16* (4), 1573–1579.

Wang, Q., Chen, C., Zhang, S., Tang, Y., Wang, H., Wong, M. S., and He, C. Q. (2022). Low back pain and its risk factors in lower limb amputee victims 10 years after the Wenchuan earthquake. *Chinese Journal of Physical Medicine and Rehabilitation, 44*(2), 168–170.

Wolf, E. J., Cruz, T. H., Emondi, A. A., Langhals, N. B., Naufel, S., Peng, G. C. Y., Schulz, B. W., and Wolfson, M. (2020). Advanced technologies for intuitive control and sensation of prosthetics. *Biomedical Engineering Letters, 10*(1), 119–128.

Wurdeman, S. R., Stevens, P. M., and Campbell, J. H. (2018). Mobility analysis of amputees (MAAT I): Quality of life and satisfaction are strongly related to mobility for patients with a lower limb prosthesis. *Prosthetics and Orthotics International, 42*(5), 498–503.

Yilmaz, M., Gulabi, D., Kaya, I., Bayram, E., and Cecen, G. S. (2016). The effect of amputation level and age on outcome: an analysis of 135 amputees. *European Journal of Orthopaedic Surgery and Traumatology, 26*(1), 107–112.

5

Earthquake Preparedness among People with and without Experience of Earthquakes and Injuries in China

Kenneth N. K. FONG
Department of Rehabilitation Sciences, The Hong Kong Polytechnic University

Peng LIAO and Cong WANG
Occupational Therapy Department, School of Rehabilitation,
Kunming Medical University

Hong ZHU
Occupational therapist, private practice, Chengdu

Qiuyun WANG
Yunnan Medical Health College

Danli WU
Yunnan University of Chinese Medicine

Cecilia W. P. LI-TSANG
Department of Rehabilitation Sciences, The Hong Kong Polytechnic University

Disaster risk management is a general approach to managing risks related to disasters. The process of the disaster risk management cycle is divided into four stages, namely, disaster response, disaster recovery, disaster prevention, and disaster preparedness. In this chapter, the authors report on a questionnaire survey which investigated the differences in responses to earthquake preparedness among people with and without experience of earthquakes and physical injuries in Sichuan and Yunnan in China. Altogether, 110 participants were recruited using convenience sampling; they were people with or without any physical injuries from an earthquake, and people who had or had not experienced an earthquake before. The survey findings showed that a majority (81%) of the participants got information about earthquake preparedness through television and 45% through the internet and smartphones. Many (73%) of them had studied how to respond to an earthquake, and 72% knew how to ensure their own safety during an earthquake. It was found that the higher the respondents' educational level, the higher the percentage of people (92%) who knew how to stay safe during an earthquake. The authors come to the conclusion that, in future, computer applications (apps) integrating capacities in disaster management and the dissemination of emergency information during an earthquake, which can be used through existing popular platforms such as WeChat, should be an effective way to improve disaster responses.

Background

A disaster is defined as "a serious disruption of the functioning of a society at any scale due to hazardous events interacting with conditions of exposure, vulnerability and capacity, leading to one or more human, material, economic and environmental losses that may exceed the ability of the affected community or society to cope using its own resources" (United Nations General Assembly, 2016, p. 13; ReliefWeb, 2008, p. 19). A natural disaster is a situation or event caused by nature that overwhelms local capacity, thereby necessitating a request to a national or international entity for external assistance; it is an unforeseen and often sudden event that causes great damage, destruction, and human suffering (Vos et al., 2010).

China is a disaster-prone country; it experiences many natural disasters every year, particularly in the form of earthquakes in recent years. China is located primarily in the southeastern part of the Eurasian plate, but the Indian plate, the Pacific plate, and the Philippine Sea plate also interact and exert an influence on the country (Beijing Earthquake Agency, 2010). A survey has shown that, although China does not experience the most serious earthquakes in the world, it is the country most affected by earthquakes. Earthquakes cause one of the highest mortality rates in China and account for 54% of the total disaster deaths worldwide. In recent years, China has experienced the 8.1 magnitude Wenchuan earthquake in 2008, the 7.0 magnitude Ya'an earthquake in 2013, and the 6.1 magnitude Ludian earthquake in 2014, three of the country's most destructive earthquakes. These earthquakes have triggered an awareness of how important disaster prevention and reduction are, and how information regarding earthquake preparedness needs to be promoted in society. These strong earthquakes have caused enormous physical losses and destruction, and numerous casualties, including from various manifestations of fear, anxiety, or mental distress (Rehdanz et al., 2015; Alexander, 2004). Earthquakes occur suddenly and violently, are unpredictable and devastating, and are difficult to prepare for and prevent. Their influence is wide and long term. They not only affect the country's economic development in direct and indirect ways, but also pose a threat to people's physical and mental health, which has a direct and negative impact on people's quality of life.

The Worldwide Scene

The following section describes the worldwide scene of disaster preparedness.

Disaster Preparedness in China

Disaster risk management includes policies, administrative decisions, and operational activities carried out by different sectors of society in regard to responding to disasters. Disaster risk management is the active preparation for a possible disaster before it happens; it is also the approach to managing risk and the process of risk avoidance (Gympie Regional Council, 2014). There are four stages in the disaster risk management cycle (Fig. 5.1): 1) disaster response (how to save lives, reduce health impacts, ensure public safety, provide humanitarian aid to victims, etc.), 2) disaster recovery (reconstruction and rehabilitation of victims' physical and mental well-being), 3) disaster prevention (evaluating the possibility of a new disaster and avoiding existing disasters and their potential impacts), and 4) disaster preparedness (public disaster education and the preparation of a plan by the government, communities, and individuals to effectively anticipate and respond to the disasters) (Gympie Regional Council, 2014; United Nations Office for Disaster Risk Reduction, 2017). Disaster risk management in China is largely carried out in the form of a top-down model, in which disaster rescue and reconstruction are mainly decided by the central government.

Figure 5.1 Disaster risk management cycle

Public education and preparation planning by the government, communities, and individuals to effectively anticipate and respond to the disasters	Disaster Preparedness	Disaster Response	How to save lives, reduce health impacts, ensure public safety, provide humanitarian aid to victims, etc.
Evaluating the possibility of a new disaster and avoiding existing disasters and their potential impacts	Disaster Prevention	Disaster Recovery	Reconstruction and rehabilitation of victims' physical and mental well-being

Disaster preparedness is the last stage of disaster risk management, in which pre-disaster preparedness and post-disaster recovery are of equal status. It aims to predict, prevent, and respond to sudden occurrences. As earthquake disaster management in China began relatively late, the provision of knowledge and education for earthquake preparedness to the public is still not in place. Comfort et al. (1999) suggest that current disaster policies are lopsided and emphasise rescue and assistance only after a disaster has occurred. Because disasters are usually unforeseeable, policymakers should focus more on disaster preparedness to reduce human vulnerability following a disaster.

Disaster preparedness should therefore be conducted in policy, planning, action, and practice at the national and regional levels, through governmental disaster management. Common preparedness measures consist of the setting of warning systems, protocols and procedures, planning, and training (Purcell, 2004; Stein, 2011). The use of educational technology to develop knowledge regarding disasters within national and local communities is the first step toward disaster readiness. A long-term plan for earthquake preparedness and earthquake risk reduction should be implemented by raising community awareness and influencing policy making. Earthquake preparedness education should include physical and psychological knowledge on how to cope with an earthquake. Disaster coping strategies will help prevent people from experiencing long-term traumatic effects as a result of disasters. Disaster victims will be assisted by different government organisations, non-governmental organisations (NGOs), and people's self-organisation, all of which play important roles in disaster management and relief (Li et al., 2015). Other strategies, such as breaking the traditional pattern of governmental predominance in disaster relief and combining victims' self-help efforts with public participation, can make earthquake disaster prevention and reduction more popular and effective in China. Disaster risk management must include people with disabilities as they are the world's largest minority—the most marginalised and vulnerable people in the community in terms of literacy, employment, and mortality rates compared to those without disabilities (United Nations, 2023).

Overseas Experiences in Disaster Preparedness

Japan and the United States have more experience than China with disaster relief, and their preparations for disaster emergencies are relatively mature (Greer, 2012). These countries focus on disaster preparedness and target children in schools, as well as residents in communities (Greer, 2012). First, they have set up well-developed regulatory systems of disaster relief policies, and programmes for disaster preparedness planning. Second, they pay particular attention to a preventive approach through earthquake education in primary and secondary schools, and the entire population participates in emergency mutual support training (Chan and Lau, 2013). Some countries focus on a remedial approach by minimising damage and taking measures to direct recovery from the damage once a disaster has occurred (Tan, 2013). In most countries, training exercises and practices for emergencies, as well as preparedness education, are provided mainly by community organisations (New Zealand Civil Defence Emergency Management, 2012). Improving earthquake preparedness education can also reduce secondary injuries that arise from people's fear. Such actions are useful for relief efforts when an earthquake disaster suddenly occurs, and may help a community avoid economic loss.

Questionnaire Survey

In order to understand the current phenomenon of disaster preparedness in China, the authors conducted a questionnaire survey in two provinces to identify the current status of people's behavioural responses to earthquakes. The survey assessed people's quality of life and physical and mental health following an earthquake in the areas of disaster prevention and mitigation. The objectives of the survey were as follows: (1) to investigate the relationship between health conditions and earthquake preparedness among people with and without earthquake experience in Yunnan and Sichuan provinces; (2) to investigate the public's knowledge and understanding of earthquakes; and (3) to compare the differences among people's responses to earthquakes with and without earthquake experience, and with and without injuries. The survey results were presented orally at the Fourth Multidisciplinary Conference of Risk, Disaster, and Crisis Management at the Center for Risk, Disaster, and Crisis Management at Nanjing University, Nanjing, China, on 5 and 6 May 2018.

Participants

All participants were selected using convenience sampling in Yunnan and Sichuan provinces. Sampling was conducted in four typical earthquake-prone areas: Yiliang in Yunnan, hit by a 5.7 magnitude earthquake in 2012; Ludian in Yunnan, affected by a 6.5 magnitude earthquake in 2014; Wenchuan in Sichuan, struck by an 8.0 magnitude earthquake in 2008; and Ya'an in Sichuan, hit by a 7.0 magnitude earthquake in 2013. The data from participants with and without injuries resulting from earthquakes were collected in hospitals in Kunming in Yunnan and Chengdu in Sichuan.

The survey recruited 110 participants who were divided into four groups: group 1 consisted of those who had suffered from injuries during an earthquake (n = 30); group 2 consisted of those who had not experienced injuries during an earthquake (n = 30); group 3 consisted of those who had never experienced either an earthquake or an injury (n = 30); and group 4 consisted of those who had never experienced an earthquake but who had experienced injuries due to other accidents (n = 20).

Instruments

The modified version of the California Earthquake Preparedness Survey (CEPS) from the University of California (Kano et al., 2009) was used to measure the behavioural responses of participants who had experienced an earthquake. Other measurement tools used to evaluate the health conditions of participants included the 12-item Short Form Health Survey (SF-12) (Lam et al., 2005), the Mini–Mental State Examination (MMSE) (Folstein et al., 1975; Luo et al., 2002), the Timed Up and Go Test (TUG) (Podsiadlo and Richardson, 1991), and the Impact of Event Scale–Revised (IES-R). They were used to assess the health condition of participants after an earthquake in terms of general health, cognition, mobility, and the presence of post-traumatic stress disorder (PTSD), respectively. All of the questionnaires and tests were administered by investigators through face-to-face interviews.

In this survey, we used five different instruments. The first is a modified version of the CEPS, used to investigate the preparedness of people with and without earthquake experience (Kano et al., 2009). The survey was first translated into Chinese by the authors and validated in terms of the appropriateness of its cultural context by a panel of five members from different disciplines: occupational therapists, social workers, rehabilitation physicians, lawyers, and university professors. It was designed to focus on the respondents' knowledge and understanding of emergency handling and their means of escape within their living environments during an earthquake, as well as their use of public resources and facilities afterward.

The second is the SF-12, a self-perceived general health status survey that has been validated in China, where a general population norm is available with international comparability (Lam et al., 2005). The SF-12 is divided into two dimensions: (1) the physical component score (PCS), which consists of physical functioning (PF, one item), role physical (RP, one item), bodily pain (BP, one item), and general health (GH, one item); and (2) the mental component score (MCS), which consists of vitality (VT, one item), social functioning (SF, one item), role emotional (RE, one item), and mental health (MH, two items). The total score combines the physical and mental health composite scores (i.e., the PCS and the MCS). The standards of the SF-12 PCS and MCS are based on the norm of the general population of the United States, with a mean score of 50, and with higher scores indicating better health.

The third instrument is the MMSE. It is a common clinical instrument used to identify individuals with mild cognitive impairments and is a global measure of cognitive function. Any score greater than or equal to 24 points (out of 30) indicates normal cognition. Scores below 24 can indicate severe (≤ 9 points), moderate (10–18 points), or mild (19–23 points) cognitive impairment. Scores below 14 indicate cognitive impairment accompanied by illiteracy. MMSE is used to examine such cognitive functions as registration, attention and calculation, recall, language, the ability to follow simple commands, and orientation (Folstein et al., 1975; Luo et al., 2002).

The fourth instrument is the TUG. It is an objective, valid, and reliable measurement of mobility that measures the time an individual takes to stand up from a standard armchair, walk for three metres, turn around, walk back to the chair, and sit down again (Podsiadlo and Richardson, 1991). The reported predictive validity and the intra- and inter-reliabilities of the test are high (Shumway-Cook et al., 2000). We used the TUG test to measure participants' walking ability and mobility in an escape response during an accident or a disaster.

The last instrument is the IES-R. It is a short, easily administered, self-report questionnaire (Weiss, 2007) containing 17 questions. In our survey, we added five more questions to the original IES in order to identify PTSD. The extended instrument was intended to measure a person's subjective response to a specific traumatic event, especially in terms of the response sets of intrusion (intrusive thoughts, nightmares, intrusive feelings and imagery, and the re-experiencing of disassociation), avoidance (degree of responsiveness and avoidance of feelings, situations, and ideas), and hyperarousal (anger, irritability, hypervigilance, difficulty concentrating, and heightened startle response). We expected it to give a total subjective stress IES-R score. A Chinese version had been standardised (Wu and Chan, 2004) and the findings of a study in Hong Kong showed that it had a moderate correlation with the General Health Questionnaire–20 among patients who had experienced a motor vehicle accident and who had visited accident and emergency departments. A Likert scale of 1–10 was designed to ask about survey participants' perceptions of the impact of an earthquake on their daily lives, school, and work, with 10 representing the greatest impact.

In the data analysis, descriptive statistics, variance analysis, correlation analysis, and regression analysis were used. All tests were two-tailed and significance was set at 0.05. All statistical procedures were completed using SPSS Statistics software.

Demographic Findings

The demographic data collected included gender, age, educational level, and geographic region. A total of 110 participants took part in this study; 45.4% were male and 54.6% were female, and 56.4% were from Yunnan province and 43.6% were from Sichuan province. Their ages ranged from 20 to 83 years, with a mean age of 40.5 ($\pm$15.1) years. Participants classified as adults comprised 87.3% of the sample, and the elderly (aged $\geq$ 65 years) comprised 12.7%. Approximately 25% of the participants had either below primary school

Table 5.1 Demographic characteristics of the participants

Characteristics	Participants (n = 110)	Group 1 (n = 30)	Group 2 (n = 30)	Group 3 (n = 30)	Group 4 (n = 20)
Gender, n (%)	110 (100.0)	30 (100.0)	30 (100.0)	30 (100.0)	20 (100.0)
Male	50 (45.4)	15 (50.0)	17 (56.6)	10 (33.3)	8 (40.0)
Female	60 (54.6)	15 (50.0)	13 (43.4)	20 (66.7)	12 (60.0)
Age, mean ± SD	40.5 ± 15.1	60.0 ± 16.7	39.5 ± 14.7	34.3 ± 10.3	33.6 ± 13.2
Educational level, n (%)	110 (100)	30 (100.0)	30 (100.0)	30 (100.0)	20 (100.0)
Illiterate	10 (9.1)	8 (26.7)	2 (13.3)	0 (0)	0 (0)
Primary school	18 (16.4)	9 (30.0)	6 (20.0)	0 (0)	3 (15.0)
Junior high school	24 (21.8)	6 (20.0)	8 (26.7)	4 (13.3)	6 (30.0)
Senior high school	12 (10.9)	5 (16.67)	3 (10.0)	2 (13.3)	2 (13.3)
College/university	37 (33.6)	2 (13.3)	10 (33.3)	17 (56.7)	8 (40.0)
Master's degree or higher	9 (8.2)	0 (0)	1 (3.3)	7 (23.3)	1 (5.0)
Geographical region, n (%)	110 (100.0)	30 (100)	30 (100.0)	30 (100.0)	20 (100)
Yunnan	62 (56.4)	15 (50.0)	14 (46.7)	15 (50.0)	18 (90.0)
Sichuan	48 (43.6)	15 (50.0)	16 (53.3)	15 (50.0)	2 (10.0)

or full primary school education, whereas 41.8% had received education at the college level or above. The demographic characteristics of the participants are listed in Table 5.1.

Ways to Obtain Preparedness Information

Figure 5.2 shows the various means by which the participants obtained earthquake preparedness information. The two most important ways were through television programmes (81%) and the internet (45%). Information was also obtained through some more traditional channels, such as through print media and the radio (26% and 28%, respectively). However, 13 participants (8%) reported that they did not have any means of getting information.

Figure 5.2 The various means by which participants obtained earthquake preparedness information

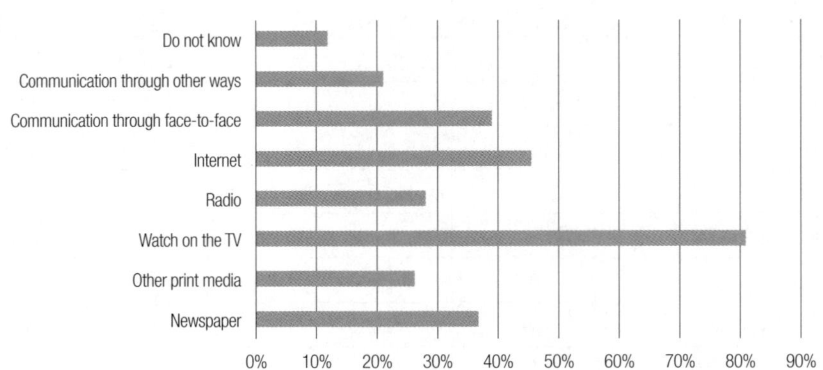

Participants' Responses to Earthquakes

Figure 5.3 shows the types of knowledge and preparations that the participants learned and used in order to respond to earthquakes. Most participants had learned how to respond to an earthquake and how to ensure their own safety (73% and 72%, respectively). One-quarter (25%) of the participants had made disaster plans before. Another quarter (approximately 26%) had made preparations for equipment and supplies that would be useful in an earthquake. However, 20 participants (18%) reported that they did not know about available information on earthquake preparedness.

Relationship between Participants' Educational Level and Preparedness

Figure 5.4 shows the relationship between the participants' educational level and their knowledge of how to stay safe during an earthquake. The results indicate that, among those who were illiterate, less than 30% knew how to keep themselves safe during an earthquake. People with a senior high school education comprised the highest percentage (91.7%) in the item "keeping safe". The second highest percentage of people with such knowledge had a college/ university level of education (78.4%).

Figure 5.3 The kinds of information and preparations participants used in their earthquake preparedness

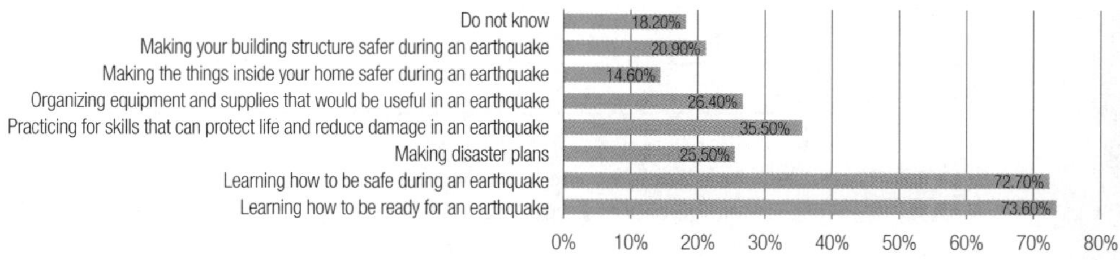

Figure 5.4 Relationship between the participants' educational levels and their knowledge of how to be safe during an earthquake

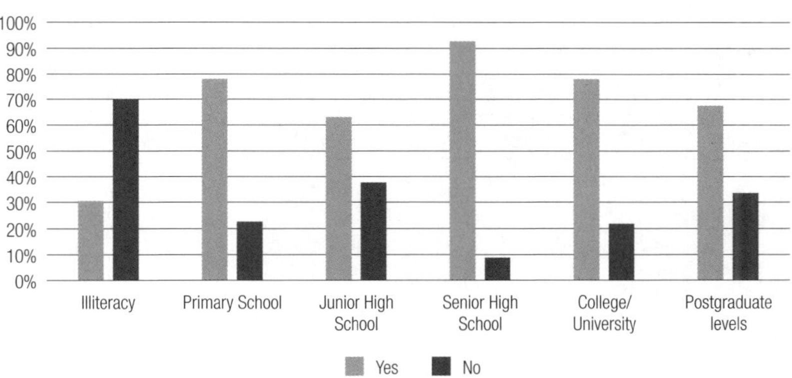

Preparedness of Participants

Table 5.2 shows the percentage of participants living in high-risk areas who had knowledge about how to stay safe during an earthquake. It shows that, in the disaster area of Ludian, only 30.0% of participants had learned how to stay safe during an earthquake.

Table 5.3 shows the percentages of participants who had taken action in regard to what they had learned about earthquake preparedness. It shows that 60.0% of the participants had learned what supplies and equipment to have on hand before an earthquake, but less than 50% of the participants had carried out the recommended actions. Only 34.6% of the participants had stored water and just 50% had stored canned or dried food in their homes or shelters.

Table 5.2 Participants living in high-risk areas who had learned how to be safe during an earthquake

	Ludian (n = 20)	Ya'an (n = 30)
Had learned, n (%)	6 (30)	29 (96.7)
Hadn't learned, n (%)	14 (70)	1 (3.3)

Table 5.3 Percentage of participants who had learned to prepare for an earthquake and percentage who had taken action

		Had (%)	Had not (%)
Knowledge	Learned what supplies and equipment to have on hand	60	40
Actions taken	Stored water	34.6	65.4
	Stored canned, dried, or other non-perishable food	50	50
	Had protective shoes in an accessible location	10	90
	Had a flashlight in an accessible location	33.6	66.4
	Kept disaster supplies in their car	11.8	88.2

Findings

Table 5.4 summarises the comparison of the subscales of the SF-12, CEPS, TUG, MMSE, and IES-R among the four groups. The results indicate that the SF-12 MCS and SF-12 PCS had strong significant differences among the four groups ($p = 0.001$). The TUG, MMSE, and IES-R subscales (PTSD: Intrusion, PTSD: Hyperarousal, PTSD: Avoidance) also had strong significant differences among groups ($p < 0.001$). Post-hoc multiple comparisons show significant differences between group 1 and group 2 and between group 1 and group 3 in the SF-12 MCS, SF-12 PCS, TUG, MMSE, PTSD: Intrusion, PTSD: Hyperarousal, and PTSD: Avoidance; between group 1 and group 4 in the SF-12 PCS, TUG, MMSE, PTSD: Intrusion, and PTSD: Avoidance; between group 2 and group 3 in PTSD: Intrusion and PTSD: Hyperarousal; and between group 3 and group 4 in the SF-12 MCS, PTSD: Intrusion, PTSD: Hyperarousal, and PTSD: Avoidance.

Table 5.4 One-way ANOVA comparisons of the differences in the SF-12, Earthquake Preparedness Questionnaire, MMSE, TUG, and IES-R scores among the four groups of participants

	Group 1 (n = 30)	Group 2 (n = 30)	Group 3 (n = 30)	Group 4 (n = 20)	F	P	Multiple comparisons
SF-12 MCS	16.60 ± 4.75	19.53 ± 3.01	19.93 ± 2.45	16.90 ± 4.79	5.806	0.001	1,2; 1,3; 3,4
SF-12 PCS	12.77 ± 1.96	10.93 ± 2.03	9.80 ± 1.75	10.90 ± 2.47	10.996	<0.001	1,2; 1,3; 1,4
TUG	14.90 ± 12.22	7.33 ± 1.77	7.87 ± 1.28	9.40 ± 2.57	8.280	<0.001	1,2; 1,3; 1,4
MMSE	22.77 ± 6.76	28.90 ± 2.14	28.83 ± 1.32	28.40 ± 2.76	16.767	<0.001	1,2; 1,3; 1,4
PTSD: Intrusion	14.90 ± 5.30	7.43 ± 5.41	3.03 ± 5.88	9.90 ± 7.88	20.147	<0.001	1,2; 1,3; 1,4; 2,3; 3,4
PTSD: Hyperarousal	10.10 ± 4.44	6.43 ± 4.81	2.13 ± 4.00	6.80 ± 5.38	15.036	<0.001	1,2; 1,3; 2,3; 3,4
PTSD: Avoidance	17.77 ± 3.84	6.57 ± 1.23	2.70 ± 5.48	7.577 ± 1.69	35.065	<0.001	1,2; 1,3; 1,4; 3,4

Table 5.5 (5a–5f) shows the results of linear regressions conducted to predict how the multiple independent variables contribute to the dependent variables. The results indicate that the MMSE (p = 0.033) and SF-12 MCS (p = 0.007) scores are significant factors that contribute to people taking actions related to earthquake preparedness. The regression correlation is 0.57, which is moderate, and these two factors explain 32.5% (R^2 = 0.325) of the total variance in "actions" (Table 5.5a).

Injury (p = 0.023) and MMSE score (p = 0.010) are significant factors that contribute to "cues" in earthquake preparedness. The regression correlation is 0.47, which is moderate, and these two factors explain 22.4% (R^2 = 0.224) of the total variance in "cues" (Table 5.5b).

The MMSE (p = 0.047) and SF-12 MCS (p = 0.018) scores are significant factors that contribute to "myths" in disaster preparedness. The regression correlation is 0.39, which is mild, and these two factors explain 15.4% (R^2 = 0.154) of the total variance in "myths" (Table 5.5c).

Gender (p = 0.001), PTSD: Intrusion (p = 0.029), MMSE (p = 0.042), and TUG (p < 0.001) scores are all significant factors that contribute to the total SF-

Table 5.5 Prediction by linear regression (method) for all participants (n = 110)

	B	SE	Sig	R	R^2
a Dependent variable: Actions					
(Constant)	−16.506	12.23	0.180	0.570	0.325
MMSE	0.50	0.23	0.033		
SF-12 MCS	0.75	0.27	0.007		
b Dependent variable: Cues					
(Constant)	−5.16	3.29	0.121	0.473	0.224
Injury	2.88	1.25	0.023		
MMSE	0.16	0.06	0.010		
c Dependent variable: Myths					
(Constant)	45.52	9.26	<0.001	0.392	0.154
MMSE	−0.35	0.18	0.047		
SF-12 MCS	−0.50	0.21	0.018		
d Dependent variable: SF-12 total score					
(Constant)	36.47	3.36	<0.001	0.672	0.452
Gender	−1.79	0.54	0.001		
PTSD: Intrusion	−0.19	0.09	0.029		
MMSE	−0.18	0.09	0.042		
TUG	−0.20	0.05	<0.001		
e Dependent variable: Impact from an earthquake					
(Constant)	0.75	2.55	0.770	0.925	0.856
PTSD: Intrusion	0.19	0.04	<0.001		
Earthquake	1.67	0.61	0.007		
Injury	2.97	0.83	0.001		
f Dependent variable: IES-R total score					
(Constant)	85.44	33.31	0.012	0.742	0.550
Injury	27.67	7.14	<0.001		
Disability	13.05	5.69	0.024		
Myths	−0.67	0.34	0.048		
SF-12 MCS	−1.78	0.69	0.012		

12 score. The regression correlation is 0.67, which is moderate, and these four factors explain 45.2% ($R^2 = 0.452$) of the total variance in the total SF-12 score (Table 5.5d).

PTSD: Intrusion ($p < 0.001$), having experienced an earthquake ($p = 0.007$), and injuries ($p = 0.001$) are significant factors that contribute to the participants' stated impact from an earthquake. The regression correlation is 0.925, which is high, and together these three factors explain 85.6% ($R^2 = 0.856$, which is high) of the total variance in the participants' stated impact from an earthquake (Table 5.5e).

Injury ($p < 0.001$), disability ($p = 0.024$), myths ($p = 0.048$), and the SF-12 MCS ($p = 0.012$) scores are significant factors that contribute to the extent to which participants are influenced by an earthquake—that is, contribute to the total IES-R score. The regression correlation is 0.74, which is moderate, and these four factors explain 55.0% ($R^2 = 0.550$) of the total variance in the participants' perception of having been influenced by an earthquake (Table 5.5f).

Comparison of Survey Results with Overseas Findings

In the United States, more than 60% of the population in earthquake-prone California have learned how to evacuate during an earthquake and about the supplies they should have on hand (California Emergency Management Agency, 2015). In general, residents in high-risk areas are more likely to have learned about how to evacuate during an earthquake. In our study, we asked two questions about the participants' disaster preparedness, focusing on their readiness to face an earthquake and their familiarity with coping procedures and recommended equipment and supplies. Our results showed that, similarly, in China, more than 60% of participants have learned earthquake preparedness. However, in one high-risk area, Ludian, 70% of the participants had not learned how to evacuate during an earthquake. This means that, after the last earthquake, the people who lived in those disaster areas did not receive effective and adequate information about earthquake preparedness.

We also found that, although 60% of the participants had learned about the kinds of supplies and equipment to have on hand, less than 50% of them had taken necessary actions. This result indicates that, in the parts of China we studied, either the current education for earthquake preparedness has not been effective, or people have not been motivated to play an active role in preparation for such a disaster. The lack of disaster readiness and disaster response is very prominent in the two earthquake-stricken provinces. For comparison, in a previous study in California, more than 80% of households were shown to have first aid kits, flashlights, and batteries in their homes. Less than 50% of households had dust masks, tools to rescue trapped people, or an extra set of emergency supplies in their car (California Emergency Management Agency, 2015). In Asia, people in Singapore and Taiwan were provided in advance with first aid kits, radios, plastic bags, water, medicine, and other supplies that were necessary for survival in emergency situations (Mukhopadhyay, 2005). However, in Yunnan and Sichuan, only 34.6% of participants had stored water and 50% had stored canned or dried food in their homes or shelters. In conclusion, people in Yunnan and Sichuan had taken insufficient action in regard to earthquake preparedness.

Faster, more accurate, and credible dissemination of information for disaster preparedness is also important. In our study, more than 85% of the participants obtained their information about earthquake preparedness from television. Relevant government departments can consider television to be the best media for disseminating information about earthquake preparedness, as television has been proven to be effective and efficient in helping people to access information, especially in rural areas, and in western China where disasters happen most frequently and the economy is less developed. Due to the low educational level of the residents and the relatively lower usage of mobile communication equipment and applications in these areas, this traditional one-way form of disaster information dissemination is therefore still the most reliable method for residents. This is no different from other places, where traditional mass media are used in one-to-many transmission during disaster communication (Andersen, 2015).

Although our study found that television programmes were the primary source from which residents got their information, multiple channels are still needed in order to reach the widest audience possible, to maintain the speed of dissemination and authenticity of the information, and for reinforcement and redundancy (Ghersetti and Odén, 2014). This is true for the most disaster-affected areas in China, especially in western China with its mountainous terrain, poor roads, disrupted communication, and slower response times for medical teams, rescuers, and hospital referrals (Redmond and Li, 2011; Burns et al., 2012). An important question remains regarding how to promote disaster communication and education that are tailored to the current situation in different areas in the most reasonable ways.

Information via the Internet

The second highest percentage of our respondents obtained their earthquake preparedness information from the internet. The internet and smartphones are now in wide use in western China (Li, 2013). With the ubiquitous presence of social media on the internet and the abundance of mobile devices in the networked world, the influence of information and communication technology on social phenomena cannot be ignored (Nilsson and Stølen, 2011). The most popular social software apps in China are QQ and WeChat, which are offered respectively through web-based and mobile phone platforms. The number of users of these software is nearly one billion (8.89 hundred million), so these two forms of communication media will continue to be significant in information transmission. The growth of socio-mobile capacities will shift crisis informatics from a top-down approach to a bottom-up interactive method through the use of social software. Social software has already changed the role of the public from being passive recipients of information to in-situ sensors and offsite volunteers. Mobile apps such as QQ and WeChat are general purpose apps that enable groups of people to send messages to each other, so they are well-suited to facilitating disaster preparedness communication and information dissemination during disasters. To further increase the usability of these apps, disaster management capacities could be integrated into existing popular platforms. For example, WeChat can extend functions for disseminating emergency information during disasters using WeChat alert functions. Compared with specialised, built-for-disaster-purpose apps, this social software approach may be more useful when disasters strike, because users are already familiar with these apps.

Use of Mobile Technology

Another kind of application that could play a role in disasters is apps built for that purpose. This kind of app is developed for five main purposes: (1) crowdsourcing; (2) collaboration; (3) alert and information dissemination; (4) information collation; and (5) user-generated notifications during disasters (Tan et al., 2017). Although China ranked among the top countries in the world with the highest number of smartphone users at more than 950 million in 2021 (Laricchia, 2022), at the moment, the built-for-disaster apps in China have less utility compared to other countries, even in the public sector. This is probably because few people know about these apps. However, these apps are currently being developed to address the emergency information needs of the public and the authorities (Schimak et al., 2015). These types of apps must be supported and endorsed by the authorities, as the access to and knowledge and usage of these apps are highly desirable in disaster preparedness education.

However, this approach often only makes sense in urban areas, where there are high levels of mobile phone usage. In rural areas, usage is less common; therefore, before planners decide on the use of mobile apps, it is essential for them to evaluate the local conditions and resources. The imbalance in development between urban and rural areas should be taken into consideration for disaster management. At the moment, mobile technology is at the forefront of innovation in regard to improving public disaster preparedness, and the use of mobile apps for disaster management will be a main trend in the future.

Conventional Communication

In our survey, two additional sources of information about earthquake preparedness were found to be newspapers (36.36% of respondents) and communication with others (29.09%). Thus, in rural areas, printed manuals and practice guidelines or pamphlets may be appropriate forms of disaster education. Advantage could be taken of rural individuals' close social networks and family ties, which could be an efficient way to spread adequate information about disaster preparedness.

In this study, our findings support the idea that the degree of effective information obtained through social networks in rural areas is relatively lower than that in urban areas (Shumway-Cook et al., 2000). Our findings show that the proportion of all respondents who had learned how to deal with an earthquake was 73.64%, and the proportion who had learned how to be safe and evacuate during an earthquake was 72.73%. These percentages are much higher than other figures. The results also indicated that less than 30% of illiterate respondents surveyed knew how to be safe during an earthquake. It is therefore suggested that oral-based educational training is very important for illiterate individuals.

Governmental Policies

There was no significant difference in "actions" among the four groups and, likewise, between the two groups with and without earthquake experience. Both results show that people in general do not have an adequate understanding of the various kinds of information about earthquakes made available to them. Further, earthquake victims are not aware of earthquake preparation. This failure to prepare may be related to a lack of information and adequate channels of communication for delivering information. After the Wenchuan earthquake, the government invested significant resources in the disaster areas, but there were no relevant departments or organisations to strengthen the dissemination of earthquake preparedness information. The authorities mainly concentrated on reconstruction and rehabilitation, and paid little attention to disaster education and disaster risk reduction. However, the government is responsible for policy making and implementing disaster risk reduction activities, so they need to provide more resources and appraise policies on public disaster management education. Governmental policies should focus on disaster preparedness, response, and relief. Otherwise, if another earthquake occurs, the probability of injury and property damage to the residents will be higher than expected. To reduce unnecessary losses, earthquake-prone areas should strengthen their promotion and training programmes for earthquake preparedness. Clearly stated follow-up actions after a disaster, in the form of systematic face-to-face training, for example, are especially beneficial and important in rural areas. In addition to this priority for government policy, community organisations could also provide face-to-face training, which is an important way to rebuild communities by consciously bringing people together.

Therefore, the first step for the government should be to educate and train professional teaching personnel, and also to set up a disaster-preparedness committee. The committee can be recruited from local volunteers and staff, who will determine efficient ways to provide the desired disaster education services in rural areas.

Effects of Literacy and Post-traumatic Stress Disorder

Both the MMSE and SF-12 MCS scores showed significant effects regarding "actions" and on "myths". In other words, if people were better educated and in a better mental state, they would do better in earthquake preparedness activities. Injury and MMSE scores also contributed to the variance in "cues". People's mobility is generally limited if they have injuries, so they will have difficulty acquiring information from their surrounding environment. We found that, although most of the respondents did not receive professional training about earthquake preparedness, some created their own earthquake preparation based on their own experiences and knowledge. We also found that, regardless of whether participants had experienced an earthquake, being in a good mental state contributed to being better prepared for an earthquake.

Our survey shows that being female, having physical disabilities, having lost relatives or friends, having sustained heavy losses of property, and having a high level of exposure to losses, human or non-human, were all main risk factors for mild mental disorders, such as PTSD (Fong et al., 2022). The study's results reveal that having experienced an earthquake, having an injury, having a disability, and SF-12 MCS scores all contribute to the variance in the total IES-R score. Having physical disabilities also has a significant impact on PTSD. Gender, PTSD: Intrusion, MMSE, and TUG scores all contribute to variance in the total SF-12 score. Being female is a significant factor predicting PTSD, which is consistent with the findings of other studies conducted in China and in other countries (Cénat and Derivois, 2014; Cofini et al., 2015; Feder et al., 2013; Kun et al., 2009). Loss of relatives and friends is significant in predicting PTSD after a disaster, which is also consistent with findings in other studies (Feder et al., 2013; Lu et al., 2021). Having physical disabilities is significantly related to being severely injured or operated on as a result of a disaster, and is also a crucial predictor of PTSD. This finding is also consistent with findings of previous studies (Zhou et al., 2013).

In general, after an earthquake, the medical services available to local residents decrease gradually during the period of recovery from the earthquake's impact. Rehabilitation treatment services may also become much scarcer. However, natural disasters frequently happen in low-income and less developed regions, where resources and humanitarian relief work are scarce and medical rehabilitation services are underdeveloped (Haig et al., 2009). Both physical and mental health have a significant impact on earthquake preparedness. In order to improve residents' physical and mental health, which may in turn benefit their earthquake preparedness at the same time, enhancing the level of medical services in less developed regions should be a priority (Kuriansky, 2006). Finally, timely psychological interventions are essential for victims suffering from PTSD, whether or not they have physical injuries from an earthquake.

Limitations

In our survey, we first found that participants' behavioural responses to earthquakes did not differ significantly between those who had experienced an earthquake before and those who had not. Second, we found that health condition had a considerable influence on the behavioural responses of people who had experienced an earthquake before, especially in terms of their mental health and cognition. Third, earthquakes had a considerable influence on PTSD, regardless of whether the participants had injuries due to an earthquake. Finally, the earthquake preparedness knowledge of participants in Yunnan or Sichuan was not sufficient.

We recognise that the sample size of our study is not large enough to represent the general population, and selection bias may exist in the data because of the use of convenience sampling. In future, we might consider adopting a random sampling method with a larger sample size in an earthquake area. The distribution of age and educational level is not even in each group. Furthermore, the Chinese version of the Modified California Earthquake Preparedness Survey lacks prior reliability and validity analysis.

Notwithstanding the limitations stated above, the findings of the survey strongly advocate for an increase in the promotion of educational efforts toward earthquake preparedness in high-risk areas, including the consideration of face-to-face education for people living in rural areas, especially for those who are illiterate. We also advocate that the internet be used to educate people living in cities about earthquake preparedness. At the very least, the public should be informed about simple strategies that they can use to cope with a disaster in the future. Government authorities should consider future policy making, management planning, as well as school education with disaster preparedness in mind.

Conclusion

Disaster risk management is a general approach to managing risks related to disasters. The process cycle is divided into four stages: disaster response, disaster recovery, disaster prevention, and disaster preparedness. This chapter presents a questionnaire survey that investigated the differences in responses to earthquake preparedness among people with and without experience of earthquakes and physical injuries in Sichuan and Yunnan in China. Altogether, 110 participants were recruited using convenience sampling; they were people with or without any physical injuries from an earthquake, and people who had or had not experienced an earthquake before. The survey findings showed that a majority (81%) of the participants obtained information about earthquake preparedness through television and 45% through the internet and smartphones. Many (73%) had studied how to respond to an earthquake, and 72% knew how to ensure their own safety during an earthquake. It was found that the higher the respondents' educational level, the higher the percentage (92%) who knew how to stay safe during an earthquake. We conclude that, in future, computer applications (apps) integrating capacities in disaster risk management and the dissemination of emergency information during an earthquake, which can be used through existing popular platforms such as WeChat, could be an effective way to improve disaster responses.

References

Alexander, D. (2004). *Planning for post-disaster reconstruction*. Paper presented at the 2004 International Conference and Student Competition on post-disaster reconstruction "Planning for reconstruction", 22–23 April 2004, Coventry, UK.

Andersen, N. B. (2015). Analysing communication processes in the disaster cycle: Complementarities and tensions. In: Rubin, O., Vendelø, M. T., and Dahlberg, R. (Eds.), *Disaster research: Multidisciplinary and international perspectives* (pp. 126–139). Abingdon: Routledge.

Beijing Earthquake Agency. (2010). *Practical guide of earthquake disaster prevention and mitigation*. Retrieved on 16 February 2022 from www.bjdzj.gov.cn/bjdzj/ztzl/302710/302716/386184/index.html.

Burns, A. S., O'Connell, C. A., and Rathore, F. (2012). Meeting the challenges of spinal cord injury care following sudden onset disaster: Lessons learned. *Journal of Rehabilitation Medicine, 44*(5), 414–420.

Cénat, J. M., and Derivois, D. (2014). Assessment of prevalence and determinants of post-traumatic stress disorder and depression symptoms in adults survivors of earthquake in Haiti after 30 months. *Journal of Affective Disorders, 159*, 111–117.

Chan, Y. W., and Lau, S. H. (2013). The effect of elementary school earthquake disaster prevention learning on parents' preparedness behavior in Japan: A case study on the Osugi-Higashi Elementary School of Tokyo. *Curriculum & Instruction Quarterly, 16*(4), 121–148.

Cofini, V., Carbonelli, A., Cecilia, M. R., Binkin, N., and di Orio, F. (2015). Post-traumatic stress disorder and coping in a sample of adult survivors of the Italian earthquake. *Psychiatry Research, 229*, 353–358.

Comfort, L., Wisner, B., Cutter, S., Pulwarty, R., Hewitt, K., Oliver-Smith, A., and Krimgold, F. (1999). Reframing disaster policy: The global evolution of vulnerable communities. *Environmental Hazards, 1*(1), 39–44.

Feder, A., Ahmad, S., Lee, E. J., Morgan, J. E., Singh, R., Smith, B. W., Southwick, S. M., and Charney, D. S. (2013). Coping and PTSD symptoms in Pakistani earthquake survivors: Purpose in life, religious coping and social support. *Journal of Affective Disorders, 147*, 156–163.

Folstein, M. F., Folstein, S. E., and McHugh, P. R. (1975). 'Mini-mental state': A practical method for grading the cognitive state of patients for the clinician. *Journal of Psychiatric Research, 12*(3), 189–198.

Fong, K. N. K., Law, Y. M., Lou, L., Zhao, Z. E., Chen, H., Ganesan, B., Lai, A. W. Y., Lee, B. H. C., Leung, A. N. T., Liu, K. Y. S., Wong, C. S. M., Li, C. W. P., Wong, M. S., and Shum, D. H. K. (2022). Post-traumatic stress disorder (PTSD) after an earthquake experience: A cross-sectional survey of Wenchuan earthquake victims with physical disabilities 10 years later. *International Journal of Disaster Risk Reduction, 80*, 103225.

Ghersetti, M., and Odén, T. A. (2014). Communicating crisis through mass media. In: Klafft, M. (Ed.), *Current issues in crisis communication and alerting* (pp. 24–33). Stuttgart: Fraunhofer Verlag.

Greer, A. (2012). Earthquake preparedness and response: Comparison of the United States and Japan. *Leadership and Management in Engineering, 12*(3), 111–125.

Gympie Regional Council. (2021). *Gympie local disaster management plan (V2.0)*. Retrieved on 20 April 2023 from www.gympie.qld.gov.au/downloads/file/3888/local-disaster-management-plan.

Haig, A., Im, J., Adewole, D., Nelson, V., and Krabak, B. (2009). The practice of physical and rehabilitation medicine in sub-Saharan Africa and Antarctica: A white paper or a black mark? *Journal of Rehabilitation Medicine, 41*(6), 401–405.

Kano, M., Wood, M. M., Kelley, M. M., and Bourque, L. B. (2009). *The study of household preparedness: Preparing California for earthquakes.* Los Angeles: University of California. Retrieved on 20 April 2023 from ssc.ca.gov/wp-content/uploads/sites/9/2020/08/cssc_09-03_the_study_of_household_preparedness_appx.pdf.

Kun, P., Han, S., Chen, X., and Yao, L. (2009). Prevalence and risk factors for post-traumatic stress disorder: A cross-sectional study among survivors of the Wenchuan 2008 earthquake in China. *Depression and Anxiety, 26,* 1134–1140.

Kuriansky, J. (2006). Working effectively with the mass media in disaster mental health. In: Reyes, G., and Jacobs, G. A. (Eds.), *Handbook of international disaster psychology: Practices and programs (vol. 1)* (pp. 127–146). Westport, Conn.: Praeger Publishers/Greenwood Publishing Group.

Lam, C. L., Tse, E. Y. Y., and Gandek, B. (2005). Is the standard SF-12 health survey valid and equivalent for a Chinese population? *Quality of Life Research, 14*(2), 539–547.

Laricchia, F. (2022). *Number of smartphone users by leading countries in 2021 (in millions)*. Statista.com. Retrieved on 20 April 2023 from www.statista.com/statistics/748053/worldwide-top-countries-smartphone-users/.

Li, L. (2013). The study of the internet and mobile phone use in urban and rural areas of West China. *China Publishing Journal, 19,* 64–68.

Li, Z., Chen, Y., and Suo, L. (2015). Impacts of social network on therapeutic community participation: A follow-up survey of data gathered after Ya'an Earthquake. *Iranian Journal of Public Health, 44*(1), 68.

Lu, B., Zeng, W., Li, Z., and Wen, J. (2021). Risk factors of post-traumatic stress disorder 10 years after Wenchuan earthquake: A population-based case–control study. *Epidemiology and Psychiatry Sciences, 30*(e25), 1–9.

Luo, Z. G., Han, J. F., and Qu, Q. M. (2002). Applicability of MMSE in West China: Who is more suitable? *Chinese Mental Health Journal, 16*(4), 246–248.

Mukhopadhyay, A. K. (2005). *Crisis and disaster management turbulence and aftermath.* New Delhi: New Age International.

New Zealand Civil Defence Emergency Management. (2012). *Group plan review: Director's guideline for civil defence emergency management groups.* Retrieved on 20 April 2023 from www.civildefence.govt.nz/memwebsite.nsf/Files/Director_Guidelines/$file/CDEM-2GP-web.pdf.

Nilsson, E. G., and Stølen, K. (2011). Generic functionality in user interfaces for emergency response. In: Paris, C., Colineau, N., Farrell, V., Farrell, G., and Huang, W. (Eds.), *Proceedings of the 23rd Australian Computer-Human Interaction Conference* (pp. 233–242). Canberra: Computer-Human Interaction Special Interest Group (CHISIG) of the Human Factors & Ergonomic Society of Australia.

Podsiadlo, D., and Richardson, S. (1991). The timed 'Up & Go': A test of basic functional mobility for frail elderly persons. *Journal of the American Geriatrics Society, 39*(2), 142–148.

Purcell, P. (2004). *Disaster prep 101: The ultimate guide to emergency readiness.* Atlanta: InfoQuest.

Redmond, A. D., and Li, J. (2011). The UK medical response to the Sichuan earthquake. *Emergency Medicine Journal, 28*(6), 516–520.

Rehdanz, K., Welsch, H., Narita, D., and Okubo, T. (2015). Well-being effects of a major natural disaster: The case of Fukushima. *Journal of Economic Behavior & Organization, 116,* 500–517.

ReliefWeb Project. (2008). *Glossary of humanitarian terms.* Geneva: ReliefWeb. Retrieved on 20 April 2023 from reliefweb.int/report/world/reliefweb-glossary-humanitarian-terms-enko.

Schimak, G., Havlik, D., and Pielorz, J. (2015). Crowdsourcing in crisis and disaster management: Challenges and considerations. In: Denzer, R., Argent, R. M., Schimak, G., and Hrebícek, J. (Eds.), *IFIP International Federation for Information Processing 2015: International Symposium on Environmental Software Systems 2015* (pp. 56–70). New York: Springer.

Shumway-Cook, A., Brauer, S., and Woollacott, M. (2000). Predicting the probability for falls in community-dwelling older adults using the Timed Up & Go Test. *Physical Therapy, 80*(9), 896–903.

Stein, M. (2011). When disaster strikes: A comprehensive guide for emergency planning and crisis survival. *International Journal of Emergency Services, 1*(2), 190–192.

Tan, N. T. (2013). Emergency management and social recovery from disasters in different countries. *Journal of Social Work in Disability & Rehabilitation, 12*(1–2), 8–18.

Tan, M. L., Prasanna, R., Stock, K., Hudson-Doyle, E., Leonard, G., and Johnston, D. (2017). Mobile applications in crisis informatics literature: A systematic review. *International Journal of Disaster Risk Reduction, 24,* 297–311.

United Nations. (2023). *Factsheet on persons with disabilities.* Retrieved on 20 April 2023 from www.un.org/development/desa/disabilities/resources/factsheet-on-persons-with-disabilities.html.

United Nations General Assembly. (2016). *Report of the open-ended intergovernmental expert working group on indicators and terminology relating to disaster risk reduction.* Document no. A/71/644. New York: United Nations.

United Nations Office for Disaster Risk Reduction. (2017). *Terminology. Disaster.* Retrieved on 16 February 2022 from www.preventionweb.net/terminology/view/475.

Vos, F., Rodríguez, J., Below, R., and Guha-Sapir, D. (2010). *Annual disaster statistical review 2009: The numbers and trends.* Brussels: Centre for Research on the Epidemiology of Disasters. Retrieved on 20 April 2023 from www.unisdr.org/files/14382_ADSR2009.

Weiss, D. S. (2007). The impact of event scale: Revised. In: Wilson, J. P., and Tang, C. S. (Eds.), *Cross-cultural assessment of psychological trauma and PTSD* (pp. 219–238). Switzerland: Springer Nature.

Wu, K. K., and Chan, S. K. (2004). Psychometric properties of the Chinese version of the Impact of Event Scale-Revised. *Hong Kong Journal of Psychiatry, 14*(4), 2–8.

Zhou, X., Kang, L., Sun, X., Song, H., Mao, W., Huang, X., Zhang, Y., and Li, J. (2013). Prevalence and risk factors of post-traumatic stress disorder among adult survivors six months after the Wenchuan earthquake. *Comprehensive Psychiatry, 54,* 493–499.

Part II

Health and Emergency Medicine:
Considerations for Hong Kong

Roles of Primary Healthcare in Major Community Events

Thomas M. C. DAO
School of Chinese Medicine, The Chinese University of Hong Kong;
Department of Family Medicine and Primary Care, The University of Hong Kong

Bean S. N. FU
The Kowloon West Cluster of the Hospital Authority;
Honorary Associate Professor, The Chinese University of Hong Kong;
Honorary Assistant Professor, The University of Hong Kong

Brendan C. Y. WU
Family medicine specialist, Assure Health Medical Centre;
Honorary Assistant Professor, The University of Hong Kong

Primary healthcare (PHC) adopts a whole-person and holistic care approach to address an individual's health needs for physical, mental, and social well-being. Most people first seek PHC in their community when they feel sick. PHC also encompasses a broader perspective on public and population health. Besides the usual and emergency care, it also has a vital role before, during, and after major community events. It plays an essential and indispensable role in the healthcare system. The first part of this chapter introduces the characteristics of PHC, how it is conceptualised in the Alma-Ata Declaration and the Astana Declaration, how it contributes to the notion of universal health coverage and the Sustainable Development Goals, and its unique role in a healthcare system. The second part illustrates the roles of PHC in a context of disease outbreak, with particular reference to the coronavirus disease 2019 (COVID-19) pandemic, including disease surveillance, diagnosis and treatment, public education, preventive care, and support for COVID-19 survivors. The last part discusses the roles of PHC in specific contexts pertaining to natural disasters and major community events, such as typhoons, floods, earthquakes, and marathons.

What is Primary Healthcare?

Primary care is the provision of integrated, accessible healthcare services by clinicians who are responsible for addressing a large majority of personal healthcare needs, developing a sustained partnership with patients, and practising in the context of family and community (Vanselow, Donaldson, and Yordy, 1995). The terms "primary care" and "primary healthcare" (PHC) are sometimes used interchangeably. To be precise, PHC encompasses a broader concept and approach to health system organisation, whereas primary care refers to the visible service-oriented element within PHC (Hone, Macinko, and Millett, 2018).

The crucial features of a PHC system are comprehensive, coordinated, continuing, person-centred, and preventive care. As stated by the World Health Organisation (WHO) and United Nations Children's Fund (UNICEF), it is a whole-of-society approach to maximise the health and well-being of individuals equitably by interventions including health promotion, disease prevention, treatment, rehabilitation, and palliative care (WHO and UNICEF, 2018). To achieve its goal, PHC has the following characteristics (Starfield, 1992; WHO, 2018).

Comprehensiveness

PHC aims to provide comprehensive care, addressing individuals' physical, psychological, and social needs as in the WHO definition of health. PHC delivers an extensive array of services for all individuals regardless of their sociodemographic factors. In contrast to highly subspecialised services, PHC provides accessible and affordable care for a wide range of health issues, from acute to chronic diseases, from paediatric to geriatric populations, from trivial to serious health problems.

Coordinated Care

PHC is one of the most cost-effective approaches to managing the population's healthcare needs by making efficient use of community healthcare resources. PHC teams can coordinate and manage healthcare services tailored to patients' needs and preferences. With more service integration, the unnecessary duplication and fragmentation of medical care can be reduced, particularly at the specialist level. Care managers and community health practitioners in PHC are professionally trained to manage patients' needs proactively through a multidisciplinary team approach.

Continuing Care

There are different healthcare needs in various stages of life. Primary care providers establish a long-term provider-patient relationship. Longitudinal continuity in PHC refers to an ongoing healthcare interaction with the same healthcare team. It is associated with high patient satisfaction, effective health resource utilisation, and desirable health outcomes, including reduced mortality. Besides longitudinal (relational) continuity, informational continuity is also essential to ensure that the most up-to-date medical records are accessible to healthcare professionals in the primary care team to provide consistent and high-quality care for patients.

Person-centredness

Person-centred care is a fundamental characteristic of PHC. In contrast to segregated, disease-based subspecialised care, PHC fosters partnerships between patients and care providers to offer comprehensive care to maintain health and well-being. Besides biomedical needs, PHC recognises the individual personhood of the patients and considers their psychological and social needs. Person-centeredness improves the quality of care, patient and provider satisfaction, health-related outcomes, and healthcare delivery efficiency. In contrast to the traditional paternalistic disease management model, person-centredness focuses more on collaborating with the patient and carers to reach a mutually satisfactory management plan after considering their ideas, concerns, and expectations.

Preventive Care

Prevention is always better than cure. Primary care health workers offer preventive care to patients in different age groups, reducing healthcare costs in both acute and chronic cases. There are four levels of prevention: primary, secondary, tertiary, and quaternary. Primary prevention refers to avoiding diseases, such as by vaccination and risk factor modification. Secondary prevention aims at identifying illness at an early stage to prevent the development of serious complications, such as cancer screening and management of hypertension to prevent cardiovascular diseases. PHC practitioners provide medical advice, health information and knowledge, investigations such as Pap smears, or prophylactic medications for travellers. Tertiary prevention includes interventions that mitigate long-term complications following an illness or injury, such as stroke and cardiac rehabilitation. According to the World Organisation of Family Doctors (2002), quaternary prevention is the action taken to prevent over-medicalisation. It protects at-risk individuals from unnecessary invasive medical procedures and promotes fair and equitable distribution of scarce medical resources.

The Alma-Ata Declaration and the Astana Declaration

The WHO Constitution states that it is a fundamental human right to have the highest attainable standard of health (International Health Conference, 2002). In 1978, the WHO and UNICEF convened an International Conference on Primary Health Care at which 134 national government members signed the Alma-Ata Declaration to recognise PHC as a policy to address health inequalities between developing and developed countries (WHO, 1978). The Declaration was one of the first international documents recognising PHC as a potential solution to improve health and reduce health inequalities. It emphasised the fullest attainment of "Health for All by 2000" and required states to commit and mobilise resources to launch and sustain PHC. PHC addresses health equity by considering social and environmental determinants of health. It is often stereotypically viewed as managing simple cases in a community clinic. In reality, PHC is inherently complex as it manages patients with all sorts of undifferentiated complaints, which poses diagnostic and therapeutic challenges to PHC providers.

Although the goal of the Alma-Ata Declaration was not entirely fulfilled after its adoption, many developing countries strove to develop PHC and achieved better population health outcomes. Forty years later, in 2018, the Astana Declaration was endorsed by more than 120 countries, reaffirming many core principles of the Alma-Ata Declaration (Hone et al., 2018). The Astana

Declaration recognised that the PHC approach is the best way to sustain a health system effectively. It reiterated the human right to health and focused on how PHC could contribute to universal health coverage (UHC) and Sustainable Development Goals (SDGs). UHC and SDGs will be further discussed below. The signatories committed to building sustainable PHC and enhancing primary care services' capacity and infrastructure with appropriate healthcare policy and financing. Bridging the gap in health service provisions is a global issue, and states should act in solidarity and leave no one behind in the pursuit of "health for all".

Universal Health Coverage and Sustainable Development Goals

UHC includes the provision of essential health services for all individuals and communities. The WHO put forward a three-part overall strategy for the progressive realisation of UHC, which involves prioritising health services, expanding coverage for high-priority services, and ensuring that disadvantaged groups are covered (WHO, 2014). Countries are making progress towards UHC by strengthening PHC within the health system. UHC also protects against the financial risks faced by the poor, including unpredictable high out-of-pocket (OOP) healthcare payments. Besides the healthcare workforce and infrastructure, affordable access to essential medicines is also important to UHC, particularly in low- to middle-income countries where OOP payments for medication constitute a significant proportion of household income of the poor. Sustainable health financing by reducing OOP payments for disadvantaged groups is therefore essential to eliminate the financial barrier to healthcare access and achieve UHC.

SDGs were developed by the United Nations and adopted by the member states in 2015 with the aim to foster global partnerships for building a sustainable environment for all. SDG 3, "Good health and well-being", is directly related to healthcare delivery. UHC is mentioned explicitly in SDG target 3.8. Although PHC is not specifically mentioned in SDGs, strong PHC could make a significant contribution to fulfilling SDG 3, including the reduction of maternal and child mortality; combating communicable diseases by disease surveillance, prevention, and treatment; managing non-communicable diseases including mental health; and controlling harmful behaviours, including the use of alcohol and tobacco. Further, PHC could contribute to other SDGs indirectly, including SDG 1 (eradication of poverty), by reducing OOP payments and providing affordable healthcare; SDG 5 (gender equality) and 10 (reduction of inequality), by advocating social justice and delivering equitable health services free of discrimination; and SDG 17 (partnership for the goals), by fostering medical-social collaboration and public-private partnerships for developing sustainable health services at the primary care level (Hone et al., 2018). These are just some examples; there are many more SDGs and targets that PHC could contribute to.

Accessibility of Primary Healthcare

Accessibility refers to the ease and timeliness of access to services in the healthcare system by a person with medical needs. Policies and infrastructures should be available to reduce the barriers to access to healthcare services for the population. Accessibility can be broken down into three domains, namely, geographical accessibility, financial accessibility, and timeliness of care. Geographical accessibility does not refer only to the location and density of community clinics and health centres but also the availability of barrier-free facilities such as accessible toilets for wheelchair users, tactile paths for the visually impaired, visual displays for the hearing impaired, and translation services to overcome language barriers. Financial accessibility refers to the cost barriers faced by those seeking medical care. OOP payments are a major determinant of financial accessibility. In PHC, OOP payments are usually lower than subspecialised services. In Hong Kong, government-funded primary care services are heavily subsidised. For each visit to a primary care physician in a general outpatient clinic, a resident is charged only HK$50 (US$6.4), medication and investigations included (Hospital Authority, n.d.). The fee is waived for patients on social security schemes and those with financial hardships to ensure health service provision to disadvantaged populations.

PHC serves as the first point of contact for patients requiring medical services. High-quality primary care can meet the majority of acute and chronic care needs. The capacity of PHC depends on the availability of effective PHC, which includes a sustainable and competent workforce that is trusted by the community. Timeliness of care is also essential to address medical needs which may require early attention, such as urgent and acute medical problems.

Community clinics with convenient operating hours, efficient appointment systems, and short waiting times can improve care access.

Role of Primary Healthcare in the Health System

There are times when the pressure on the healthcare system is tremendous, such as during infectious disease outbreaks, natural disasters, and major community events. PHC supports the system via strategies to prevent crises from happening (e.g., health promotion and education) or mitigate the risk of further harm (e.g., disaster preparedness planning, disease surveillance, and management). Strong PHC can improve resilience and prevent collapses in the health system when facing huge healthcare demand.

The strength of PHC within a health system is also associated with better health outcomes. According to an epidemiological study in the United States, for every 10 additional primary care physicians per 100,000 population, it was associated with a 51.5-day increase in life expectancy and a 0.9–1.4% reduction in mortality in cases of cardiovascular diseases, respiratory diseases, and cancer (Basu et al., 2019). PHC is also a means of cost saving. An evaluation study of a patient-centred primary care home programme in Oregon showed that with every dollar spent on PHC, US$13 were saved on in-patient or specialty services (Gelmon, Wallace, Sandberg, Petchel, and Bouranis, 2016). The strength of PHC relates to the accessibility of primary care services provided to the population.

In summary, the unique characteristics of PHC make it a practical and sustainable means to bridge the inequalities in health service delivery. PHC plays a significant role in both acute and chronic care. Evidence has shown that strong PHC can lead to improved mortality and morbidity and the population's overall health. In the following section, the authors will explore how PHC has contributed to combating the COVID-19 pandemic.

Role of Primary Care in Disease Outbreaks

Primary care providers frequently manage infectious diseases. These diseases range from simple upper respiratory tract infections to complex human immunodeficiency virus (HIV) infections requiring a multidisciplinary approach. The most common infectious diseases seen in PHC are respiratory infections, followed by gastroenteritis or skin infections. An infectious disease outbreak can progress towards a public health disaster if the chosen containment strategies fail to limit its propagation. In fact, the PHC strategy is always engaged in fighting infectious disease outbreaks. The essence of primary care is managing a person at any time point of their illness in the community, in contrast to hospital specialists, who treat relatively sick patients in an institutional setting. Comprehensive PHC involves early detection, diagnosis, management (from initial management to post-recovery care), public education, disease prevention, and surveillance. In this section, the role of PHC in disease outbreaks is illustrated with reference to the COVID-19 pandemic.

Definition of Outbreak and Novel Infectious Diseases

Novel infectious diseases are the major cause of mortality in an outbreak. A novel infectious disease is one caused by a new pathogen appearing in humans, and, most of the time, health professionals have little knowledge of it. There are various infectious agents, the majority of which are viruses, such as influenza, Ebola, Zika and, the most well-known in recent years, coronaviruses (CoV). A sudden increase in the incidence of a particular disease is defined as an outbreak. In epidemiology, alternatively, the term "epidemic" refers similarly to the occurrence of more cases of a disease than expected within a population in a certain geographic area over a given period of time. A pandemic occurs with the wide spread of the infectious agent across different geographic regions. In 2009–2010, the swine flu pandemic caused an estimated 0.7–1.4 billion infections and 151,700–575,400 deaths (Dawood et al., 2012; Donaldson et al., 2009).

COVID-19: Epidemiology and Virology

On 30 January 2020, the WHO declared a public health emergency of international concern in response to the coronavirus disease identified in 2019 (COVID-19). It is now known that COVID-19 is attributed to a novel strain of the *Coronaviridae* family—severe acute respiratory syndrome coronavirus 2 (SARS-CoV-2). Previous outbreaks of severe acute respiratory syndrome (SARS) in

2002 and Middle East respiratory syndrome in 2012 were caused by viruses of the same family. SARS-CoV-2 is an enveloped single-stranded positive-sense RNA virus belonging to the *Betacoronavirus* genus of the *Coronaviridae* family (Fernandes et al., 2022). COVID-19 presents as a syndrome characterised by fever, cough, fatigue, muscle pain, pneumonia, and acute respiratory distress. It is mainly transmitted by respiratory droplets and aerosols in extreme conditions. As of 23 July 2022, more than 500 million confirmed COVID-19 cases and over 6 million related deaths had been recorded in the world.

Furthermore, mutations during viral replication have led to the emergence of variants. Of these, Alpha, Beta, Gamma, Delta, Epsilon, and the most prevalent recently, Omicron were defined as variants of concern by the WHO, based on the risk posed to public health globally. In Hong Kong, a territory in the WHO Western Pacific Region, a tremendous upsurge of confirmed cases was observed from February 2022, with a daily peak of over 70,000 confirmed cases in March. As of 29 January 2023, there had been 2,876,106 confirmed cases and 13,333 deaths in Hong Kong (Centre for Health Protection, 2023).

Disease Surveillance

PHC serves as the first point of contact with the healthcare system. Numerous infectious diseases present with mild symptoms and can be successfully managed in the PHC setting. As such, disease surveillance in the PHC setting can frequently provide early warning of an impending outbreak of an infectious disease. Various countries across the globe with a well-established primary care system perform disease surveillance in the primary care setting. For example, the influenza surveillance system in Australia consists of general practice and hospital sentinel systems, with laboratory-confirmed notifications and a community-based online self-reported data system. In Hong Kong, regular disease surveillance for influenza and gastroenteritis is undertaken locally by the Department of Health. It is achieved by collecting data from the Clinical Management System of the Hospital Authority, representing the primary care system in the public sector, and from private primary care physicians by invitation of the Department of Health.

Following the COVID-19 pandemic, national primary care guidelines were established in many countries in response to the demands of the outbreak. As a public health function, many countries have set up surveillance systems in primary care settings (e.g., Canada, China, Ethiopia, India, Malaysia, Nigeria, and the United Kingdom; Haldane et al., 2020). This system can ensure early detection of a possible outbreak in a certain geographical region and combative measures can be implemented in time.

Early Diagnosis and Management

Early diagnosis of a highly transmissible disease is crucial for subsequent infection control measures. Hospitals and specialist clinics are also easily paralysed by the outbreak of an infectious disease with a rapid upsurge of suspected cases requiring diagnosis and management. This will negatively impact the healthcare system and, most of the time, resources will be inappropriately consumed. Mitigating measures to alleviate pressures on hospitals and specialist services are thus essential in medical emergencies and outbreaks.

In Singapore, a national policy has been established for public access to diagnosis by primary care physicians. Individuals with mild coryzal symptoms can consult their primary care doctors for assessment and diagnosis, either face-to-face or via telemedicine. With the use of rapid antigen tests of high sensitivity and specificity, an early diagnosis of COVID-19 can be confirmed within minutes. Polymerase chain reaction (PCR) tests are reserved for high-risk individuals (e.g., the elderly and immunocompromised) and those with severe symptoms for a definite diagnosis. In Italy, guidance for managing suspected and confirmed COVID-19 cases in the primary care setting was published in November 2020 (Lopes et al., 2020). Similar policies for diagnosis by primary care physicians have been adopted in various other countries, too. For example, the National Health Service (NHS) of the United Kingdom coordinates primary care, and the Department of Health and Aged Care of the Australian Government supports general practitioners in its states and territories.

In Hong Kong, the rapid upsurge of the Omicron variant in the fifth wave of COVID-19 in early 2022 posed an enormous challenge to the local healthcare system. After the SARS outbreak in 2003 and the Ebola outbreak in 2013, the role of primary care physicians in risk reduction and preparedness locally for medical emergencies quickly gained recognition. Primary care physicians in the public sector (i.e., general outpatient clinics) are involved in early assessment of confirmed cases awaiting isolation facilities. The remaining 90% of primary care physicians in the private sector focus on the early diagnosis of the disease.

People approach primary care workers when they or a member of their family have symptoms of COVID-19. Patients' clinical condition, mostly stable or with mild upper respiratory symptoms, are assessed. Doctors' most important task is to confirm diagnosis of COVID-19 by either rapid antigen or PCR tests with nasal or oropharyngeal swabs. Primary care doctors can offer advice or perform tests for patients. Managing patients' common symptoms and avoiding the spread of infectious diseases are the top priorities of primary care practice, as well as triage and referring patients who may need specialist care. Many patients also need doctors' documentation and certificates of vaccination or infection to fulfil requirements in their community.

Support in Community Treatment Facilities

Community treatment facilities are community-based premises offering medical care, but not to the level of a standard hospital setting. These facilities range from polyclinics comprising different disciplines (e.g., primary care, physiotherapy, dietetics, podiatry, etc.) to medical centres offering basic hospital-level care. These facilities are usually found in less populated areas, serving as a bridge between primary care and hospital specialists. Most are operated by primary care professionals and thus are also referred to as primary care facilities. For example, in Iran, a country prone to natural disasters, each "health house" serves about 1,200 inhabitants with a healthcare worker called a *behvarz* (Yari et al., 2021). There are also larger rural PHC facilities staffed by a physician and a team of up to 10 healthcare workers providing a more comprehensive range of services in areas such as maternal and child healthcare, reproductive health, and mental health, to a population of up to 7,000 people.

In the COVID-19 pandemic, community treatment facilities serve diversified purposes. These facilities often serve as a triage point that provides readily accessible care, diagnosis, and initial management for people suspected of having or confirmed to have COVID-19. The spread of the disease can be thus contained and reduced across the community. Vaccination can be provided to the community in these facilities. In addition, the burden on hospitals can be alleviated by these facilities through medication refill programmes. Patients with chronic diseases in the community can refill their medications and have their conditions reviewed by primary care physicians.

In Hong Kong, the primary care system mainly involves testing and vaccination for COVID-19. Community testing and community vaccination centres are primarily operated by private enterprises or private hospitals.

Public Education

Providing anticipatory care to patients is an essential component of primary care. With the unique role of primary care in the provision of continuous and comprehensive care and as the first point of contact with the healthcare system, primary care physicians can offer patients appropriate and tailor-made preventive advice. In the context of COVID-19, patient education and health literacy in infection outbreaks can be integrated into the continuity of care model and achieved in day-to-day consultations. The public can be informed easily of protective measures such as regular handwashing, the use of face masks, and avoiding crowds by primary care physicians well trained in dealing with patients and behaviour modification.

COVID-19 not only poses physical health risks but also has negative psychological impacts. With stringent infection control measures such as social distancing, prohibition of gatherings, travel restrictions, and lockdowns, people often feel isolated and unsupported and may fall into anxiety and depression. Primary care physicians can enhance public awareness by educating people about these associated mental health problems, and manage the affected people in the community.

Preventive Care: Vaccination

Vaccination represents the most cost-effective primary preventive strategy for combating infectious diseases. Apart from reducing morbidity and mortality, preventing infectious diseases through vaccination has financial benefits because of lowering hospitalisation rates, prevention of long-term disability, and increased productivity. Primary healthcare providers are well known to be involved in national vaccination programmes, promoting and providing vaccinations to people according to their age group. The seasonal influenza vaccine is the largest-scale global vaccination programme and most influenza vaccinations are performed in the primary care setting.

The role of promoting and offering vaccines has been maintained in the COVID-19 pandemic. Current evidence shows that mass vaccination has reasonable efficacy and safety (Fathizadeh et al., 2021). In most countries, vaccination against COVID-19 is conducted through the PHC system. For example, in Australia and the UK, vaccines are administered by general practitioners. In Hong Kong there is a mixed model involving community vaccination centres, which are mainly operated by private primary care enterprises, and primary care physicians.

Supporting the Physical and Mental Needs of Survivors and Families

COVID-19 survivors may have long-term physical and psychological problems. Post-COVID symptoms, also known collectively as "long COVID", are defined as symptoms persisting more than four weeks after the infection. Long COVID occurs not only amongst patients hospitalised with severe symptoms but also amongst those who were asymptomatic or had only mild symptoms (Vance et al., 2021). Post-COVID symptoms can be respiratory, cognitive, and neurological, and include chronic fatigue, dysautonomia, and anosmia. In countries with huge numbers of confirmed cases, hospital specialists cannot take care of all discharged patients. In the US and Spain, guidelines were established for managing post-COVID symptoms in primary care (Sisó-Almirall et al., 2021). These guidelines focus on not only prolonged physical symptoms resulting from infection but also the management of psychological disorders, such as psychological distress, post-traumatic stress disorder (PTSD), anxiety, and depression (Wright, Gnanapragasam, Downes, and Bisson, 2021).

As the unique specialism providing holistic care, primary care has always played an important role in managing carer stress. In one study, 46.1% of family members of COVID-19 survivors admitted to the intensive care unit (ICU) had mental health symptoms three months post-ICU and 38.8% after 12 months, respectively. These represented psychological distress, anxiety, depression, and PTSD symptoms. Primary care physicians are best placed for intervention, with reference to the dynamic between survivors and their care.

Role of Primary Care in Specific Contexts: Natural Disasters and Community Events

As the first point of medical contact, it is essential to maintain primary care functions during disasters. Disaster plans should maximise universal coverage and the accessibility of PHC. People may have multiple injuries or trauma. Infectious diseases may spread among victims quickly. Preparation begins with anticipation of the risk of incidents according to local context and weather forecasts. The healthcare infrastructure should be designed and built according to the risks of disasters in the specific location. The system should consistently increase resilience to flooding, wind damage, heat stress, power outages, and other physical harm.

In this section, the roles of primary care during the preparatory, response, and recovery phases of specific natural disasters are discussed. During and after the disasters, the healthcare needs of victims and their families increase. Many have PTSD, psychosomatic symptoms, and other somatic symptoms. Studies have also demonstrated lower immune functions in victims, leading to various illnesses (Segerstrom and Miller, 2004). Primary care providers can offer evidence-based collaborative care for patients with physical, social, and psychological problems. A primary care team can provide clinical assessment, minor operations and medication management, and brief cognitive behavioural therapy to patients as soon as possible. The preventive medicine practice, comprehensive care, and coordinator role of PHC can be pragmatically demonstrated in the below events or disasters.

Hurricanes/Typhoons/Cyclones

Hurricanes, typhoons, and cyclones commonly occur in the summer to fall seasons. A tropical cyclone is a collective term for a cyclonically rotating flux of heat derived from the ocean. Tropical storms are tropical cyclones with maximum sustained winds between 17 and 32 m/s. Those with winds of 33 m/s or more are called hurricanes in the Atlantic and Northeastern Pacific basins and typhoons in the Northwestern Pacific. Tropical cyclones in the Indian Ocean and South Pacific are called simply cyclones.

Primary care workers can assist the victims in planning, action, and follow-up activities of a structured programme, like the US Veterans Health Administration Home Based Primary Care programme targeted at community-dwelling medically vulnerable older adults (Wyte-Lake, Der-Martirosian, Chu, Johnson-Koenke, and Dobalian, 2020). The preparatory phase starts before the tropical cyclone season. Social workers and primary care workers register a list of high-risk older people, particularly those who need special medical devices and have poor mobility and poor caregiver support. There are constant reviews of emergency plans, transportation, and shelter support. The response phase begins when a tropical cyclone approaches landfall. When the evacuation response begins, staff call patients immediately to provide help. Staff are often required to engage in outreach with patients in severely damaged areas. There is usually a surge of medical need in the post-hurricane phase, especially among patients who are dependent on electrical medical equipment. Primary care workers take care of most of patients' physical and mental health needs. They can also coordinate special care referrals for patients who cannot manage at the primary care level.

Flooding

Floods are a common threat to areas below sea level or along riverbanks. Flooding causes floodwater mortality and morbidity, such as drowning, hypothermia, and physical injuries. It may cause diseases due to exposure to pollutants, water-borne (such as diarrhoea and cholera) or vector-borne infections (such as dengue and malaria), and shortages of food and clean water. The associated psychological problems can last for months to years. During floods, the commonest diseases encountered include dermatitis, bacterial and fungal skin infections, conjunctivitis, digestive complaints, and diarrhoea, which are readily manageable by primary care physicians. Due to limited facilities and access to specialists, surgical operations may only be available in limited centres (Van Minh et al., 2014).

In Vietnam, the key documents for flood policies and strategies are the Ordinance on Prevention and Control of Floods and Storms; the National Strategy for Natural Disaster Prevention, Response and Mitigation to 2020 from

2007; and the National Target Program in response to climate change from 2008. The governance structure is designated to the provincial, district, and commune levels. They developed a plan for prevention, control, and response to the consequence of the floods and storms that occur each year. All records and information regarding the prevention and treatment activities carried out by local community health centres and district health centres are adequately stored.

In district health centres, community health centres, and village health worker networks, information is communicated via community meetings and public loudspeaker announcements before, during, and after floods (Van Minh et al., 2014). Stakeholders in district hospitals start preparing flood-related health risk activities. These include first-aid services, disinfection techniques after hazardous events, ambulance, water, sanitation, and nutrition support during the disaster. According to a standardised protocol, the village health worker networks provide primary medicine and health equipment. The response teams at different levels must perform regular disaster simulation exercises. The first-aid training topics for healthcare staff include underwater rescue, first aid, and transportation of victims. Specialist medical training covers emergency care and diagnosis and management of injuries, drowning, and snake bites. Primary care can offer preventive medicine such as counselling services and vaccination against various diseases (e.g., diphtheria, tetanus, pertussis, poliomyelitis, measles, and tuberculosis).

A survey in Sri Lanka showed staff absenteeism due to flooding, and subsequent failure to provide essential daily healthcare services (Van Minh et al., 2014). Apart from the provincial, district, and hospital levels, they have primary medical care units that offer first-line care and implement preventive health programmes.

Most of the programmes focus chiefly on response rather than prevention. To further improve primary care's capacity to respond to floods, specific job descriptions of health facilities, a clear role of primary care healthcare, and the budgets for health emergency plans for handling storm- and flood-related health problems should be enacted.

Earthquakes

Buildings collapse during earthquakes, causing physical trauma and injuries. The destruction of sanitary and water systems triggers communicable diseases. Population migration after earthquakes causes problems of access to safe food and water supply.

The 2011 Great East Japan Earthquake in Tohoku was followed by a tsunami. It resulted in large numbers of dead (15,879) and missing people (2,700), but relatively small numbers of injured (6,130) (Ushizawa et al., 2013). The Tokyo Medical and Dental University Hospital Disaster Medical Assistance Teams provided medical care to the victims. People received resuscitation, trauma management, and surgical care in the first week after the earthquake. After that, primary care health workers provided minor medical care for around 47% of patients, such as treatment of mild respiratory infections. They also supported mass screening and transportation of patients from radiation-affected areas.

The Singapore Armed Forces team embarked on a humanitarian assistance and disaster relief (HADR) mission after the 2015 Nepal earthquake (Ho et al., 2016). The earthquake centred in the eastern district of Lamjung measured 7.8 on the Richter scale and killed 8,600 people and displaced more than 450,000 (Roy, Sathian, and Banerjee, 2015). The HADR provided primary care, basic resuscitation, and minor procedures for victims. The top five most common earthquake-related problems were musculoskeletal, respiratory, gastrointestinal, dermatological, and psychiatric (Ho et al., 2016). The HADR brought essential equipment and drugs to provide wound and fracture and dislocation management. All procedures were performed in well-lit conditions with moderate sedation or local anaesthesia. These two examples from Japan and Singapore via Nepal demonstrate the essential role of primary care after earthquakes.

Marathons and Ultramarathons

Apart from disasters, primary care workers also support community events involving crowds and mass gatherings. Marathons and ultramarathons have become popular worldwide. Traditionally, marathon participants run 26.2 miles or 42.195 km mostly on flat roads. The ultramarathon race starts from 50 km and goes up to 100 miles (~160 km), usually in a natural environment, such as mountains or deserts. Typical ultramarathon races are divided into different stages or days. Long-distance runners may suffer from acute musculoskeletal changes and injuries or illnesses in convalescence.

The medical support offered by PHC practitioners begins in participants' pre-race education and health declaration. People with unstable pre-existing medical conditions, such as recent cardiovascular events, seizures, or asthma, should not participate. Education via pre-race briefings, information sessions, or electronic communications can be delivered to runners.

Conclusion

PHC treats individuals, their families, and the community in the first instance when they are sick. It is the most fundamental and accessible service for all. PHC can lead, coordinate, and cooperate with multidisciplinary healthcare teams. PHC doctors can provide outpatient consultation for whole-person health problems, emergency care, and rehabilitation in community events. With the universal health coverage and Sustainable Development Goals proposed by the WHO and the United Nations, respectively, health inequalities, particularly among low-income populations, can be addressed. Provision of adequate PHC during disease outbreaks, natural disasters, and community events is essential for residents and their families. PHC practitioners support people's physical, social, and mental well-being. In the COVID-19 pandemic, PHC staff perform disease surveillance, diagnosis and treatment, public education, preventive care, vaccination, and support for COVID-19 survivors. All governments must support the development of strong PHC teams to serve the community, particularly deprived populations.

References

Basu, S., Berkowitz, S. A., Phillips, R. L., Bitton, A., Landon, B. E., and Phillips, R. S. (2019). Association of primary care physician supply with population mortality in the United States, 2005–2015. *JAMA Internal Medicine, 179*(4), 506–514.

Centre for Health Protection. (2023). *Latest situation of COVID-19 (as of 29 January 2023)*. www.chp.gov.hk/files/pdf/local_situation_covid19_en.pdf.

Dawood, F. S., Iuliano, A. D., Reed, C., Meltzer, M. I., Shay, D. K., Cheng, P., Bandaranayake, D., Breiman, R. F., Brooks, W. A., Buchy, P., Feikin, D. R., Fowler, K. B., Gordon, A., Hien, N. T., Horby, P., Huang, Q. S., Katz, M. A., Krishnan, A., Lal, R., Montgomery, J. M., Mølbak, K., Pebody, R., Presanis, A. M., Razuri, H., Steens, A., Tinoco, Y. O., Wallinga, J., Yu, H., Vong, S., Bresee, J., and Widdowson, M. (2012). Estimated global mortality associated with the first 12 months of 2009 pandemic influenza A H1N1 virus circulation: A modelling study. *The Lancet Infectious Diseases, 12*(9), 687–695.

Donaldson, L. J., Rutter, P. D., Ellis, B. M., Greaves, F. E. C., Mytton, O. T., Pebody, R. G., and Yardley, I. E. (2009). Mortality from pandemic A/H1N1 2009 influenza in England: Public health surveillance study. *BMJ, 339*, b5213.

Fathizadeh, H., Afshar, S., Masoudi, M. R., Gholizadeh, P., Asgharzadeh, M., Ganbarov, K., Köse, Ş, Yousefi, M., and Kafil, H. S. (2021). SARS-CoV-2 (Covid-19) vaccines structure, mechanisms and effectiveness: A review. *International Journal of Biological Macromolecules, 188*, 740–750.

Fernandes, Q., Inchakalody, V. P., Merhi, M., Mestiri, S., Taib, N., Moustafa Abo El-Ella, D., Bedhiafi, T., Raza, A., Al-Zaidan, L., and Mohsen, M. O. (2022). Emerging COVID-19 variants and their impact on SARS-CoV-2 diagnosis, therapeutics and vaccines. *Annals of Medicine, 54*(1), 524–540.

Gelmon, S., Wallace, N., Sandberg, B., Petchel, S. J. N., and Bouranis, N. (2016). *Implementation of Oregon's PCPCH Program: Exemplary practice and program findings*. Portland: Portland State University.

Haldane, V., Zhang, Z., Abbas, R. F., Dodd, W., Lau, L. L., Kidd, M. R., Rouleau, K., Zou, G., Chao, Z., and Upshur, R. E. (2020). National primary care responses to COVID-19: A rapid review of the literature. *BMJ Open, 10*(12), e041622.

Ho, M. L. L., Lim, J. Z. M., Tan, M. Z. W., Kok, W. L., Zhang, J. R., Tan, M. Y., and Tan, A. C. B. (2016). Humanitarian assistance and disaster relief mission by a tripartite medical team led by the Singapore Armed Forces after the 2015 Nepal earthquake. *Singapore Medical Journal, 57*(8), 426.

Hone, T., Macinko, J., and Millett, C. (2018). Revisiting Alma-Ata: What is the role of primary health care in achieving the Sustainable Development Goals? *Lancet, 392*(10156), 1461–1472.

Hospital Authority (n.d.) *Fees and charges*. Retrieved on 29 March 2023 from www.ha.org.hk/visitor/ha_visitor_index.asp?Content_ID=10045&Lang=ENG.

International Health Conference. (2002). Constitution of the World Health Organization. *Bulletin of the World Health Organization, 80*(12), 983–984.

Lopes, N., Vernuccio, F., Costantino, C., Imburgia, C., Gregoretti, C., Salomone, S., Drago, F., and Lo Bianco, G. (2020). An Italian guidance model for the management of suspected or confirmed COVID-19 patients in the primary care setting. *Frontiers in Public Health, 8,* 572042.

Roy, B., Sathian, B., and Banerjee, I. (2015). Nepal earthquake 2015—An overview. *Journal of Biomedical Sciences, 2*(1), 1–2.

Segerstrom, S. C., and Miller, G. E. (2004). Psychological stress and the human immune system: A meta-analytic study of 30 years of inquiry. *Psychological Bulletin, 130*(4), 601.

Sisó-Almirall, A., Brito-Zerón, P., Conangla Ferrín, L., Kostov, B., Moragas Moreno, A., Mestres, J., Sellarès, J., Galindo, G., Morera, R., and Basora, J. (2021). Long Covid-19: Proposed primary care clinical guidelines for diagnosis and disease management. *International Journal of Environmental Research and Public Health, 18*(8), 4350.

Starfield, B. (1992). *Primary care: Concept, evaluation, and policy.* Oxford University Press.

Ushizawa, H., Foxwell, A. R., Bice, S., Matsui, T., Ueki, Y., Tosaka, N., Shoko, T., Aiboshi, J., and Otomo, Y. (2013). Needs for disaster medicine: Lessons from the field of the Great East Japan Earthquake. *Western Pacific Surveillance and Response Journal, 4*(1), 51.

Van Minh, H., Anh, T. T., Rocklöv, J., Giang, K. B., Trang, L. Q., Sahlen, K., Nilsson, M., and Weinehall, L. (2014). Primary healthcare system capacities for responding to storm and flood-related health problems: A case study from a rural district in central Vietnam. *Global Health Action, 7*(1), 23007.

Vance, H., Maslach, A., Stoneman, E., Harmes, K., Ransom, A., Seagly, K., and Furst, W. (2021). Addressing post-COVID symptoms: A guide for primary care physicians. *Journal of the American Board of Family Medicine, 34*(6), 1229–1242.

Vanselow, N. A., Donaldson, M. S., and Yordy, K. D. (1995). A new definition of primary care. *JAMA, 273*(3), 192.

WONCA Europe. (2002). *The European definition of general practice/family medicine.* Barcelona: WONCA Europe.

World Health Organisation. (1978). *Primary health care: Report of the international conference on primary health care, Alma-Ata, USSR, 6–12 September 1978.* Geneva: World Health Organisation.

World Health Organisation. (2014). *Making fair choices on the path to universal health coverage: Final report of the WHO Consultative Group on Equity and Universal Health Coverage.* apps.who.int/iris/handle/10665/112671.

World Health Organisation. (2018). *From Alma-Ata to Astana: primary health care: reflecting on the past, transforming for the future: interim report from the WHO European Region* (No. WHO/EURO: 2018-3313-43072-60283). Copenhagen: WHO Regional Office for Europe.

World Health Organisation and United Nations Children's Fund. (2018). *A vision for primary health care in the 21st century: Towards universal health coverage and the Sustainable Development Goals.* apps.who.int/iris/handle/10665/328065.

Wright, L. A., Gnanapragasam, S., Downes, A. J., and Bisson, J. I. (2021). Managing COVID-19 related distress in primary care: Principles of assessment and management. *BMC Family Practice, 22*(1), 1–6.

Wyte-Lake, T., Der-Martirosian, C., Chu, K., Johnson-Koenke, R., and Dobalian, A. (2020). Preparedness and response activities of the US Department of Veterans Affairs (VA) home-based primary care program around the fall 2017 hurricane season. *BMC Public Health, 20*(1), 1–9.

Yari, A., Zarezadeh, Y., Fatemi, F., Ardalan, A., Vahedi, S., Yousefi-Khoshsabeghe, H., Boubakran, M. S., Bidarpoor, F., and Motlagh, M. E. (2021). Disaster safety assessment of primary healthcare facilities: A cross-sectional study in Kurdistan province of Iran. *BMC Emergency Medicine, 21*(1), 1–9.

7

Training and Preparedness for Major Events, Massive Accidents, and Natural Disasters
A Hong Kong Report

Yukie Y. K. LAM
Department of Medicine and Therapeutics, The Chinese University of Hong Kong

Cynthia K. C. WAI
Auxiliary Medical Service; Yan Chai Hospital

Jonathan H. O. WAI
Auxiliary Medical Service; Hong Kong Disaster Medicine Association;
Precious Blood Hospital

Kin-kwan LAM
Auxiliary Medical Service; Hong Kong Disaster Medicine Association;
Hospital Authority

Natural and human-caused disasters in crowded cities such as Hong Kong can lead to serious human, social, and economic losses. In Hong Kong, government bodies have established emergency protocols to deal with these incidents. When a disaster occurs in Hong Kong, trained medical personnel and well-equipped facilities will be mobilised in a timely fashion according to plan. In order to provide timely responses to disasters, both the government and community organisations conduct training for professional personnel and carry out regular call-and-response drills. This preparation work is illustrated, with examples, in this chapter. To reduce the impacts of and losses caused by disasters, individuals in the community should also be prepared, and should know how to respond when a disaster strikes. Here, the particular focus is on the preparatory efforts individuals can contribute to disaster management. This chapter provides examples of how government and non-governmental bodies work in collaboration with local communities to prepare people to face challenges arising from disasters.

Professional Training of Personnel for Major Events in Hong Kong

Common disasters in Hong Kong include typhoons and landslides (natural), transportation accidents (human-caused), and territory-wide major events, and government bodies have established emergency protocols to deal with these events (Cocks, 2000). When a disaster occurs in a well-conceived or civilian event in Hong Kong, trained medical personnel and well-equipped facilities will be mobilised in a timely fashion according to plan, and appropriate care will be provided to all victims. In order to provide a timely response to disasters, government and community organisations conduct training for professional personnel and carry out regular drills and call-and-response exercises.

Take large-scale sports events as an example. The aims of preparation work are to promote safety, prevent injuries, and provide medical care to athletes on site. It is necessary to put into place appropriate measures and logistic support to enable swift responses to the medical needs of the sick and injured at the venue. The overall planning of such events should incorporate a medical disaster plan. The planning and implementation of disaster management and medical support measures in two large-scale sports events in Hong Kong are described below.

The Hong Kong Marathon

The Hong Kong Marathon (formally called the Standard Chartered Hong Kong Marathon (SCHKM), n.d.) is a large-scale international event that has been awarded Gold Label status by World Athletics. The Major Sports Events Committee under the Sports Commission of the Hong Kong Special Administrative Region (SAR) government also gave "M" status to the SCHKM 2021 (The Government of the Hong Kong Special Administrative Region, 2021). Standard Chartered bank began sponsoring the event in 1997, when about 1,000 participants took part in the race. Over the years, the number of participants has increased, up to 40,000 in 2006. In the past few years, the quota was set at 75,000 participants, with an estimated 10,000 overseas runners.

During the preparation period, the organiser, the Hong Kong Association of Athletics Affiliates (HKAAA, n.d.), provides athletes and emergency responders with knowledge about the event in general, and informs them about the rules and regulations of the races, as well as how to help prevent injuries among participants. The organiser conducts training courses on the management of sports injuries and exercise drills for medical personnel. It also coordinates logistical arrangements for first aid and other medical services, and holds briefing sessions shortly before the event. This preparatory work is essential in enhancing the smooth operation of the emergency services in response to any incidents that may occur.

On the day of the event, coordination among the related operational network of emergency services, such as the Hong Kong Police Force, the Fire Services Department, and the accident and emergency (A&E) departments at local hospitals, is maintained. An Incident Coordinating Centre (ICC) is set up at the venue to collect data and pass on reports to involved parties responsible for handling incidents. The logistics and support of medical services include transfer arrangements and the mobilisation of medical workforces and equipment along the race route.

When the event is finished, medical teams are asked to stand down. All reports of medical cases and incidents encountered during the event at all posts are collected and stored. Critical or unusual cases are reviewed and discussed at a future debriefing meeting, which allows relevant parties to share experience and comments with the management, to help them to improve in the future.

As the scale of events has become larger and larger over the years, there is an increase in resources allocated for planning and support, as well as in the collaborative efforts among participating organisations. The Organising Committee of the SCHKM is led by the HKAAA, as the chief organiser. It is joined by other government and non-governmental organisations (NGOs), which include the Auxiliary Medical Service, the Auxiliary Police Volunteer Services Cadre, the Civil Aid Service, the Environmental Protection Department, the Fire Services Department, the Food and Environmental Hygiene Department, the Hong Kong Girl Guides Association, the Highways Department, the Home Affairs Department, the Information Services Department, the Hong Kong Police Force, the Hong Kong Tourism Board, the Leisure and Cultural Services

Department, Route 3 (CPS) Company Limited, the Scout Association of Hong Kong, the Transport Department, Tsing Ma Control Area operator, and Western Harbour Tunnel Company Limited. Each supporting organisation plays a different role, and some have explicit response plans for emergencies. The role of the Auxiliary Medical Service at the event is described in detail below.

The Auxiliary Medical Service

The provision of first aid and medical support throughout the marathon is carried out by the Auxiliary Medical Service (AMS) of the Hong Kong government. The participating members of the AMS during the event are volunteers trained in medical first aid and disaster management skills. The AMS provides first aid and ambulance services for the SCHKM, with the aim of "guarding everyone on the marathon track". Over time, a special committee, Medical and Professional Committee on Major Events (MPCOME), was formed under the AMS to coordinate all issues related to the provision of medical services for large-scale events. Its duties include logistical planning for both fixed and mobile first aid posts on the race route; the design of large medical posts (sick bays) at certain strategic areas and the finish line; the planning of evacuation exits on the route; workforce estimates for deployment; the preparation of equipment lists; stocking drugs; and the provision of special training courses for all members deployed to the event. Shortly before the event, extra drills and training are provided to members, particularly in regard to the handling of sports injuries, resuscitation for critical conditions, the use of special equipment, ambulance loading and transfer, telecommunication, and reporting data to the ICC.

A total of 75,294 runners took part in the 2019 SCHKM, which was held on 17 February. More than 900 AMS members, 15 town ambulances, four motorcycles, and 22 bicycles were deployed by the AMS (Auxiliary Medical Service, 2019). During the event, critical cases were treated and observed in sick bays or at medical posts, or transported to the A&E departments of hospitals after initial stabilisation. In the same year, the AMS established a new Medical Services and Operation Policy Committee to enhance the capabilities of AMS officers and members of medical teams in handling the sick and injured during large-scale events. The AMS hence organised a series of targeted training courses, such as the Communication and Dispatch Training Course,

Radio Communication Training Workshop, Major Incident Management and Command Course, Simulation Training on First Aid Cases, First Aid Skills Training for Rescuing the Critically Injured, Training of Mobile First Aid Squads, and Advanced Cardiac Life Support (ACLS) training. In addition, in response to the coronavirus disease 2019 (COVID-19) pandemic, training courses on gowning-up and de-gowning in relation to personal protective equipment, and on preventive measures against the transmission of COVID during high-risk aerosol generating procedures, such as cardiopulmonary resuscitation and bag-valve-mask ventilation, were also organised. As the 2021 marathon was held in the warmer month of October instead of cooler February, training on heat-related illnesses was also provided. More details of these training courses can be found in the chapter appendix.

The recruitment of doctors and nurses for the event is centrally managed by AMS headquarters. These medical practitioners are deployed by the Medical Coordinator of the event to different medical posts along the race route. A commanding officers' meeting is held a few months before the event. Near the event day, operation briefings are organised for the officers and members, who include doctors and nurses. During the briefings, there is first a comprehensive introduction by the race manager of the HKAAA regarding the marathon route and the locations of medical posts along the route. Then, an officer from AMS headquarters gives a briefing on the deployment of members, nurses, and doctors to the first aid and medical posts along the route, the operation of the ICC, and the locations of ambulances, motorcycles, mobile bicycle teams, and mobile on-foot teams. There is also a run-through of the operations communication and dispatch system, the collection of patient treatment data, and the half-hourly submission of data to be compiled into statistical reports. Transport arrangements for members deployed to remote posts along the race route are also explained.

These briefing sessions for the officers-in-charge and members of the first aid teams are useful in that they ensure all duty members are prepared on the event day, and remind them of the reporting times, transport arrangements, uniform, and other important information, such as the weather forecast. Logistical arrangements regarding equipment (which may be adjusted according to the weather forecast) are checked one day before the event. It is important that the checked equipment is delivered to the correct locations on the race route. Portable radio telephones are supplied for communication in each of the first aid posts; they ensure messages or data from each post are received by the ICC. All these preparatory actions are essential for the smooth execution of swift emergency medical services.

Debriefings are held about two weeks after the event to review and evaluate the operations. The AMS headquarters coordinate the collection of all reports and comments from the officers and members of different parties. Feedback is collected from the officers-in-charge of the first aid posts, and doctors- and nurses-in-charge of the medical posts. This is useful in terms of identifying problems and devising measures for future improvement. If found to be necessary, the organiser is advised to make changes to the number of medical tents, the locations of first aid posts, the emergency routes for the ambulances, and the quantity of consumables and other supplies.

Anti-COVID Measures Implemented for the 2021 SCHKM

The 2021 SCHKM was one of the most iconic sports events in Hong Kong, as it was the first major occasion with mass public participation since the COVID-19 pandemic began (SCHKM, 2021). It demonstrated to the world Hong Kong's capability in organising major sports events under extremely challenging circumstances and greatly boosted the spirit of the local community. It also strengthened Hong Kong's position as a centre for major international sports events. Bearing in mind that the 2020 SCHKM was called off at the last minute because of the COVID-19 pandemic, the HKAAA, the organiser of the 2021 SCHKM, adopted a number of stringent infection prevention and control measures. The total quota for runners in 2021 was markedly reduced to 18,500, which included 8,000 participants in the 10-km race, 6,500 in the half marathon, and 4,000 in the full marathon. All participating runners were required to have received all doses of the COVID-19 vaccination at least 14 days before the race, and to obtain a negative result from a COVID-19 nucleic acid test within 72 hours before the race day.

On the race day, runners had to wear face masks before crossing the starting line and again immediately after crossing the finishing line, and wear designated race wristbands and race bibs at all times during the race. During the race, no eating was allowed in designated areas in Victoria Park, the finishing area. In addition, a "rolling start" was employed for non-elite participants, to reduce the risk of infection from close contact; these runners started in small groups at short intervals within a designated time period. In addition, participants were advised to leave the finishing area as soon as possible to avoid blocking runners who were arriving at the finishing line and to avoid overcrowding. Runners who failed temperature checks, did not wear their wristband and race bib properly, or did not comply with other forms of anti-pandemic requirements laid out by the Hong Kong government were not allowed to participate in the race.

The 2016 FIA Formula E HKT Hong Kong ePrix

The first Hong Kong ePrix (formally, the 2016 FIA Formula E HKT Hong Kong ePrix) was held on 8 and 9 October 2016 in the central harbourfront area. It was organised by Formula Electric Racing (Hong Kong) Limited, co-organised by the Hong Kong Automobile Association (HKAA), and supported by various government departments. The event consisted of an electric motor race and a number of other entertainment activities.

Support from the Auxiliary Medical Service

During the event, the duties of the AMS were to provide medical first aid coverage and ambulance stand-by services to the racers and crew members at the track area. The MPCOME of the AMS is responsible for planning and expert input during the recruitment, training, and deployment of volunteers, who are professional doctors, nurses, and paramedics (Lam et al., 2017). During meetings with the Security Bureau and Tourism Commission of the Hong Kong government, the MPCOME of the AMS discussed matters related to emergency medical services in the circuit and for spectators. The MPCOME also deliberated with the HKAA over matters related to the layout and set-up of a medical centre and first aid posts, the preparation of special medical equipment under the Fédération Internationale de l'Automobile (FIA), and specific training courses for AMS members during this new sports event. In addition, the committee held discussions with the Hospital Authority on subjects such as designated hospitals for racers, event staff, and spectators, and communication between the chief medical officer of the event, A&E departments, and the Major Incident Communication Centre of the Hospital Authority.

The Role of the Chief Medical Officer

A chief medical officer (CMO) was appointed by the HKAA to take responsibility of the overall control of the organisation and administration of medical services within the racing circuit. He was Dr Kin-kwan Lam, a co-author of this chapter, who was also appointed as coordinator of the AMS medical team. In preparation for the race, he assured the FIA that he had contacted the designated hospitals regarding the event and obtained their support. Two months prior to the event, he completed and submitted to FIA motorsport management a medical services questionnaire, which contained information about equipment to be stored at the medical centre and medical intervention cars; functional data and premises for doping tests; trackside equipment; medical centre personnel, including medical specialists and paramedics; trackside doctors, including doctors on foot and inside medical intervention cars and ambulances; doctors in extrication teams; and details of hospitals for injured drivers. Information about the extrication teams, electrical energy recovery devices, firefighting provisions, and dis-incarceration facilities was also included. There was a contingency plan in case of a major disaster beyond normally foreseeable scenarios, and when demands exceed the capacity of the medical services on site.

Medical Equipment

The FIA requires a list of medical intervention equipment to meet its car racing requirements, including equipment to secure the clearance of the human upper airway; equipment for ventilation, circulatory support, and cervical spine support; dressings; medications; scissors to cut through harnesses and overalls; and survival blankets and splints. It also requires additional mandatory equipment, such as oxygen reserves, casualty immobilisers, surgical instruments, inflatable devices for the setting and retention of fractures, cervical collars, otoscopes, reflex hammers, urinary catheters, equipment for gastric lavage, and stitching materials and needles. Thus, the complete list of equipment for FIA motorsport management is quite comprehensive and can handle all types of severe trauma, including injuries sustained in an explosion. As there are electrical risks in Formula E racing, special blankets for insulation and rubber gloves are needed, and these are provided by the Formula E extrication teams.

Intensive Training for Medical Officers, Paramedics, and Other Stakeholders

The training of rescue team members is of utmost importance to the international ePrix event, especially when held for the first time in Hong Kong. First, training on circuit safety for marshals, medical officers, and paramedics was held one month before the event. It consisted of a three-hour course on scene safety, racing regulations, and flag symbolisation. Second, a four-hour intensive ambulance aid training session on special equipment familiarisation, scenario training in car racing or mild cognitive impairment situations, and patient care journeys and handing over was held in the month before the race. Third, the Motorsport Medicine Incident Management Course, a nine-hour course specifically designed for the event, was held in the simulation centre at the Hong Kong Academy of Medicine. It included trackside care simulations, ambulance care simulations, medical room care simulations, and command and coordination of the race. Fourth, the Emergency Escort Exercise was used to familiarise the emergency escorts of the ambulances with the route from the race track to the nearest hospital. It was conducted by the Police Force. Fifth, an Interdepartmental Formula E Joint Communication Exercise was conducted three weeks before the race at the then newly built and well-equipped Fire and Ambulance Services Academy in Tseung Kwan O, to familiarise all stakeholders with the operational tactics of handling emergencies during the event. This 10-hour exercise examined the effectiveness of flag marshals; tested a dry run of the casualty handling and conveyance and "first attending" procedures; practised communication among the Race Control Centre, the Joint Agency Control Centre, the security management, and other liaison posts on-site; and tested crowd control and the security response.

An operational briefing session was held one week before the race day, and was attended by the officers-in-charge, doctors, and nurses stationed at the duty posts. The aim of the briefing was to familiarise participants with the plan for the venue layout, the location of medical support at the 10 turning points, the parking sites for the five ambulances, and emergency vehicle access. During the briefing, the operation order of command, communication, reporting time and location, the assembly of ambulances, and the dress code of those on duty were decided.

Debriefing

A debriefing session was held about two weeks after the event. It was attended by both the CMO and the deputy CMO, as well as doctors- and officers-in-charge of the posts. The aim of the session was to review and evaluate the FIA Formula E Hong Kong ePrix operations of the AMS. It is customary that, after a major event, the AMS headquarters collects all reports and comments from officers-in-charge and members of different AMS groups. Feedback collected from officers in charge of mobile posts, ambulance posts, and medical posts is crucial in identifying problems and devising measures for improvement in future events in regard to the safety of staff, the supply of food and drinks for frontline workers, the deployment of equipment, and the use of radio telephones for better communication.

The Aim of Medical First Aid During Major Events

Medical first aid at the "disaster scene" of major events intends to provide triage for the injured, and give appropriate care and management on the field. It is not intended to act as a full-scale emergency room providing definitive treatment; it only treats mild injuries, while stabilising and transferring those in need to hospitals, thus avoiding overloading A&E departments with non-urgent cases. During large-scale international events, such as the SCHKM and FIA Formula E HKT Hong Kong ePrix, adequate preparation in regard to medical support is necessary to cope with expected incidents.

Disaster Preparedness in Hong Kong:
The Survival Skills and Knowledge of Individuals

On the one hand, Hong Kong has a high risk of natural disasters due to its geographical location. It is particularly vulnerable to tropical cyclones, rainstorms, floods, and landslides. On the other hand, human-caused disasters, such as fires, explosions, and traffic and industrial accidents, are also common in Hong Kong due to its dense population, busy and compact transportation network, and industrialisation. There is also COVID-19, which was still a worldwide event affecting every single person in the world at the time this chapter was written. Therefore, Hong Kong people are at risk in regard to various types of disasters. It is thus important for every Hong Kong resident to have the knowledge and skills necessary to cope with potential disasters and their consequences.

Are Hong Kong people prepared for disasters? The Hong Kong Jockey Club Disaster Preparedness and Response Institute (HKJCDPRI), together with a number of collaborators, carried out an extensive survey with different stakeholders in Hong Kong on the subject of disaster preparedness in Hong Kong (HKJCDPRI, 2016). In the survey, 99% of interviewees were interested in receiving more information about disaster preparedness, but many of them reported that they did not know where to access such information. One-third of the participants thought Hong Kong was adequately prepared for disasters, while a similar proportion disagreed. In another study, the Hong Kong Red Cross, through its Consumer Search Group, conducted its Public Resilience Survey with Hong Kong people in 2018 and 2021. A total of 1,200 interviewees took part in the 2021 study (Hong Kong Red Cross, 2021). The studies show that the general public had a notably low level of readiness for disasters or emergencies. In the 2018 study, only 12.9% of the respondents indicated that their households were prepared for disasters or emergencies. Although the figure rose to 24.3% in 2021, the latter study reveals that over 75% were still not prepared for disasters or emergencies. A great deal more effort is still needed to equip the public to adequately face disasters and emergencies.

Disasters are sometimes inevitable, but adequate preparation can help to reduce casualties and property loss. Work to prepare individuals for disasters can be carried out at the individual, community, and governmental levels.

The Preparedness of Individuals

Key Steps to Developing Preparedness

Three key steps have been introduced by the Hong Kong Red Cross to guide individuals to better equip themselves for potential disasters (Hong Kong Red Cross, n.d.).

Step one is to "be informed". Knowledge of potential disasters is established based on research and experience. Relevant knowledge and up-to-date news of potential disasters should be made readily available and easily accessible to individuals so they can be informed and get prepared. This is especially important for people living in susceptible localities and for high-risk groups. For instance, residents of subdivided flats are prone to fires and communicable diseases in view of their crowded living spaces. Certain areas, such as Lei Yue Mun, are highly susceptible to floods and landslides. Tai O also has a substantially higher risk of floods when compared to other districts. Ongoing climate change is causing a gradual rise in sea levels, as well as frequent and severe typhoons and heavy rain; these phenomena will likely pose a more detrimental threat of disasters in the near future. In order to "be informed", one should anticipate the types of disasters or emergencies that are likely to happen in specific areas, and identify effective means of communication to receive the most up-to-date information possible from related authorities, such as the Hong Kong Observatory. While emergency and disaster warning systems should disseminate clear and wide-reaching messages when a disaster occurs, every individual should be vigilant and prepared, and know the risks well.

Step two is to "make an emergency plan". In a household, after identifying possible threats, residents are advised to formulate an emergency plan so that individual members of the family will know what to do when a crisis occurs. The emergency plan should include the allocation of roles and responsibilities to each individual, so that the whole family works as a team. Each individual should know evacuation routes and meeting areas, and be familiar with the emergency plan. The plan should be tailored to the household environment. An emergency plan in a high-rise apartment building in the city is very different from one in a low-rise house in the suburbs. Similarly, emergency plans must also be prepared for institutions and workplaces. For areas susceptible to floods or tropical cyclones, such as waterfront buildings, specific emergency protocols for these natural disasters can reduce the loss of lives and property.

Step three is to "get a survival kit". Essential items and supplies should be packed into a kit in advance. Items in the kit should include but not be limited to identification documents, keys, spare mobile phones and chargers, extra batteries, flashlights and a whistle, water, food, money, a first aid kit, and emergency medication. Some items specific to individuals, such as eyeglasses and prescription medications, should also be included. Suggestions for the contents of an emergency kit can be found on the webpages of the Hong Kong Red Cross, the Security Bureau, and various government departments. The kit should be placed in an easy-to-reach location that every family member knows and can access. It should provide essential supplies that can ensure survival and emergency contact for a few days.

Psychological Preparedness

Adequate disaster preparedness includes not only physical but also psychological components. Psychological preparedness helps individuals manage a disaster and its impact, and reduces the resulting psychological distress (Zulch, 2019). It enables individuals to anticipate and identify their feelings, and to manage their emotional responses, resulting in better coping mechanisms. Individuals under stress are more vulnerable when hazards or emergencies occur. Stress impairs one's ability to think and act properly, so much so that one may not be able to respond logically when facing an emergency. Situational preparedness and psychological preparedness complement one another. Situational preparedness, such as disaster drills, and making available resources and emergency support services, emergency contacts, emergency kits, and water and food supplies in the household, all contribute to better perceived preparedness and support. With situational preparedness in place, an individual can feel calm and more focused on managing the emergency when it arises.

Experiencing emergencies and disasters can lead to long-term health problems and risks, such as substance abuse, insomnia, phobias, amnesia, and anxiety. An individual's recovery process is also affected by his or her mental status. Post-traumatic stress disorder (PTSD), acute stress disorder, depression, and other mental illnesses are examples of the more severe psychological manifestations after disasters. In a real-life example, a young social worker was left with a long scar on her face after an unfortunate traffic accident. Thereafter, she suffered from insomnia and often experienced images of the accident flashing through her mind at night. She also found it hard to focus on her work during the daytime and became easily irritated. She was referred to a psychiatry service and was eventually diagnosed with PTSD. This is just one common case in which the victim needed long-term mental and social support. Furthermore, psychological distress can arise from grievances related to family or property loss, which can indirectly lead to emotional disturbance, fatigue, and burnout.

Psychological or mental preparedness involves maintaining a healthy mental status and developing good coping mechanisms. Research on the interplay between stress and coping with stress have identified three coping styles: adaptive emotion coping, avoidance coping, and task-focused coping (Pooley et al., 2013). People who have developed adaptive emotion coping strategies respond and recover better in a disaster situation. They tend to seek assistance, and are better able to accept and tolerate sudden changes. In contrast, maladaptive coping strategies, such as the suppression or avoidance of emotions, lead to problems such as heightened distress or even substance abuse. Task-focused coping aims to eliminate sources of stress or work with the stressors themselves. Identifying more emotionally vulnerable individuals and helping them develop better coping strategies can reduce injuries and psychological impacts during disasters. It is essential to anticipate, identify, and manage stress or emotions that may arise from disasters. Incorporating psychological preparedness into existing disaster preparedness policies and practices help individuals cope with psychological distress during or after a disaster, and foster long-term resilience. People will show more positive psychological responses and be confident coping with the situation at hand. The Hospital Authority has a website on disaster psychosocial services, with detailed information in this area at the individual, community, disaster worker, and organisational levels (Disaster Psychosocial Services, 2019).

Preparedness through Community Work

Preparation for and the management of disaster responses require structured organisation and adherence to protocols set up by the government, as well as strong community engagement by individuals and non-governmental organisations. In the community, preparing local people for disasters comprises drills and education in schools, institutions, and workplaces. For example, in Japan, regular earthquake drills are conducted in schools to prepare schoolchildren and staff for earthquakes, to which the country is geographically prone. Self-protection skills, emergency exit routes, assembly spots, and roll-call protocols are regularly practised. There are also collaborations with local fire services for earthquake simulations, and practice sessions using devices such as fire extinguishers and emergency chutes.

In Hong Kong, institutions such as schools and hospitals hold regular fire drills. The drills aim to familiarise everyone in these institutions with emergency exit plans. In hospitals, protocols are established for evacuating patients who are bedbound. Knowledge of fire safety precautions and various community-based fire extinguishing devices is also regularly updated for staff. Other organisations, such as the HKJCDPRI, the Hong Kong Red Cross, the Collaborating Centre for Oxford University and the Chinese University of Hong Kong Disaster and Medical Humanitarian Response (CCOUC, n.d.), and the Hong Kong Disaster Medicine Association (HKDMA), have established a number of programmes to enhance disaster preparedness and response. This effort from NGOs is particularly important in the provision of disaster preparedness and response work at the community level.

Tai O is one of the most common flooding black spots in Hong Kong, as it has a large floodplain but an inadequate drainage system. The HKJCDPRI collaborated with two local organisations, Carbon Care InnoLab and Tai O Sustainable Development Education Workshop, to launch a "Flood Preparedness and Climate Change Awareness Enhancement Campaign" in Tai O in 2016. During the campaign, Tai O residents were encouraged to join educational talks, workshops, and exhibitions to better prepare themselves for natural hazards (Carbon Care InnoLab, 2016). Workshops on flood preparedness and responses targeted at local young adults and teenagers were held and, after the workshops, the participants further disseminated knowledge on flood preparation to other community members. With support from the Hong Kong Observatory, virtual reality (VR) games and video clips were also produced for residents in the district to educate local people on how to anticipate and respond to natural hazards.

The Hong Kong Red Cross, in collaboration with the HKJCDPRI, launched a community campaign on disaster resilience for subdivided flat residents and ethnic minorities in the Yau Tsim Mong District in 2019 (HKJCDPRI, 2019). The subdivided flat communities were particularly at risk for fires and outbreaks of communicable diseases. Home visits, fire station visits, and workshops featuring VR games on fire responses were organised by the Hong Kong Red Cross for the residents. The campaign also engaged and empowered grassroots welfare service centres in the implementation process. Through the campaign, underprivileged and vulnerable residents and ethnic minority populations, who might not have had access to fire safety information before, were able to receive such an education. Various NGOs also worked with kindergartens and primary and secondary schools to advocate disaster response and preparation. Apart from the direct but passive transmission of fire safety knowledge to schoolchildren, education in participatory formats was also provided. The latter included drama and drawing competitions focused on disaster knowledge, risk concepts, and attitudes toward emergencies in schools and the community. Through these participatory means, the concept of disaster preparedness was spread to the next generation (HKJCDPRI, n.d.).

Conferences on disaster preparedness and responses have been organised by parties such as the HKJCDPRI and the HKDMA (Hong Kong Disaster Medicine Association, n.d.). Government officials, professionals, and renowned individuals involved in disaster management were invited to the conferences to share their views on working toward a resilient and sustainable community. The HKDMA also organised workshops in conjunction with authorities in mainland China and Taiwan to share experiences in disaster management and disaster drilling.

The Work of the Hong Kong Government

The Security Bureau of the Hong Kong government is responsible for emergency response management and has developed detailed contingency plans for disasters and emergencies (Security Bureau, n.d.). The plans provide effective and efficient responses to all emergency situations that threaten life, property, and public security. A system is designed to handle three main phases of emergency response: namely, response, recovery, and restoration. The Emergency Support Unit of the Security Bureau and all related bureaus and departments have adopted the concept of "prior risk assessment", whereby they conduct pre-disaster risk assessments and carry out risk reduction control measures to minimise potential threats to the community and city infrastructure. For example, the adequacy and effectiveness of plans for typhoons are fully validated, and drills are thoroughly tested before the typhoon season. The government also invites NGOs to provide suitable training on emergency awareness and self-help knowledge to the community. In addition, a set of simple guidelines on disaster management are made available on the Security Bureau website. The guidelines provide information the general public can use to respond to disasters such as tropical cyclones, hill fires, and tsunami and nuclear emergencies, as well as where to obtain emergency assistance. Hong Kong people can also search for updates regarding disaster situations, safety tips, and response and recovery information from various forms of media.

Conclusion

Disaster prevention and management constitute a collaborative form of work involving both government authorities and non-governmental bodies. Every individual in society has a role to play in preparing for potential and emerging disasters. Advocating what individuals can do is as important as the establishment of government policies and a management structure. Members of society should obtain up-to-date information, gather practical preparation tips and necessary skills, and be mentally prepared for disasters. Lessons learned from previous disasters and the presently evolving pandemic should better equip the community for future challenges.

References

Auxiliary Medical Service. (2019). Hong Kong Standard Chartered Marathon 2019 Duty Album. *Auxiliary Medical Service News, 1,* 2–8. www.ams.gov.hk/files/news2019-q1.pdf.

Carbon Care InnoLab. (2016). *Tai O community campaign on disaster resilience.* Retrieved on 20 March 2022 from www.ccinnolab.org/en/TaiOCommunityCampaign.

Cocks, R. A. (2020). The medical management of civil disasters in Hong Kong. *Hong Kong Journal of Emergency Medicine, 7*(3), 179–184.

Collaborating Centre for Oxford University and the Chinese University of Hong Kong Disaster and Medical Humanitarian Response. (n.d.). *Home.* Retrieved on 20 March 2022 from ccouc.org.

Disaster Psychosocial Services. (2019). *Home.* Retrieved on 20 March 2022 from hadps.ha.org.hk/en_index.aspx.

Hong Kong Association of Athletics Affiliates. (n.d.). *Home.* Retrieved on 20 March 2022 from hkaaa.com.

Hong Kong Disaster Medicine Association. (n.d.). *Home.* Retrieved on 20 March 2022 from www.hkdma.org.

Hong Kong Jockey Club Disaster Preparedness and Response Institute. (n.d.). *Community engagement.* Retrieved on 20 March 2022 from www.hkjcdpri.org.hk/community-engagement-1.

Hong Kong Jockey Club Disaster Preparedness and Response Institute. (2016). *Disaster preparedness in Hong Kong: A scoping study.* www.hkjcdpri.org.hk/download/research/ScopingStudy.pdf.

Hong Kong Jockey Club Disaster Preparedness and Response Institute. (2019). *Hong Kong Red Cross: Community campaign on disaster resilience for sub-divided flat residences in Yau Tsim Mong district.* 14 January 2019. www.hkjcdpri.org.hk/hong-kong-red-cross.

Hong Kong Red Cross. (n.d.). *3 steps for disaster preparedness.* www.redcross.org.hk/sites/redcross/files/media/irs_files/Local%20Projects/DP_3step.pdf.

Hong Kong Red Cross. (2021). *Hong Kong Red Cross releases result of "Public Resilience Survey" and appeals to individuals and institutions to develop disaster preparedness plan as 75% households are not prepared for disasters* [Press release]. 15 October 2021. www.redcross.org.hk/en/press_room/press_release_2021/20211015.html.

Lam, K. K., Ng W. W. Y., and Lau, T. L. (2017). *Auxiliary Medical Service Formula E Circuit Medical Service: Recruit, training and deployment of professional volunteers.* Paper presented at CPCE Health Conference 2017, 16 January 2017, The Hong Kong Polytechnic University, Hong Kong.

Pooley, J. A., Cohen, L., O'Connor, M., and Taylor, M. (2013). Post-traumatic stress and post-traumatic growth and their relationship to coping and self-efficacy in

Northwest Australian cyclone communities. *Psychological Trauma: Theory, Research, Practice, and Policy, 5,* 392–399.

Security Bureau. (n.d.). *Emergency response management.* Retrieved on 20 March 2022 from www.sb.gov.hk/eng/emergency/index.html.

Standard Chartered Hong Kong Marathon. (n.d.). *Home.* Retrieved on 20 March 2022 from www.hkmarathon.com.

Standard Chartered Hong Kong Marathon. (2021). *Runner's guide.* Retrieved on 20 March 2022 from www.hkmarathon.com/runners_guide.

The Government of the Hong Kong Special Administrative Region. (2021). *"M" Mark status awarded to Standard Chartered Hong Kong Marathon 2021* [Press release]. 21 October 2021. www.info.gov.hk/gia/general/202110/21/P2021102100256.htm.

Zulch, H. (2019). *Psychological preparedness for natural hazards: Improving disaster preparedness policy and practice.* Contributing paper to GAR 2019. www.preventionweb.net/files/66345_f357zulchpsychologicalpreparednessf.pdf.

Appendix
Targeted Training by the Auxiliary Medical Service

1. The Communication and Dispatch Training Course covers basic radio usage, radio communication skills, the functions of the communication and dispatch centre, and the use of mobile whiteboards. In addition to classroom knowledge and theory, the course allows participants to practise the skills they have learned during simulated scenarios. In this way, participants can apply the knowledge of radio communication gained from the classroom. Through this practical session, participants further understand the key points of communication in pre-hospital emergencies, the operations of the communication and dispatch centre, and the entire process of dispatching ambulance services.

2. The Radio Communication Training Workshop aims to provide better medical services during large-scale events by enhancing the efficiency of communication. It is organised by the government's Communication and Information Technology Section. The contents include an introduction to wireless communication methods, recognition of common pitfalls in the use of radio communication, and standard operating methods for radio

communication. After the theory classes, participants are divided into groups for large-scale training, which includes simulations of the deployment of ambulances, the operation of control rooms, the use of trunked radio networks, and setting up control room action boards. During the training, the trainer sends simulated messages to the trainees to test their responses and adaptation to different positions during an operation.

3. The Major Incident Management and Command Course is organised for senior officers of Rank 4 or above, to enable them to master the management of major incidents. It deepens their knowledge and enhances their skills in disaster medical support and management. The course covers basic knowledge and rescue techniques at both operational and technical levels, with particular emphasis on skills execution under pressure. Based on a model of large-scale accidents, the lecturer teaches participants how to coordinate and communicate with other regular rescue forces, such as the Ambulance Command of the Fire Services Department and the Hong Kong Police. By mastering management and command skills in the control centre, senior officers become capable of providing appropriate support at the scene of an accident. They also learn how to organise drills to train team members in regard to disaster management in their own regions. After taking the course, these supervisors overwhelmingly find the content is substantial and beneficial.

4. Simulation Training on First Aid Cases is conducted for members of the Operation Wing ahead of the Standard Chartered Hong Kong Marathon. The theoretical sessions that make up the course teach members a dynamic team approach to first aid and the key points in handling different types of first aid cases at the scene. After learning about this theory, participants attend group practice sessions to engage in observation and comment on one another's performances. In this way, participants have the chance to strengthen their skills through practice. At the same time, they practise and familiarise themselves with the use of face masks, fingertip pulse oximeters, and other equipment in the emergency box, as well as the newly designed trauma backpack and resuscitation backpack. Team members become more proficient in providing first aid through this training.

5. The First Aid Skills Training for Rescuing the Critically Injured is carried out based on four demonstration videos. They are "patient with no breathing, no pulse", "bystander CPR steps", "comatose patient", and "patient with chest pain and shortness of breath". These videos help members to master essential skills and become psychologically prepared to deal with emergencies. Members can also repeatedly view the videos using their own smartphones. The headquarters issues a timetable and specifies a list of training items, so all units of the Operation Wing can carry out training systematically. During the month before the Standard Chartered Hong Kong Marathon, simulated training for first aid cases is conducted for members of various districts of the Operation Wing, the motorcycle team of the Transport Section, and the emergency bicycle teams. Officers also participate in the training as observers and provide assistance in the process as needed. Members find that, after the training, their confidence and, hence, their performance in regard to handling the sick and injured improve when they are under pressure during actual large-scale emergency operations.

6. Training of Mobile First Aid Squads in the use of newly designed emergency rucksacks is an essential course for mobile teams because they are the first responders to emergency situations. A mobile first aid team works in pairs, one person carrying the trauma backpack and another carrying the resuscitation backpack. The trauma backpack is used to examine and evaluate the wounded, clean and dress wounds, and splint fractures. Inside the trauma backpack, there is a fingertip digital oximeter, a tympanic thermometer, a wrist-type electronic sphygmomanometer, and a foldable splint, among other instruments and tools. The resuscitation backpack includes an automatic external defibrillator, a pocket mask, a bag-valve-mask resuscitator, and a manual suction device.

7. Advanced Cardiac Life Support (ACLS) training for doctors and nurses is conducted by trainers who are experienced specialists in emergency medicine, intensive care, or cardiology, or by nursing consultants. During the course, doctors and nurses learn the cardiac arrest algorithm and practise resuscitation on mannequins using different simulated scenarios. Participants also rotate to other stations that cover other topics from the

course, including airway management and endotracheal intubation, the use of mechanical cardiopulmonary resuscitation (CPR) devices, and automated external defibrillators.

8. In response to the COVID-19 pandemic, training has been organised on gowning-up and de-gowning in relation to personal protective equipment (PPE), and preventive measures against the transmission of COVID during high-risk aerosol generating procedures, such as the use of high flow oxygen, cardiopulmonary resuscitation, and bag-valve-mask ventilation. During the course, there are theoretical sessions on the epidemiological triangle of infectious diseases, different modes of transmission of infectious diseases, standard precautions against infectious diseases, and additional transmission mode-based precautionary measures. These sessions are followed by a practical session, which starts with a video demonstration on alcohol hand rubbing and the gowning-up and de-gowning of PPE. Participants in the course then practise using PPE under the supervision of nurses. Finally, they are tested individually by nurses on how to use the standard PPE marking sheet. Participants must pass the PPE examination before they are eligible to take part in major events during the COVID-19 pandemic.

9. Training on heat-related illnesses has been carried out since the 2021 Standard Chartered Hong Kong Marathon, which was held in the warmer month of October instead of cooler February. Members are trained to differentiate between heat stroke and heat exhaustion. They learn to understand the rationale of different cooling methods, which help to dissipate heat through conduction, convection, evaporation, and radiation. The key points of cooling down a person are covered during the course, including placing instant ice packs on the axillar and groin areas of the person to aid heat loss through conduction, the use of water sprays after wiping away excessive sweat, and using fans to enhance heat loss through evaporation.

8

Management of COVID-19 in Hong Kong

Leon Wai LI
Hong Kong College of Community Health Practitioners

Percy W. T. HO
Hong Kong College of Community Health Practitioners

Sandra Wing Yi CHAN
School of Nursing and Health Studies, Hong Kong Metropolitan University

Billy S. H. HO
Hong Kong Institute of Integrative Medicine,
The Chinese University of Hong Kong

Simon C. LAM
School of Nursing, Tung Wah College

Coronavirus disease 2019 (COVID-19) is caused by a new coronavirus called SARS-CoV-2 first identified in December 2019. It developed into a pandemic and dominated different countries worldwide, which significantly affected and altered individuals' daily lives. With a high morbidity and infection rate, COVID-19 had claimed over 6 million lives and infected over 500 million people at the end of 2021. To contain the spread of COVID-19, different countries had adopted various infection control measures including surveillance, quarantine, and social distancing. Nevertheless, the emergence of COVID-19 variants caused the situation to remain unpredictable. All countries should take an integrated approach to monitor and review public health interventions, including public health and community measures, vaccination, enhanced diagnostics ability, and resilience implementation. Hong Kong, a special administrative region of the People's Republic of China, is a highly populated city with approximately 6,800 people per square kilometre (total population ~7,420,000; land area ~1,085 km²) and is a regional travel hub to the world. Although these risk factors made Hong Kong a vulnerable region to the pandemic, Hong Kong still managed to contain the spread of COVID-19 effectively with around 12,500 confirmed cases (0.16%) and 210 deaths (0.002%) in 2021. Nevertheless, in late January 2022, the fifth wave of the COVID-19 outbreak in Hong Kong put great pressure on the public healthcare system with an overwhelming number of infections and deaths which also cast a shadow over the community. Hence, the analysis of measures in the management of COVID-19 in Hong Kong can identify any enhancements that can be made to current infection control strategies for future outbreaks.

The COVID-19 Pandemic

Coronavirus disease 2019 (COVID-19) was declared a pandemic by the World Health Organisation (WHO) in March 2020 and was a public health emergency in Hong Kong and many places around the world. According to the WHO dashboard, over 500 million people worldwide have been diagnosed with COVID-19 and it has claimed more than 6 million lives since it was first reported in December 2019 (WHO, 2021b). COVID-19 is caused by a pathogen named severe acute respiratory syndrome coronavirus 2 (SARS-CoV-2). It affects the respiratory and other organ systems, and causes mild to severe symptoms such as fever, cough, fatigue, shortness of breath, sore throat, gastroenteritis, anosmia, ageusia, and clinical signs of pneumonia or respiratory failure (WHO, 2021d; Nalbandian et al., 2021). The pathogen is spread through respiratory droplets and transmitted through contact with these particles. The incubation period ranges from one to 14 days, and the symptoms usually appear in five to six days (WHO, 2020a).

To contain the spread of COVID-19, most governments around the world have implemented a variety of restrictive and non-pharmaceutical interventions, including increased surveillance, social distancing, advice on personal protective measures, travel restrictions, and national/regional lockdowns (Haug et al., 2020). With the emergence of variants, in addition to the current control measures, information sharing and access, imminent research on potential impacts, management guidance, technical practice in testing and healthcare planning, and systemic communication are also vital for designing appropriate public health and social measures.

Hong Kong, a special administrative region (SAR) of the People's Republic of China, is one of the most densely populated cities in the world, with approximately 6,800 people per square kilometre in a land area of around 1,085 square kilometres (total population ~7,420,000) as reported by the Census and Statistics Department in 2021. It also plays the role of an international travel hub, making it a vulnerable region during the pandemic. Nevertheless, with previous experiences of tackling severe acute respiratory syndrome (SARS) in 2003, Hong Kong had learned lessons and maintained a robust infection control plan. Together with the local community's stringent precautionary measures such as practising proper hand hygiene and wearing face masks, the city successfully maintained relatively low morbidity (around 12,500 confirmed cases, ~0.16% of the total population) and mortality rates (around 210 deaths, ~0.002% of the total population) during the four waves of COVID-19 outbreaks from 2019 to 2021 (Kwok et al., 2020; The Government of the Hong Kong Special Administrative Region (HKSAR), 2021c). The fifth wave of the COVID-19 outbreak in 2022 brought an unprecedented impact to the community and local healthcare system with skyrocketing confirmed cases and deaths due to the highly infectious Omicron variants (HKSAR, 2022a). The previous infection control strategies had to be adjusted to mitigate the rapidly worsening situation and provided another valuable lesson for the Hong Kong government when facing future infectious disease outbreaks.

In this chapter, the local infection control strategies will be explored and analysed with reference to measures implemented in other countries to show how the COVID-19 epidemic could be contained in such a small, highly populated city. In light of the ever-changing COVID-19 situation, such as the emergence of virus variants, the effect of temporal changes in strategic planning for general and personal resilience will also be examined with recommendations on preventive measures and public responses.

Infection Control Strategies in Selected Countries

COVID-19 coping strategies and measures adopted by the United States of America (US), United Kingdom (UK), India, Philippines, Singapore, and mainland China during this unprecedented global pandemic were reviewed according to the countries' demographics, COVID-19 situations, and their connectivity to Hong Kong (Table 8.1). The reviews of public health measures, epidemiological data, and resilience plans are based on policy information retrieved from national documents, official press releases, and response plans to COVID-19 from related authorities' webpages or academic papers. As the measures implemented by different countries change continuously to adapt to the evolving COVID-19 situation, a cut-off date for the compared measures was set on 31 December 2021.

Table 8.1 Overview of COVID-19 in the US, UK, Philippines, India, Singapore, Mainland China, Hong Kong SAR (as of 31 December 2021)

	US	UK	Philippines	India	Singapore	Mainland China	Hong Kong SAR
Population	331,002,651	67,886,011	109,581,078	1,380,004,385	5,453,600	1,411,778,724	7,428,300
No. of confirmed cases	54,497,728	13,641,524	2,861,119	35,018,358	287,243	134,399	12,560
COVID-19 infection rate (%)	16.5	20.1	2.61	2.54	5.27	0.01	0.16
No. of deaths	812,000	148,941	51,604	482,551	838	5,699	213
Case fatality rate (%)	1.47	1.09	1.8	1.38	0.29	4.24	1.7
Persons receiving at least one dose of vaccine	241,208,244	51,801,494	61,066,594	859,026,846	4,853,704	1,259,967,000	5,087,074
Persons fully vaccinated	199,796,085	47,332,158	49,626,599	617,226,608	4,744,632	1,207,413,000	4,712,831
Vaccination rate (%)	60.3	69.7	45.3	44.7	87	85.5	63.4

The United States of America

The United States of America is the country with the most confirmed COVID-19 cases: approximately 54 million confirmed cases with more than 800,000 cumulative deaths from 2019 to 2021 (WHO, n.d.). It has a high infection rate (16.5%) and a high fatality rate (1.47%). Close to 60% (about 200 million people) of the US population has been fully vaccinated, though the vaccination rates across states vary, with only New Hampshire (95.0%), Massachusetts (91.5%), and Hawaii (90.0%) having over 90% of the population vaccinated with at least one dose, while seven states have less than 60% coverage with at least one dose (Tennessee (59.1%), Alabama (58.9%), Indiana (58.2%), Louisiana (57.2%), Mississippi (56.2%), Wyoming (56.2%), and Idaho (52.4%)) (Centers for Disease Control and Prevention (CDC), 2021).

The National Center for Health Statistics reported that since the beginning of COVID-19 in January 2020, the US has experienced the most significant single-year decline in life expectancy, from 78.8 years in 2019 to 77.0 years in 2020. Moreover, by some estimates, the actual number of deaths from COVID-19 was at least 31% higher than the officially reported figure, as there is often a delay in reporting COVID-19 deaths because of low diagnostic rates of causality and incorrectly issued death certificates, which adversely affected local and national responses (Gill and DeJoseph, 2020; Stephenson, 2022; Stokes et al., 2021; Woolf et al., 2020). Hence, in studying US strategies for the COVID-19 pandemic, it is vital to identify the shortcomings in surveillance measures, communication, and public health actions, so as to avoid a major outbreak in Hong Kong.

The United Kingdom

In the United Kingdom, confirmed COVID-19 cases skyrocketed in October 2021 and peaked at the end of December 2021. The UK has around 13.6 million confirmed cases in total, and the administrative regions in England recorded more than 130,000 deaths during this period (Office for National Statistics, 2022). The UK government estimated the infection rate of COVID-19 to be 20.1%, which meant one in five people in the country had been infected by COVID-19 in 2021. Although approximately 69.7% of the UK population has been fully vaccinated—almost 52 million people have received a first dose and over 80% have received a second jab (WHO, 2021a)—hospitalisation of patients due to infection with COVID-19 was still rising significantly in late December 2021. At this point, there were more than 2,000 cases daily, which was likely caused by the emergence of viral variants and the easing of lockdown restrictions for Christmas (GOV.UK, 2021a).

In view of the fact that most imported cases in Hong Kong came from the UK, and some local cases had travelled to the UK during the incubation period (Centre for Health Protection (CHP), 2022a), it is worthwhile for Hong Kong to study the strategies and measures adopted in the UK, as these could help prevent emerging viral variants from spreading dangerously in the local community and could provide a useful point of reference for the design of local resilience plans.

The Philippines

The Philippines had 2.86 million confirmed cases of COVID-19 with more than 51,604 deaths. The Philippines' pandemic peaked in September 2021, causing about 20,000 infections per day and leading to nearly 300 deaths. Under the rapidly worsening situation, only 45.7% of people were fully vaccinated, and 55.7% had received the first dose of vaccine at the end of 2021 (Department of Health, Republic of the Philippines, 2021).

There are more than 200,000 Filipinos working as domestic helpers in Hong Kong, and this number has increased significantly in the past few years (Office of the Government Chief Information Officer, 2019; Census and Statistics Department, 2017). The Philippines are thus the source of the second largest number of imported cases to Hong Kong (CHP, 2022a). Therefore, a study of infection control measures implemented in the Philippines is important for identifying potential public health and social impacts on Hong Kong due to the country's high connectivity to Hong Kong's households and community activities.

India

India is the second most populous country in the world, and is the second most affected country with over 35 million confirmed cases and 480,000 deaths (WHO, 2021b). Only 44.7% of people in India were fully vaccinated despite the high infection and mortality rates from 2019 to 2021 (WHO, 2021a).

According to the 2016 Population By-census Thematic Report: Ethnic Minorities published by the Census and Statistics Department (2017), Indians are one of the major ethnic minority populations in Hong Kong. The majority of ethnic minorities in Hong Kong are Usual Residents (98.7% in 2016), while only 1.3% are Mobile Residents. Since India was reported to have imported the third highest number of infected cases to Hong Kong (CHP, 2022a), it is important to study the country's infection control measures to see if local infection control practices can be improved.

Singapore

Singapore was one of the first countries outside China to report a confirmed COVID-19 case, on 23 January 2020. This was followed by local transmissions identified on 4 February (Young et al., 2020). As of December 2021, Singapore had registered over 280,000 confirmed cases (about 5% of the total population) and over 800 deaths (about 0.29% of the total confirmed cases) (Ministry of Health, Singapore, 2021a), figures comparable to those of Hong Kong.

Singapore is a city-state in Southeast Asia that is demographically similar to Hong Kong, in that it has a multi-ethnic population, is densely populated (total population: 5,450,000; population density: 7,000 per km^2) (Department of Statistics, Singapore, 2021; Urban Land Institute, Singapore, and Centre for Liveable Cities, Singapore, 2013), has high connectivity to the rest of the world via travel and economic activities, and is also a key location that experienced the 2003 SARS outbreak (Chotirmall, Wang, and Abisheganaden, 2020).

Although there was a proposal to establish a bilateral air travel bubble between Hong Kong and Singapore in the second half of 2020, the scheme did not materialise and the idea was abandoned in view of the upsurge of confirmed cases in early July 2021 and mid-September 2021, respectively, as well as a gradual divergence of COVID-19 coping strategies in the two regions (CHP, 2021b; HKSAR, 2021a; Ministry of Health, Singapore, 2021b). On 6 December 2021, Hong Kong further designated Singapore as a "high-risk" place from which inbound travellers would be subject to the strictest risk-based air flight boarding and compulsory quarantine requirements on arrival (Ministry of Foreign Affairs, Singapore, 2021). So, an analysis and comparison of the outbreak management strategies between Hong Kong and Singapore helps to understand the rationales of both places in containing viral transmission in populated regions and their pursuit of "COVID-19 resilience" in local community activities and international connectivity.

Mainland China

As the first country in the world struck by COVID-19 from December 2019 through the Chinese New Year holidays when large population movements were occurring, China had to rapidly contain the pandemic without clear aetiology and available pharmaceutical countermeasures (Bogoch et al., 2020; Xu et al., 2020). Although a surge of confirmed COVID-19 cases and high case fatality rate was demonstrated by a more than 200-fold increase from around 40 cases in early January to the peak with over 10,000 cases in late January 2020 (WHO, 2021c), China managed to slow down transmission in February 2020 with a series of strict containment measures, including citywide lockdowns, the establishment of nationwide screening, intensive epidemiologic and aetiologic investigations, mobilising healthcare teams, advanced contact tracing, active case surveillance and quarantine, community health education, etc. (Chen et al., 2021).

As Hong Kong is a special administrative region of China and aimed to resume quarantine-free travel between the two places (HKSAR, 2021d), Hong Kong should have infection control measures that could complement mainland

Table 8.2 Overview of infection control strategies (as of 31 December 2021)

Infection control strategy	US	UK	Philippines
Country/citywide lockdown	O Stay-at-Home Order	O	✓ Granular lockdown
Border control and travel scheme	✓ Traveller health declaration; proof of vaccination/proof of vaccine exception; negative viral test result before departure; quarantine measures	✓ Passenger locator form; proof of vaccination/proof of vaccine exception; negative viral test result before departure; quarantine measures	✓ Different measures for green list and yellow list countries; all travel prohibited from red list countries
Contact tracing mobile app	✗	✓ NHS COVID-19	✓ TRAZE
Surveillance in community	✓ Acute febrile illness surveillance systems	✓ PCR test/rapid lateral flow test for susceptible individuals	✓ Active surveillance of suspected, probable, or confirmed cases
Other pandemic prevention and control measures	O Social distancing ✓ Face mask mandates ✓ Temporary closure of premises such as schools, sport centres, gymnasiums, restaurants, bars, etc. ✓ Vaccination	O Social distancing ✓ Face mask mandates ✓ Temporary closure of premises such as schools, sport centres, gymnasiums, restaurants, bars, etc. ✓ Vaccination	✓ Social distancing ✓ Face mask mandates ✓ Temporary closure of premises such as schools, sport centres, gymnasiums, restaurants, bars, etc. ✓ Vaccination

Key: ✓ Implemented measures; ✗ Never implemented; O Lifted measures

China's "zero tolerance" measures to facilitate the process and effectively control local cases at low numbers or even null. Therefore, it is crucial to highlight the effectiveness of China's control measures and identify the tactics that could also be applied in Hong Kong (Silver, 2021).

Hong Kong's Infection Control Strategies in Comparison with Other Countries

Public health containment measures and infection control strategies implemented in the following areas will be discussed: country/citywide lockdown, border control measures, travel scheme, quarantine measures, surveillance, and pandemic prevention and control measures (Table 8.2).

...ndia	Singapore	Mainland China	Hong Kong SAR
○ Nationwide lockdown	○ "Circuit-breaker" lockdown	✓ Wuhan and Xi'an lockdown	✗
✓ Self-declaration form; negative viral test result before departure; quarantine measures	✓ Safe travel lanes scheme and Category I/II/III/IV health measure framework	✓ Port health quarantine; medical screening of travellers	✓ Group A–C health measures with different boarding and quarantine requirements
✓ Aarogya Setu	✓ TraceTogether	✓ Health Code	✓ LeaveHomeSafe
○ Mandatory testing for contacts of confirmed cases	✓ Active community-wide multisector surveillance	✓ Active community-wide multisector surveillance	✓ Universal Community Testing Programme, Targeted Group Testing Scheme, and operation of Community Testing Centres
✓ Social distancing ✓ Face mask mandates ✓ Temporary closure of premises such as schools, sport centres, gymnasiums, restaurants, bars, etc. ✓ Vaccination	✓ Social distancing ✓ Face mask mandates ✓ Temporary closure of premises such as schools, sport centres, gymnasiums, restaurants, bars, etc. ✓ Vaccination	✓ Social distancing ✓ Face mask mandates ✓ Temporary closure of premises such as schools, sport centres, gymnasiums, restaurants, bars, etc. ✓ Vaccination	✓ Social distancing ✓ Face mask mandates ✓ Temporary closure of premises such as schools, sport centres, gymnasiums, restaurants, bars, etc. ✓ Vaccination

Lockdown Measures and Travel Restrictions

Hong Kong never implemented a complete citywide lockdown when facing COVID-19, though previous research has suggested that strict travel restrictions may have little and unreasonable impact on pandemic dynamics (Russell et al., 2021). In fact, most confirmed cases were imported cases in Hong Kong, with continuous growth in the number of tourists who visited Hong Kong at the end of 2021 (Hong Kong Tourism Board, 2021). The Hong Kong community is exposed to the relatively higher risk of a COVID-19 variant invasion from foreign countries (Lam et al., 2022). While Singapore adopted the "COVID-19 resilience" approach to transitionally resume social activities and live with COVID-19 (Ministry of Health, Singapore, 2021b), the Philippines, mainland China, and Hong Kong still kept social distancing and gathering restrictions in place in some high-risk states or regions with the emergence of viral variants and increasing confirmed cases (Inter-agency Task Force for the Management of Emerging Infectious Diseases, Republic of Philippines, 2021; HKSAR, 2021d; Silver, 2021).

All the selected countries allowed limited international flights with various levels of screening and quarantine measures. Hong Kong followed similar strategies as the selected countries with region-specific restrictions by classifying all foreign countries into Groups A–C based on the severity of COVID-19. Hong Kong also specifically implemented the "Return2HK" and "Come2HK" schemes, in which both residents and non-residents who had not travelled outside Guangdong province or Macao within 14 days prior to arrival could be exempted from quarantine measures. All travellers through these schemes should upload a valid negative real-time polymerase chain reaction (RT-PCR) nucleic acid test result to the electronic health declaration system of the Department of Health through "Yuekang Code" or "Macao health code" (HKSAR, 2021d). Singapore had a similar strategy named "Vaccinated Travel Lanes" for inbound travellers who were Singapore citizens and permanent residents, Long Term Pass Holders, or immediate relatives of Singapore citizens. They were exempt from quarantine, but Singapore required all travellers to be fully vaccinated along with a valid electronic health declaration and different levels of health measures applied depending on travel history and according to the "Category I/II/III/IV health measure framework" (Immigration and Checkpoints Authority, n.d.). Though Hong Kong had assigned high-risk and medium-risk countries/regions into Groups A and B, health measures applied to travellers from these places would also differ based on vaccination status, which could facilitate the management of frontline operations and capability in adapting the strategic plan to the fluctuating COVID-19 situation (Yau et al., 2021).

Contact Tracing and Quarantine Measures

To monitor the activities of travellers and prevent the transmission of the virus if an individual was a potential carrier, contact tracing and quarantine were essential measures in outbreak control. With the widespread use of smartphones nowadays, all the selected countries, except the US, developed and established contact tracking and contact notification applications that were mandatory for foreign travellers and local residents to increase efficacy in curbing the spread of COVID-19 (Liu and Graham, 2021; Seto, 2021). The Hong Kong government developed and established the LeaveHomeSafe app in November 2020 for contact tracing by assessing exposure risk and identification of confirmed cases. Beginning on 9 December 2021, all premises under the Prevention and Control of Disease (Requirements and Directions) (Business and Premises) Regulation should require customers or users to scan a designated QR code with the app before entry (Information Services Department, 2021). LeaveHomeSafe lacked a Global Positioning System (GPS) tracking function that could locate individuals' positions, and all the scan records would only be stored in the users' phones and were automatically eliminated after 31 days to protect users' privacy. This app additionally provided access to electronic vaccination records and could be further connected with the Hong Kong Health Code system to ease the health declaration procedure on arrival and facilitate the resumption of quarantine-free travel to the Mainland and Macao (Office of the Government Chief Information Officer, 2021). With nearly 6 million smartphone users in Hong Kong, such mobile phone applications could enhance the pandemic control capacity to protect the public (Census and Statistics Department, 2021a). Similarly, in China, the Health Code System could control and monitor actions by identifying and generating different coloured QR codes based on the user's risk level, such as confirmed or suspected cases, travel history, time spent in high-risk areas, and relationship with potential contacts. The QR codes had to be scanned before entering public places not just for catering businesses and restaurants, but also metro stations and shopping malls. The total number of registered accounts for WeChat and Alipay was approximately 2.1 billion, and many users supported the Chinese government in synchronising health codes with digital wallets (Yang et al., 2020).

To better monitor people under quarantine, the Hong Kong government developed another application named StayHomeSafe which was mandatorily installed by a quarantined person. This application could track the activities of an individual when linked with a wristband with Bluetooth and geofencing technology to prevent him/her from leaving the containment facilities. Such tracking features and technology was similar to those in China and India (Government of India, n.d.; Norton Rose Fulbright, 2021). Although travellers from mainland China, Macao, Taiwan, and medium-risk countries/regions would be quarantined at home or in a designated quarantine hotel, this arrangement raised concerns about potential disease transmission to family members and hotel staff, though a regional study illustrated that modest relaxation of control measures for inbound travellers from areas with low infection rates would not result in a higher import risk (Yang et al., 2021). Zhu and Tan (2021) further pointed out the effect of home isolation was not much different from that of hotel isolation, but the government should have considered strengthening the enforcement of mandatory home isolation. Meanwhile, the high-quality infection control training and strict compliance by hotel staff in Hong Kong successfully prevented intra-hotel transmission (Li et al., 2021).

Surveillance

The Hong Kong government also put great effort into surveillance from border control to the local community. The first mass testing scheme launched in September 2020 was the Universal Community Testing Programme to identify asymptomatic patients and break the transmission chain of the third pandemic wave, with 32 of the 1,783,000 specimens identified as confirmed cases (HKSAR, 2020). In addition, to minimise the risk after the easing of social distancing measures, the Hong Kong government established Community Testing Centres to implement the Targeted Group Testing Scheme from late

October 2021. This provides more frequent and regular virus testing services for people with high exposure risk, such as staff of catering businesses, healthcare staff, foreign domestic helpers, construction site personnel, and those who were unfit for vaccination because of health reasons (HKSAR, 2021b). This approach of targeted group testing could identify infected persons as early as possible to cut the transmission chains. This can ensure a safe working environment among high-risk occupational groups while protecting visitors and customers (Mutambudzi et al., 2020; US Department of Labor, 2020).

Apart from enhanced surveillance, the Hong Kong government also established individual and community-wide mitigation measures intermittently under the Prevention and Control of Disease Ordinance (Cap. 599) based on the outbreak severity including social distancing, stay home advice, vaccination, and compulsive testing (Wong et al., 2021; Shen et al., 2021). Nevertheless, it was not easy to maintain a social distance of 1.5 metres. Therefore, Hong Kong additionally adopted the practice of mass masking / universal masking and all residents showed great compliance with the initiative (Leung et al., 2020; Cheng et al., 2020; Tam et al., 2020). An observational study conducted by the Faculty of Medicine of The University of Hong Kong showed that surgical masks were effective in reducing the transmission of coronavirus and seasonal influenza in symptomatic patients (Leung et al., 2020). Another experimental study in which hamsters were separated by surgical masks also confirmed that masks could reduce the infection rate and severity of SARS-CoV-2 (Chan et al., 2020). Most authoritative organisations in the world and many systematic reviews have consistently stated that face masks were effective infection control measures for containing the coronavirus (CDC, 2020b). Hong Kong's response to the early stage of the COVID-19 pandemic served as a good model internationally (Wong et al., 2020).

Improvement of Occupational Safety and Protection in Clinical Settings

Hong Kong has a reputable record in fighting against novel pathogenic diseases such as H5N1, H9N2, and H7N1 influenza. During the outbreak of SARS in 2003, there were around 1,800 confirmed cases in Hong Kong, and nearly 300 deaths including eight medical staff. This pandemic raised awareness and showed the urgent need for a response plan for large-scale disease outbreaks (WHO, 2015). Seventeen years had passed, but the outbreak of COVID-19 was quick to refresh Hong Kong people's painful memories of SARS. The Hong Kong government and the healthcare sector were highly alert in advance to the possible impact on medical and healthcare staff and patients this time. The outbreak management measures in hospitals and clinics under the Hospital Authority (HA) had been greatly enhanced in preparation for such a severe outbreak.

Before 2003, the Hong Kong government and the HA had used two different response systems to manage infectious diseases according to their severity and impact on the community. However, the two-system approach was found to be inadequate in cross-sectoral emergency responses during SARS. Therefore, from July 2006, the HA drew up its three colour-coded (green/yellow/ red) alert system following the government's three-tier system to ensure the contingency plan could be rolled out with greater effectiveness and efficiency. A three-tier risk response system had already been adopted by the government. The response levels are differentiated into three gradings: "alert" indicates low risk, "serious" for moderate risk, and "emergency" for high and imminent risk (CHP, 2020). Details of the system are given in Table 8.3.

Table 8.3 Three-tier risk response system in Hong Kong

	Three-tier response levels		
	Alert	**Serious**	**Emergency**
Risk impact on community health	Low	Moderate	High and imminent
Intention	To prevent the importation of disease	To limit transmission	To contain the wide spread of serious infections
Remarks	Unusual cause of infectious disease outbreak in a hospital Coordinated by the Health Bureau	Activated and lowered by the Secretary for Health	Activated and lowered by the Chief Executive

From late December 2019 to 4 January 2020, with the global development of the COVID-19 situation, the government's response level was initially raised to "serious" from "alert", then further advanced to the "emergency" level two days after the first confirmed infection was recorded in Hong Kong. Only the Chief Executive of Hong Kong can activate or lower the "emergency" level, based on the risk impact (Chief Infection Control Officer Office, 2022).

Case Reporting Mechanism

On 8 January 2020, Hong Kong announced that COVID-19 was to be included among the statutorily notifiable diseases under the Prevention and Control of Disease Ordinance (Cap. 599) (Chief Infection Control Officer Office, 2020). All suspected or probable cases should be reported to the Central Notification Office under the Centre for Health Protection (CHP) and the HA Head Office. Case reporting criteria in Hong Kong involved clinical presentation and other epidemiological criteria. Any patient who met the criteria must be isolated at a local hospital.

Enhanced Measures in Public Hospitals and Clinics

Under the "emergency" response level, a series of actions were implemented to enhance infection control measures and to ensure occupational safety.

Improving Ventilation in Hospitals and Clinical Settings

Evidence has shown that viral transmission of SARS-CoV-2 occurs mainly through contact and droplet transmission (WHO, 2020a). However, there have also been suggestions that the virus can spread through short-distance airborne transmission and even over long distances in poorly ventilated areas. To minimise airborne transmission of SARS-CoV-2, it is important to enhance ventilation in hospitals and clinics, especially in high-risk and crowded patient areas (WHO, 2020a). Enhancements including increased fresh air exchange by the widest opening fresh air dampers and add-on mobile high-efficiency particulate air (HEPA) devices to improve total air exchange have been applied in hospital and clinical settings (CHP, 2022b).

Due to the high risk of airborne transmission when performing aerosol-generating procedures (AGPs), all AGPs had to be performed under airborne precautions, preferably in a negative pressure airborne infection isolation room (AIIR) for high-risk patients. If AIIR was not available in patient areas, AGPs would be performed in a negative pressure single room with no less than 12 air changes (ACH) per hour, or in a well-ventilated area with at least six ACHs and the use of a portable HEPA filter operating nearby (CHP, 2022b). To ensure adequate removal of airborne contaminants after AGPs, and to reduce the risk of infection for medical staff, after patients had been discharged, the patient area would be adequately ventilated before any cleaning and disinfection work.

Reviewing and Updating Personal Protective Equipment Stockpile

After the 2003 SARS epidemic, the HA followed the recommendations of three review panels and pledged to maintain at least a three-month stockpile of personal protective equipment (PPE) in anticipation of risks. In view of increased PPE demands, the HA tried to increase the stockpile from three months to six in the early stages of COVID-19. However, due to global shortages and restrictions in worldwide procurement, there was only one-month PPE stock in early 2020. Although PPE supplies became more stable later, the stock was still not readily available, and judicious use of PPE was advocated.

In view of the development of the COVID-19 situation, the HA formed a Central Committee on Infectious Diseases and Emergency Response (CCIDER) to oversee the pandemic, and to provide strategic recommendations on infectious disease management, infection control, and contingency plans for potential outbreaks of the disease. The CCIDER consisted of representatives from the CHP, coordinating committees, and central committees of relevant specialisms, the HA Head Office, as well as infection control and infectious disease experts from the HA. Guidelines for the HA's staff on the use of PPE for COVID-19 were formulated based on international guidelines, particularly those released by the CDC and the WHO. At the beginning of the COVID-19 outbreak, due to limited knowledge about the disease, PPE specifications of the highest standard were employed. With better understanding of the virus, the CCIDER revised its PPE guidelines for all HA sectors (Chief Infection Control Officer

Table 8.4 CCIDER's PPE recommendations (since 19 February 2020)

	AIIR for suspected/ confirmed COVID-19	Triage station/ fever room at GOPC	Surveillance ward	Aerosol-generating procedures	General wards/other patient areas	Other areas with no direct patient contact
Types of precautions	Standard precautions ± Transmission-based precautions for all patients (Standard precautions + Airborne precaution + Droplet precaution + Contact precaution for all confirmed COVID-19 cases)					
Mask	N95	Surgical mask/N95	Surgical mask/N95	N95		Surgical mask
Isolation gown	AAMI level 1	AAMI level 1	AAMI level 1	AAMI level 1	According to mode of transmission	✗
Disposable gloves	✓	Risk dependent	Risk dependent	✓		✗
Eye protection	✓	✓	✓	✓		✗
Hair cover	Optional	Optional	Optional	Optional	Optional	✗

Key: AAMI Level 1, Minimum level of liquid barrier protection established by the Association for the Advancement of Medical Instrumentation

Office, 2022). Table 8.4 shows the revised recommendations in place since 19 February 2020.

Infection Control Beds and Facilities

The three review panels set up after the 2003 SARS epidemic also identified the problem of insufficient isolation facilities for patient care and reducing the risk of cross-infection during infectious disease outbreaks. The panels' proposed solutions were an increase of isolation beds to 1,440 in 14 acute care hospitals under the HA, and setting up three infectious diseases centres with around 100 isolation beds each. However, the Legislative Council believed that the chosen sites for the three centres were too close to residential buildings and rejected the proposal. Eventually, only one centre was built at Princess Margaret Hospital.

In early January 2020, when COVID-19 was in rapid development, only 480 of the proposed 1,440 isolation beds in hospitals under the HA were ready for use. To cope with demand, more second-tier isolation wards were deployed to accommodate confirmed cases, and a community treatment facility was set up at the AsiaWorld-Expo for stable COVID patients. A newly constructed infectious disease centre, the North Lantau Hospital Hong Kong Infection Control Centre (HKICC), began operation on 26 February 2021. As of 3 January

2022, 1,200 first-tier isolation beds and 660 second-tier isolation beds in public hospitals under the HA, as well as 500 isolation beds in community treatment facilities and 800 isolation beds in the HKICC, were in operation (Department of Justice, 2022).

Vaccination and Regular Compulsory Testing Scheme for High-risk Groups

To prevent nosocomial transmission of COVID-19, the Hong Kong government rolled out its COVID-19 vaccination programme on 26 February 2021. The HA is the largest employer in Hong Kong's public health sector, and the HA plays a crucial role in promoting COVID vaccines and encouraging all healthcare workers and other high-risk working groups to get vaccinated. HA staff who were vaccinated were granted a day of vaccination leave for each dose. As of 29 August 2021, 93.3% of full-time HA staff were vaccinated.

Additionally, to ensure patient and staff safety, the HA also introduced rapid antigen test kits for frontline staff in May 2021. They needed to conduct a weekly self-test and upload the result to the HA database via the HA staff mobile app. From 1 September 2021, the HA extended the testing scheme to cover all HA staff, and staff who had not received two doses of vaccination had to perform self-financed PCR-based nucleic acid tests biweekly outside working hours (Civil Service Bureau, Education Bureau, Social Welfare Department, and Hospital Authority, 2021).

Communication Strategies

The integrated use of multidisciplinary data has played a critical role in studying clinical care and catastrophic events (Rooney et al., 2014; Zhang, Qing, Huang, and Li, 2015). In 2017, in response to public health emergencies at that time, the WHO called on all countries to develop resilient and integrated systems to prepare for potential emergencies in clinical and public health systems (WHO, 2017). COVID-19 not only poses challenges to healthcare systems, it also presents difficulties for risk communication strategies. Although the WHO's COVID-19 global research database and studies related to COVID-19 have been made freely available to the public and all scientific researchers, thus improving data transparency and sharing (Cunningham, Smyth, and Greene, 2021), Porter and Hook (2020) found that international collaboration on COVID-19 research was lower than expected. This might be due to additional communication costs in search and coordination, political image, and social stability, all of which make multidisciplinary cross-border teamwork more difficult (Zhang, Li, and Chen, 2020). Mindful of the gaps in communication and data sharing, the Hong Kong government has worked hard to promote cooperation between institutions and the community to ensure the effectiveness of infection control actions.

Establishment of Expert Advisory Group and Workgroups

In Hong Kong, a steering committee-cum-command centre was set up in 2020 to formulate timely and targeted strategies and measures responding to the changing situation of the epidemic, and to achieve effective epidemic prevention and control. The committee was chaired by the Chief Executive and it had an expert advisory group and four workgroups: the Workgroup on Disease Prevention and Control, the Workgroup on Responses and Actions, the Workgroup on Public Participation, and the Workgroup on Communications (Home Affairs Bureau, 2020).

The Workgroup on Disease Prevention and Control was responsible for the development of strategies to manage infected cases and for maintaining close contact with relevant departments in mainland China. Hong Kong and the Mainland established a special team for anti-epidemic work which included the operation and cross-referencing of the health code systems used by both regions, the enhancement of the control cooperation mechanism at ports, and coordination for the resumption of quarantine-free travel.

Coordinating Multidisciplinary Actions

The Workgroup on Responses and Actions helped to coordinate work across various sectors. The Health Bureau (formerly known as the Food and Health Bureau) arranged for experts from mainland China to exchange views and to strengthen the management of high-risk populations. The Innovation, Technology and Industry Bureau introduced the implementation plan of the

Hong Kong Health Code system so that people in Hong Kong were able to try it out prior to the implementation of quarantine-free travel to the Mainland.

Encouraging and Empowering the Community to Participate in Mitigation Work

Due to the high transmissibility and varying severity of the COVID-19 variants, there was an unprecedented need to enhance the role of risk communication and community engagement in breaking the chains of transmission and mitigating the impact of the pandemic (WHO, 2021a). Governments need to devote sufficient time and resources to build community relationships, to empower people to participate in COVID-19 control measures, and to help identify locally appropriate and community-centred solutions (WHO, 2020b). On the other hand, an individual with higher compliance can foster interest and engagement in potential participants to widen community participation. Working with the community and involving community groups in operations helps governments to obtain community support, to improve trust in the government, and to boost communication effectiveness (Bonevski et al., 2014).

In the early stages of COVID-19, there was a shortage of PPE in both clinical and community settings (Lam, Suen, and Cheung, 2020). Civil society initiated a wide range of activities to compensate for the shortage by sharing and distributing surgical masks and hand sanitisers to people in need and to vulnerable groups (Wan et al., 2020). Hong Kong people also adopted self-protection measures such as enhanced personal hygiene and refrained from travel to reduce the chances of infection (Kwok et al., 2020). However, Mena et al. (2021) found that people of low socioeconomic status and marginalised groups were less likely to have access to health knowledge or adopt preventive behaviours during public health emergencies. Therefore, to build closer relationships with the community, the Workgroup on Public Participation encouraged the community to participate in activities to combat the virus. Support from the government to strengthen individuals' responsibility for their actions and to empower businesses, schools, and other agencies to adopt appropriate measures was found to prevent transmission and maintain a healthy environment (CDC, 2020a).

Enhancing Transparency of Government Information

A tremendous amount of information about COVID-19 is circulated on the internet, especially via social media. A study indicated that nearly 90% of the general public received health-related information via social media (Marar, Al-Madaney, and Almousawi, 2019). Unfortunately, not all of this information is true. Fake news, disinformation, and myths related to COVID-19 infection abound on social media (Sahoo, Padhy, Ipsita, Mehra, and Grover, 2020). For example, there were myths about COVID-19 vaccines altering people's DNA or causing the spread of variants. Such misleading information went viral on some social media platforms, which can pose a public health threat (Waszak, Kasprzycka-Waszak, and Kubanek, 2018).

The Hong Kong government's Workgroup on Communications ensured that the most up-to-date and accurate information was conveyed to the public promptly and effectively. The effectiveness of the government's communication strategy in general depends on a certain level of public trust and confidence in the government (Siegrist and Zingg, 2014). Therefore, it is necessary that the government makes use of an appropriate channel to disseminate information to the public (Hyland-Wood, Gardner, Leask, and Ecker, 2021). During the COVID-19 pandemic, the Hong Kong government provided a detailed, useful, transparent, and reliable source of information in its thematic website *Together, We Fight the Virus* (HKSAR, 2021e). This website contained lists of buildings and transportation services which had been visited or used by people who later tested positive for COVID-19, together with the time of the visit. People who had been to the same place around the same time were required to undergo a compulsory test within a fixed period of time, so that infected people could be identified and quarantined. Updates on health advice, travel advice, and latest local COVID-19 news are clearly provided on the website using a dynamic dashboard. From January 2020, officials of government health departments and hospitals held daily press conferences to report on the local COVID-19 situation and to answer questions of public concern (HKSAR, 2021d; Wong et al., 2020).

Strategic Approaches to Building Resilience

In order to safeguard public health and to hasten the resumption of normal activities, the Hong Kong government launched its free COVID-19 vaccination programme to all Hong Kong residents. The programme was a public-private partnership, where private doctors and medical organisations were invited to provide vaccination services. The types of vaccines used were CoronaVac (Sinovac) and Comirnaty (BNT162b2 mRNA vaccine; BioNTech). The venues used for vaccination include community vaccination centres, designated private clinics, residential care homes, nursing homes, COVID-19 vaccination stations in some hospitals, mobile vaccination stations, outreach vaccination services, designated general outpatient clinics (GOPCs) of the HA, as well as designated clinics of the Department of Health (HKSAR, n.d.). When the spread of COVID-19 was seen to be under control, the Hong Kong government adopted the strategic COVID-19 resilience approaches of widening vaccination coverage and reopening catering businesses and premises such as gymnasiums and schools.

Mental Well-being and COVID-19

Xiang and colleagues opined that mental well-being was a pressing concern during the COVID-19 pandemic, and deserved global attention (Xiang et al., 2020). After reviewing data from several local studies, Choi, Hui, and Wan (2020) found that depressive symptoms during the pandemic decreased with age. People aged 18 to 34 exhibited the highest incidence of depressive symptoms (56.0–57.0%), and this age group was most vulnerable to severe depressive symptoms (8.8–11.4%) (Fig. 8.1). Depressive symptoms were associated with a higher probability of arousing suicidal thoughts in an individual (Choi et al., 2020).

A research team from The Hong Kong Polytechnic University (PolyU) together with a dozen overseas scholars collected data on over 20,000 residents in nine countries through an online questionnaire during the first wave of the COVID-19 outbreak (Cheung et al., 2021). It was found that 46.7% of people in North America, 42.2% in Asia, 31.8% in South America, and 21.5% in Europe had depressive symptoms as measured by Patient Health Questionnaire – 9

Figure 8.1 Depressive symptom prevalence by age group in Hong Kong

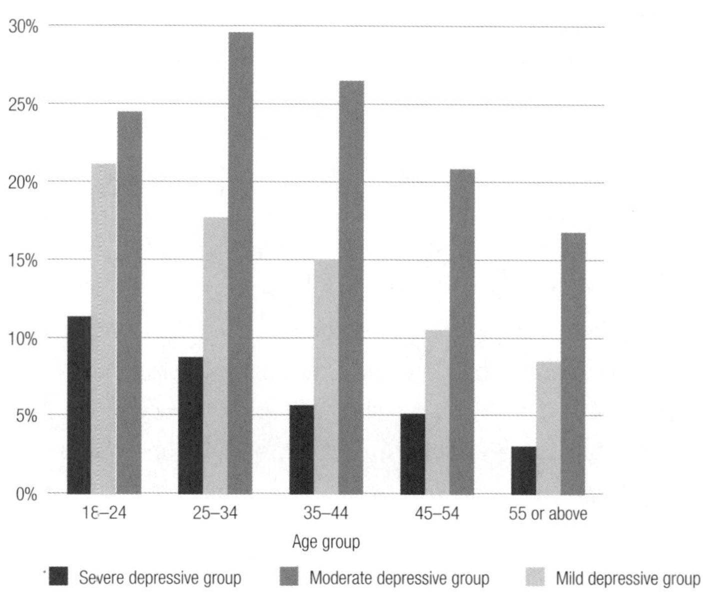

Adapted from 林清、陳信、黃韻芝、張綽芝、林建邦、何思穎、楊穎輝、韓正玉、孫桂萍、項玉濤 [Lam et al.] (2020).

(PHQ-9). These figures were four to six times the norm before the pandemic in the respective regions. The PolyU research team also collected data from more than 10,000 Hong Kong adults aged 18 to 59. The study found that 46.5% of the population presented different degrees of depressive symptoms (Bressington et al., 2020). Among them, the tendency to reuse masks, the frequent wearing of face masks, and the perception of being highly susceptible to COVID were found to be factors more likely to cause depressive symptoms. In another local study, it was found that inadequate supply of surgical masks was a factor that led to mental problems with signs of depression and anxiety (Choi et al., 2020). However, people with higher cues to action, more knowledge of COVID-19, and higher self-efficacy showed a lower degree of depressive symptoms.

Under such a large-scale public health emergency, it was observed that prolonged sleep disturbance increased the likelihood of developing mental health problems. In a web-based cross-sectional study, another PolyU research team collected sleep data from more than 1,000 adults. The results indicated that between 29.1% and 38.3% of people reported unsatisfactory sleep quality, insufficient sleep time, and difficulty falling asleep, while about 30% had insomnia (Yu et al., 2020b). It was also found that people with an insufficient stock of face masks at home were more likely to suffer from insomnia. A longitudinal follow-up study on 339 participants during the third and fourth waves of the COVID-19 pandemic indicated that the weighted prevalence of insomnia, anxiety, and depression was 33.6%, 15.3%, and 22.0%, respectively (Lam et al., 2021). Similar results were found in another vulnerable group, healthcare staff. A survey conducted during the first wave compared the mental health of frontline healthcare workers in Hubei province, Guangdong province, and Hong Kong (Lam et al., 2020). The results revealed that 50.4% of Hong Kong healthcare workers had depressive symptoms (PHQ-9), and that the perceived lack of protective equipment in the workplace was a significant contributing factor. In late September 2020 (i.e., the third wave in Hong Kong), the Hong Kong Overall Happiness Index 2020 survey also explored symptoms of depression. The findings showed that more than 45% of the 2,000 respondents had mild to severe depressive symptoms (HK.WeCARE, 2021). It was observed that several parameters related to mental well-being had persisted and there was no sign of improvement.

To minimise the impacts of the pandemic, the United Nations has recommended that governments should (a) apply a whole-of-society approach to promote, protect, and care for mental health; (b) ensure widespread availability of emergency mental health and psychological support; and (c) support recovery from COVID-19 by building mental health services for the future (United Nations Sustainable Development Group, 2020). Before the COVID-19 pandemic, Hong Kong's Food and Health Bureau (now known as the Health Bureau) had already launched a territory-wide mental health promotion and public education initiative called "Shall We Talk" to eliminate stigmatisation of people with mental health issues. In addition to promotion and awareness activities, there was a one-stop website disseminating relevant information and providing channels to assist those in need of mental healthcare. These establishments are useful in maintaining the mental well-being of people affected by the pandemic.

Although Hong Kong's control strategies and measures had been effective in preventing a large outbreak up until the fifth wave of COVID-19, the strict restrictions inevitably affected people's daily lives and the economic activities of the city. Negative impacts of the measures included an increase in the unemployment rate, deterioration of mental health among young people, and difficulties experienced by older people in communicating with their social support groups. In order to lessen hardships and to show support for COVID-19 control measures, an Anti-epidemic Fund was set up by the government and contributed to by both the government and private companies to promote the physical and mental health of Hong Kong people through the provision of financial aid. Examples of the use of the fund include a relief package offered to individuals and subsidised designated quarantine hotel schemes (HKSAR, 2021c). However, the outbreak of the Omicron variant in December 2021 significantly restricted the delivery of effective mental health services, which may remain a long-term challenge for the government and the community.

Lessons from the Fifth Wave in Hong Kong

In late January 2022, the rapid development of the COVID-19 situation in Hong Kong due to the Omicron variants marked the beginning of the fifth wave of the epidemic (HKSAR, 2022a). Table 8.5 shows the significant evolving epidemic in Hong Kong from 31 December 2021 to 31 March 2022. The epidemic curve in Figure 8.2 also demonstrates the upward trend of positive cases in Hong Kong after late January 2022. The weekly confirmed cases of fewer than 5,000 increased by threefold to over 18,000 (CHP, 2022a).

To contain recurrent cases with the high transmissibility of the Omicron variants, the Hong Kong government launched a series of tightened social distancing measures in mid-February 2022 for all catering business and scheduled premises, and specifically mandated the compulsory use of the LeaveHomeSafe mobile application. Customers needed to have received at least one dose of vaccine before entering catering premises for dine-in service, and all catering premises should cease operation from 18:00 to 04:59. In addition, all mass events/group gatherings including multi-household gatherings in private premises were prohibited (HKSAR, 2022b). To provide substantial support to

Figure 8.2 Epidemic curve of cases testing positive for SARS-CoV-2 virus by nucleic acid tests in Hong Kong from 31 December 2021 to 31 December 2022

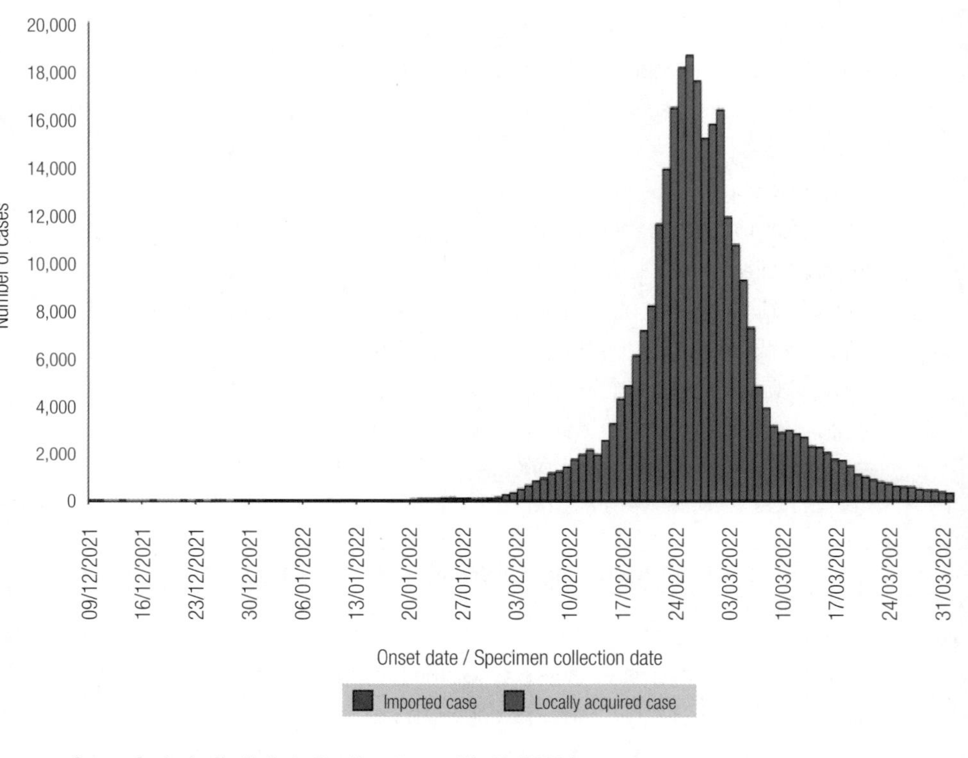

Source: Centre for Health Protection, Department of Health (2022a)

Table 8.5 Comparison of reported COVID-19 cases between December 2021 and March 2022 in Hong Kong (as of 31 March 2022)

	December 2021	March 2022
No. of confirmed cases	12,560	1,144,784 (722,514 (nucleic acid tests) + 422,270 (rapid antigen tests))
No. of deaths	213	7,612
% increase in confirmed cases during the period	9,014.5%	
% increase in deaths during the period	3,473.7%	

the premises affected by the tightened measures, the government immediately established the sixth round of the Anti-epidemic Fund that cost $27 billion to benefit around 6,700 businesses and over 750,000 individuals (HKSAR, 2022c).

Nevertheless, the abruptly worsening situation exposed the unpreparedness of the Hong Kong government. There were reports about overwhelmed hospitals and quarantine centres full of COVID-19 patients (Lindberg, Marlow, Tam, and Hong, 2022; Wong and Tin, 2022). In view of the intense demands on manpower and resources, the government requested support from the Chinese central government in mid-February 2022. The central government promptly responded with resources to support the anti-epidemic efforts and daily necessities in Hong Kong. A National Health Commission task force was also sent to Hong Kong to share anti-epidemic experiences in the Mainland and to provide advice and guidance on local COVID-19 strategies. Moreover, immediate construction of extra isolation and treatment facilities to accommodate over 10,000 patients was begun. The construction showed good progress with the Tsing Yi isolation facility first completed in late February 2022 (HKSAR, 2022d; Information Services Department, 2022).

With insufficient testing capacity to handle surging demands in surveillance, the Hong Kong government adopted a new risk-based testing strategy in late February 2022 by distributing rapid test kits based on the risk levels of districts instead of issuing compulsory testing notices, targeting more higher-risk buildings to conduct restriction-testing declaration operations. Unlike the past arrangement where rapid antigen test (RAT) positive persons were required to submit samples to specimen collection points for further confirmation by nucleic acid tests, the RAT positive results were recognised as positive cases by registering the results through a designated online system which was launched on 7 March 2022 (HKSAR, 2022f). Moreover, samples preliminarily testing positive at outsourced laboratories were no longer required to be sent to the Public Health Laboratory Services Branch of the Department of Health for further review with confirmatory results (HKSAR, 2022e). The revised arrangements were meant to avoid resource duplication and time delays in reporting test results to residents.

In view of the tremendous increases in confirmed cases and deaths from 2021 to 2022, monitoring efforts and control measures should be maintained in a vigilant manner. If and when an appropriate time is reached to launch the shelved "Compulsory Universal Testing" plan, manpower and resources should be well-prepared for the most efficient and effective execution in order to achieve zero infection. By reviewing mainland China's successful experience and knowledge shared by Chinese experts, the Hong Kong government should firstly integrate the different online electronic systems, like the Electronic Health Record Sharing System (eHealth), LeaveHomeSafe, Declaration System for Individuals Tested Positive for COVID-19 Using Rapid Antigen Test, COVID-19 Electronic Testing Record, and so on, into a single electronic platform to allow all residents to access the necessary platforms and information easily. This will help to improve compliance in the community and enhance community organisation in a public health emergency response (Car et al., 2017).

Recommendations

Vaccination is one of the main strategies to mitigate the impact of COVID-19 outbreaks (Moghadas et al., 2020), but Hong Kong still has a relatively low community vaccination rate compared to Singapore and mainland China. Especially in people aged 60 or above, who were the major vulnerable population to be hospitalised in critical condition or die during the fifth wave of COVID-19, evidence has shown that the fatality rate was at least 5 times lower for those who had received two doses of vaccine (CHP and HA, 2022). With increasing efforts to promote vaccination by the Hong Kong government, the vaccination rate will hopefully rise. In the US and the UK, where vaccination rates are at a moderate level, there is still a need for continued compliance with non-pharmaceutical interventions and pandemic prevention and control measures in the community in order to overcome COVID-19 and emerging variants (WHO, 2021b). These active protective measures include frequent and thorough hand washing, wearing face masks in public or crowded areas, avoiding social activities or mass events, and maintaining social distancing (Wong et al., 2020). There is also a need to assure the quality of face masks available in the market, as a local research team found that many did not meet the American ASTM F2299-03 standard (i.e., a standard test method which measures the particle filtration efficiency (PFE) of various materials used for medical face masks). The team tested a total of 160 brands of surgical masks manufactured in different regions of the world. The results showed that 48.8% of the masks were of poor quality (0.3 particulate PFE, mean = 47%), and 42.6% did not meet the standards on the packaging (e.g., ASTM level 1) (Lam et al., 2020). Public education about good practices when wearing face masks is deemed helpful in fending off the virus. Examples are avoid wearing unfitted masks, try wearing a disposable mask underneath a cloth mask to enhance respiratory protection, and try other face mask fits such as placing pantyhose over the mask and head (CDC, 2020b; O'Kelly et al., 2022), which has been proven to be an effective way to improve fit while reducing side flow leakage.

Private clinics in the community also serve a crucial role in reporting suspected cases of COVID-19 since they are the first line of contact for patients (CHP, 2021a; Food and Health Bureau, 2010). Hence, primary care settings should also be given resources and responsibilities in outbreak control (e.g., provision of PPE and rapid diagnostic testing kits). Family doctors should be able to assume the role of a sentinel and provide an additional response to future pandemics (Yu et al., 2020a). This pandemic also serves as an evident point to strengthen the development of community-based primary healthcare which can divert Hospital Authority patients with non-critical conditions for consultations and follow-ups with primary care providers, and telehealth services to alleviate the pressure on quarantine facilities (Wong et al., 2021; The Legislative Council Commission, 2021). More discussion on primary healthcare can be found in chapter 6.

Although the thorough lifting of international restrictions on COVID-19 has not yet occurred, a transitional phase to move towards COVID-19 resilience in the future has already begun. In 2021, Hong Kong proposed quarantine-free travel to the Mainland (HKSAR, 2021d). China previously adopted a "zero-tolerance" approach to COVID-19, so Hong Kong's compliance with China's Health Code System of medical monitoring and contact tracing was necessary before quarantine-free travel to and from the Mainland could be resumed. Hong Kong must review its preparedness and have a response plan for novel infectious diseases with a more structural and stepwise framework that conforms to China's strategies for COVID-19 resilience (State Council Information Office of the People's Republic of China, 2020).

At present, Hong Kong has a three-tier response system for pandemics. It grades the risk of any novel infectious disease affecting Hong Kong and its health impact on the community. The system ensures a contingency plan and response measures, and effective communication of information about the disease to the public by relevant agencies, companies, and organisations. However, the current plan lacks guidance on the easing of social restrictions. In the Disease Outbreak Response System Condition (DORSCON) framework adopted in Singapore, there are four levels of responses across three different phases—alert, containment, mitigation—which show some similarity to Hong Kong's current response plan. Nevertheless, the most severe level of DORSCON is red, at which time the government fully concentrates its efforts on mitigating the disease outbreak with strict social distancing and containment measures. When the disease is contained, the lowering of the response level starts with a relaxation of restrictive measures while maintaining high vigilance on border control, and surveillance and containment of local cases (Ministry of Health, Singapore, 2014). Therefore, the Hong Kong government should review its current strategic preparedness and response plan, and reconsider the balance between strict public health measures and the impact on the community to see if there is room for greater flexibility in the responses in each unique scenario of pandemic developments. In the social and economic challenges posed to the community, people have experienced enormous frustration because of sudden disruptions to their normal lives due to fluctuating COVID-19 situations. Clearer guidance for pandemic response can boost public compliance with COVID-19 public health measures (Hung and Lin, 2021).

Conclusion

Generally, Hong Kong has shown an efficient and timely response to COVID-19 with mass community surveillance, rigorous quarantine and monitoring measures for inbound travellers, advanced contact-tracing techniques, rapid epidemic prevention and control measures within the community, and high community compliance with the use of face masks, social distancing, and other community-wide mitigation measures. Thanks to the experience of the

2003 SARS epidemic, the whole-of-government planning and response plan also secured interdisciplinary actions in adopting necessary initiatives to curb the spread of COVID-19, particularly in clinical settings which are the frontline battlefields to the disease, to safeguard the delivery of quality care to patients with strict infection control measures simultaneously. This cannot be achieved without the high professional standard of Hong Kong healthcare workers. With the improvement in interdisciplinary communication and experience in handling the rapid outbreak of the fifth wave of COVID-19, the Hong Kong government should be able to optimise the current infection control and public health strategies to tackle imminent outbreaks in future.

As global society is now highly interconnected, especially in an international city like Hong Kong with a special demographic structure including foreign domestic helpers and ethnic minorities, it will be a continuous challenge for Hong Kong to maintain effective border control measures while not affecting local community activities and the needs of local households. Another challenge will be the prolonged post-COVID-19 syndrome / long COVID that has raised concerns regarding long-term impacts to the healthcare system (Menges et al., 2021). The health services and management strategies to respond to the needs of these patients should be addressed in future resilience plans, especially the preparedness for possible recurrence of domestic cases.

With the large-scale impact of COVID-19 globally, countries may consider more advanced coping strategies. Future analysis and research are needed to explore the potential benefits and risks of all public health interventions, which can take into account the local specific circumstances when adopting public health measures. Until that time, communities should embrace the new normal with high precautions in terms of personal hygiene and social distancing until an effective way to detect asymptomatic transmission of SARS-CoV-2 and a concrete extent of vaccine protection can be found.

References

Bogoch, I. I., Watts, A., Thomas-Bachli, A., Huber, C., Kraemer, M. U. G., and Khan, K. (2020). Pneumonia of unknown aetiology in Wuhan, China: Potential for international spread via commercial air travel. *Journal of Travel Medicine, 27*(2).

Bonevski, B., Randell, M., Paul, C., Chapman, K., Twyman, L., Bryant, J., Brozek, I., and Hughes, C. (2014). Reaching the hard-to-reach: A systematic review of strategies for improving health and medical research with socially disadvantaged groups. *BMC Medical Research Methodology, 14*, 42.

Bressington, D. T., Cheung, T. C. C., Lam, S. C., Suen, L. K. P., Fong, T. K. H., Ho, H. S. W., and Xiang, Y. T. (2020). Association between depression, health beliefs, and face mask use during the COVID-19 pandemic. *Frontiers in Psychiatry, 11*, 1075.

Car, J., Tan, W. S., Huang, Z., Sloot, P., and Franklin, B. D. (2017). eHealth in the future of medications management: Personalisation, monitoring and adherence. *BMC Medicine, 15*, 73.

Census and Statistics Department. (2017). *Hong Kong 2016 population by-census – Thematic report: Ethnic minorities.* www.censtatd.gov.hk/en/EIndexbySubject. html?pcode=B1120100&scode=459.

Census and Statistics Department. (2021a). *Use of information technology – Table E572: Usage of information technology.* www.censtatd.gov.hk/en/ EIndexbySubject.html?scode=590&pcode=D5600572.

Census and Statistics Department. (2021b). *Population estimates.* Retrieved on 24 January 2022 from www.censtatd.gov.hk/en/scode150.html.

Centers for Disease Control and Prevention. (2020a). *Implementation of mitigation strategies for communities with local COVID-19 transmission.* Retrieved on 31 January 2022 from www.cdc.gov/coronavirus/2019-ncov/community/ community-mitigation.html.

Centers for Disease Control and Prevention. (2020b). *Your guide to masks.* Retrieved on 11 February 2022 from www.cdc.gov/coronavirus/2019-ncov/prevent-getting-sick/about-face-coverings.html.

Centers for Disease Control and Prevention. (2021). *COVID data tracker - COVID-19 vaccinations in the United States.* Retrieved on 31 December 2021 from covid. cdc.gov/covid-data-tracker/#vaccinations_vacc-people-onedose-pop-5yr.

Centre for Health Protection. (2020). *Preparedness and response plan for novel infectious disease of public health significance.* www.chp.gov.hk/files/pdf/ govt_preparedness_and_response_plan_for_novel_infectious_disease_of_ public_health_significance_eng.pdf.

Centre for Health Protection. (2021a). *Appeal to offer coronavirus disease 2019 (COVID-19) testing for all symptomatic patients.* www.chp.gov.hk/files/pdf/ letters_to_doctors_20211231.pdf.

Centre for Health Protection. (2021b). *Latest local situation of COVID-19.* Retrieved on 31 December 2021 from www.chp.gov.hk/files/pdf/local_situation_covid19_ en.pdf.

Centre for Health Protection. (2022a). *Latest situation of COVID-19 (as of 31 March 2022)*. Retrieved on 31 March 2022 from www.chp.gov.hk/files/pdf/local_situation_covid19_en.pdf.

Centre for Health Protection. (2022b). *Recommended personal protective equipment (PPE) in hospitals/clinics under serious/emergency response level coronavirus disease (COVID-19)*. Retrieved on 25 March 2022 from www.chp.gov.hk/en/features/102742.html.

Centre for Health Protection and Hospital Authority. (2022). *Statistics on 5th Wave of COVID-19*. Retrieved on 6 March 2022 from www.covidvaccine.gov.hk/pdf/5th_wave_statistics.pdf.

Chan, J. F. W., Yuan, S., Zhang, A. J., Poon, V. K. M., Chan, C. C. S., Lee, A. C. Y., Fan, Z., Li, C., Liang, R., Cao, J., Tang, K., Luo, C., Cheng, V. C. C., Cai, J. P., Chu, H., Chan, K. H., To, K. K. W., Sridhar, S., and Yuen, K. Y. (2020). Surgical mask partition reduces the risk of noncontact transmission in a golden Syrian hamster model for coronavirus disease 2019 (COVID-19). *Clinical Infectious Diseases, 71*(16), 2139–2149.

Chen, H., Shi, L., Zhang, Y., Wang, X., Jiao, J., Yang, M., and Sun, G. (2021). Comparison of public health containment measures of COVID-19 in China and India. *Risk Management and Healthcare Policy, 14*, 3323–3332.

Cheng, V. C. C., Wong, S. C., Chuang, V. W. M., So, S. Y. C., Chen, J. H. K., Sridhar, S., To, K. K. W., Chan, J. F. W., Hung, I. F. N., Ho, P. L., and Yuen, K. Y. (2020). The role of community-wide wearing of face mask for control of coronavirus disease 2019 (COVID-19) epidemic due to SARS-CoV-2. *Journal of Infection, 81*(1), 107–114.

Cheung, T., Lam, S. C., Lee, P. H., Xiang, Y. T., and Yip, P. S. F. (2021). Global imperative of suicidal ideation in 10 countries amid the COVID-19 pandemic. *Frontiers in Psychiatry, 11*, 588781.

Chief Infection Control Officer Office, Hospital Authority. (2020). *Enhanced surveillance and control measures in public hospitals for "severe respiratory disease associated with a novel infectious agent".* icidportal.ha.org.hk/Home/File?path=/Training%20Calendar/145/Ms_MY_KONG_IC_Forum.pdf.

Chief Infection Control Officer Office, Hospital Authority. (2022). *Hospital Authority community kit – coronavirus disease 2019 (COVID-19) formerly named novel coronavirus (nCoV) version 7.21.* www.ha.org.hk/haho/ho/pad/Comkit.pdf.

Choi, E. P. H., Hui, B. P. H., and Wan, E. Y. F. (2020). Depression and anxiety in Hong Kong during COVID-19. *International Journal of Environmental Research and Public Health, 17*(10), 3740.

Chotirmall, S. H., Wang, L., and Abisheganaden, J. A. (2020). Letter from Singapore: The clinical and research response to COVID-19. *Respirology, 25*(10), 1101–1102.

Civil Service Bureau, Education Bureau, Social Welfare Department, and Hospital Authority. (2021). *Vaccination of government and key public service sector employees* [Paper for discussion by Legislative Council Panel on Public Service]. www.csb.gov.hk/english/info/files/20210920_Vaccination_e.pdf.

Cunningham, E., Smyth, B., and Greene, D. (2021). Correction: Collaboration in the time of COVID: A scientometric analysis of multidisciplinary SARS-CoV-2 research. *Humanities and Social Sciences Communications, 8*, 264.

Department of Health, Republic of the Philippines. (2021). *Updates on COVID-19 vaccines.* Retrieved on 31 December 2021 from doh.gov.ph/vaccines.

Department of Justice. (2022). *Cap. 599 prevention and control of disease ordinance.* Retrieved on 31 December 2022 from www.elegislation.gov.hk/hk/cap599!en-zh-Hant-HK?INDEX_CS=N.

Department of Statistics, Singapore. (2021). *Singapore population.* Retrieved on 31 December 2021 from www.singstat.gov.sg/modules/infographics/population.

Food and Health Bureau. (2010). *Primary care development in Hong Kong: Strategy document.* www.fhb.gov.hk/download/press_and_publications/otherinfo/101231_primary_care/e_strategy_doc.pdf.

Gill, J. R., and DeJoseph, M. E. (2020). The importance of proper death certification during the COVID-19 pandemic. *Journal of the American Medical Association, 324*(1), 27.

Government of India. (n.d.). *Aarogya Setu.* Retrieved on 31 December 2021 from www.aarogyasetu.gov.in/.

GOV.UK. (2021a). *Living safely with respiratory infections, including COVID-19.* Retrieved on 16 January 2022 from www.gov.uk/guidance/covid-19-coronavirus-restrictions-what-you-can-and-cannot-do#what-has-changed.

GOV.UK. (2021b). *COVID-19 response: Autumn and winter plan 2021.* Retrieved on 16 January 2022 from www.gov.uk/government/publications/covid-19-response-autumn-and-winter-plan-2021/covid-19-response-autumn-and-winter-plan-2021.

GOV.UK. (2021c). *COVID-19 response: Roadmap out of lockdown.* www.gov.uk/government/publications/covid-19-response-spring-2021/covid-19-response-spring-2021-summary.

Haug, N., Geyrhofer, L., Londei, A., Dervic, E., Desvars-Larrive, A., Loreto, V., Pinior, B., Thurner, S., and Klimek, P. (2020). Ranking the effectiveness of worldwide COVID-19 government interventions. *Nature Human Behaviour, 4*(12), 1303–1312.

HK.WeCARE. (2021). 整體開心指數 *2020* [Overall happiness index 2020]. Retrieved on 11 February 2022 from www.hkwecare.hk/happiness_index/general_happiness_index_2020/.

Home Affairs Bureau. (2020). *Workgroup on public participation: Together, we fight the virus.* Retrieved on 24 January 2022 from www.hyab.gov.hk/en/policy_responsibilities/District_Community_and_Public_Relations/working_group.htm.

Hong Kong Tourism Board. (2021). *Monthly report – visitor arrival statistics: Nov 2021.* partnernet.hktb.com/filemanager/LatestStatistics/30/Tourism%20 Statistics%2011%202021.pdf.

Hung, L., and Lin, M. (2021). Clear, consistent and credible messages are needed for promoting compliance with COVID-19 public health measures. *Evidence Based Nursing, 25*(1), 22.

Hyland-Wood, B., Gardner, J., Leask, J., and Ecker, U. K. H. (2021). Toward effective government communication strategies in the era of COVID-19. *Humanities and Social Sciences Communications, 8*, 30.

Immigration and Checkpoints Authority, Singapore. (n.d.). *Travelling to Singapore.* Retrieved on 31 December 2021 from safetravel.ica.gov.sg/arriving/ overview#lanelist.

Information Services Department. (2021). *LeaveHomeSafe app rule to expand* [Press release]. 6 December 2021. www.news.gov.hk/eng/2021/12/20211206/20211 206_175552_090.html.

Information Services Department. (2022). *Tsing Yi isolation facility set* [Press release]. 28 February 2022. www.news.gov.hk/eng/2022/02/20220228/202 20228_174638_064.html.

Inter-agency Task Force for the Management of Emerging Infectious Diseases, Republic of the Agree. (2021). *Guidelines on the nationwide implementation of alert level system for Covid-19 response.* doh.gov.ph/sites/default/files/ health-update/Guidelines-Alert-Level-System-for-COVID-19-Response.pdf.

Kwok, K. O., Li, K. K., Chan, H. H. H., Yi, Y. Y., Tang, A., Wei, W. I., and Wong, S. Y. S. (2020). Community responses during early phase of COVID-19 epidemic, Hong Kong. *Emerging Infectious Diseases, 26*(7), 1575–1579.

Lam, C. S., Yu, B. Y. M., Cheung, D. S. T., Cheung, T., Lam, S. C., Chung, K. F., Ho, F. Y. Y., and Yeung, W. F. (2021). Sleep and mood disturbances during the COVID-19 outbreak in an urban Chinese population in Hong Kong: A longitudinal study of the second and third waves of the outbreak. *International Journal of Environmental Research and Public Health, 18*(16), 8444.

Lam, H. Y., Lau, C. C. A., Wong, C. H., Lee, K. Y. K., Yip, S. L., Tsang, K. L. A., Cheng, K. C. P., Au, K. W. A., Ng, H. L. K., Chuang, S. K., and Lam, M. K. R. (2022). A review of epidemiology and public health control measures of COVID-19 variants in Hong Kong, December 2020 to June 2021. *IJID Regions, 2*, 16–24.

Lam, S. C., Arora, T., Grey, I., Suen, L. K. P., Huang, E. Y. Z., Li, D., and Lam, K. B. H. (2020). Perceived risk and protection from infection and depressive symptoms among healthcare workers in Mainland China and Hong Kong during COVID-19. *Frontiers in Psychiatry, 11*, 686.

林清、陳信、黃韻芝、張綽芝、林建邦、何思穎、楊穎輝、韓正玉、孫桂萍、項玉濤 [Lam, S. C., Chan, S., Huang, E. Y.-z., Cheung, T., Lam, H. K. B., Ho, H. S. W., Yeung, J. W. F., Hon, C. Y., Suen, L. K. P., and Xiang, Y.-T.]. (2020). 知識專欄：抗疫中的精神狀態 (頁120–125)。港島東醫院聯網醫護編。《COVID-19抗疫之路：香港醫護的心路歷程》 [Knowledge section: Mental state during the period of the pandemic. In: Healthcare Professionals from Hong Kong East Cluster of Hospital Authority (Eds.), *The Road to Fight against COVID-19: The Journey of Healthcare in Hong Kong* (pp. 120–125)]. 香港：聯合出版（集團） [Hong Kong: Sino United Publishing (Group)], p. 122.

Lam, S. C., Suen, L. K. P., and Cheung, T. C. C. (2020). Global risk to the community and clinical setting: Flocking of fake masks and protective gears during the COVID-19 pandemic. *American Journal of Infection Control, 48*(8), 964.

Leung, C. C., Lam, T. H., and Cheng, K. K. (2020). Mass masking in the COVID-19 epidemic: People need guidance. *Lancet, 395*(10228), 945.

Li, X., Chen, H., Lu, L., Chen, L. L., Chan, B. P. C., Wong, S. C., Cheng, V. C. C., Yuen, K. Y., Chan, K. H., and To, K. K. W. (2021). High compliance to infection control measures prevented guest-to-staff transmission in COVID-19 quarantine hotels. *Journal of Infection, 84*(3), 418–467.

Lindberg, K. S., Marlow, I., Tam, O., and Hong, J. (2022). "Chaos at Hong Kong quarantine camp leaves some detainees without food and power." *Bloomberg.* 14 January 2022. www.bloomberg.com/news/articles/2022-01-14/chaos-at-hong-kong-quarantine-camp-leaves-some-detainees-trapped.

Liu, C., and Graham, R. (2021). Making sense of algorithms: Relational perception of contact tracing and risk assessment during COVID-19. *Big Data & Society, 8*(1).

Marar, S. D., Al-Madaney, M. M., and Almousawi, F. H. (2019). Health information on social media. *Saudi Medical Journal, 40*(12), 1294–1298.

Mena, G. E., Martinez, P. P., Mahmud, A. S., Marquet, P. A., Buckee, C. O., and Santillana, M. (2021). Socioeconomic status determines COVID-19 incidence and related mortality in Santiago, Chile. *Science, 372*(6545).

Menges, D., Ballouz, T., Anagnostopoulos, A., Aschmann, H. E., Domenghino, A., Fehr, J. S., and Puhan, M. A. (2021). Burden of post-COVID-19 syndrome and implications for healthcare service planning: A population-based cohort study. *PLOS ONE, 16*(7), e0254523.

Ministry of Foreign Affairs, Singapore. (2021). *Hong Kong.* Retrieved on 28 December 2021 from www.mfa.gov.sg/Countries-Regions/H/Hong-Kong/Travel-Page.

Ministry of Health, Singapore. (2014). *Being prepared for a pandemic.* Retrieved on 21 January 2022 from www.moh.gov.sg/diseases-updates/being-prepared-for-a-pandemic.

Ministry of Health, Singapore. (2021a). *COVID-19 situation report.* Retrieved on 31 December 2021 from www.moh.gov.sg/covid-19/statistics.

Ministry of Health, Singapore. (2021b). *Resuming our transition towards COVID resilience* [Press release]. 20 November 2021. www.moh.gov.sg/news-highlights/details/resuming-our-transition-towards-covid-resilience.

Ministry of Home Affairs, India. (2021). *MHA Order dated 27 December 2021.* www.mha.gov.in/sites/default/files/MHAOrder_27122021.pdf.

Moghadas, S. M., Vilches, T. N., Zhang, K., Wells, C. R., Shoukat, A., Singer, B. H., Meyers, L. A., Neuzil, K. M., Langley, J. M., Fitzpatrick, M. C., and Galvani, A. P. (2020). The impact of vaccination on COVID-19 outbreaks in the United States. *medRxiv.* Published online 2 January 2021.

Mutambudzi, M., Niedzwiedz, C., Macdonald, E. B., Leyland, A., Mair, F., Anderson, J., Celis-Morales, C., Cleland, J., Forbes, J., Gill, J., Hastie, C., Ho, F., Jani, B., Mackay, D. F., Nicholl, B., O'Donnell, C., Sattar, N., Welsh, P., Pell, J. P., Katikireddi, S.V., and Demou, E. (2020). Occupation and risk of severe COVID-19: Prospective cohort study of 120 075 UK Biobank participants. *Occupational and Environmental Medicine, 78*(5), 307–314.

Nalbandian, A., Sehgal, K., Gupta, A., Madhavan, M. V., McGroder, C., Stevens, J. S., Cook, J. R., Nordvig, A. S., Shalev, D., Sehrawat, T. S., Ahluwalia, N., Bikdeli, B., Dietz, D., Der-Nigoghossian, C., Liyanage-Don, N., Rosner, G. F., Bernstein, E. J., Mohan, S., Beckley, A. A., Seres, D. S., Choueiri, T. K., Uriel, N., Ausiello, J. C., Accili, D., Freedberg, D. E., Baldwin, M., Schwartz, A., Brodie, D., Garcia, C. K., Elkind, M. S. V., Connors, J. M., Bilezikian, J. P., Landry, D. W., and Wan, E. Y. (2021). Post-acute COVID-19 syndrome. *Nature Medicine, 27*(4), 601–615.

Norton Rose Fulbright. (2021). *Contact tracing apps in Hong Kong - A new world for data privacy.* www.nortonrosefulbright.com/-/media/files/nrf/nrfweb/contact-tracing/hk-contact-tracing.pdf.

Office of the Government Chief Information Officer. (2019). *Statistics on the number of foreign domestic helpers in Hong Kong (English).* Retrieved on 31 December 2021 from data.gov.hk/en-data/dataset/hk-immd-set4-statistics-fdh/resource/b983aa1d-2617-4051-9ec1-dc5ca281b117.

Office of the Government Chief Information Officer. (2021). *LeaveHomeSafe – How it works.* Retrieved on 31 December 2021 from www.leavehomesafe.gov.hk/en/.

Office for National Statistics. (2022). *Coronavirus (COVID-19) latest insights.* Retrieved on 19 July 2022 from www.ons.gov.uk/peoplepopulationandcommunity/healthandsocialcare/conditionsanddiseases/articles/coronaviruscovid19latestinsights/deaths.

O'Kelly, E., Arora, A., Pirog, S., Pearson, C., Ward, J., and Clarkson, P. J. (2022). Face mask fit hacks: Improving the fit of KN95 masks and surgical masks with fit alteration techniques. *PLOS ONE, 17*(2), e0262830.

Porter, S. J., and Hook, D. W. (2020). *Report: How COVID-19 is changing research culture.* London: Digital Science.

Rooney, J., Byrne, S., Heverin, M., Tobin, K., Dick, A., Donaghy, C., and Hardiman, O. (2014). A multidisciplinary clinic approach improves survival in ALS: A comparative study of ALS in Ireland and Northern Ireland. *Journal of Neurology, Neurosurgery & Psychiatry, 86*(5), 496–501.

Russell, T. W., Wu, J. T., Clifford, S., Edmunds, W. J., Kucharski, A. J., and Jit, M. (2021). Effect of internationally imported cases on internal spread of COVID-19: A mathematical modelling study. *The Lancet Public Health, 6*(1), e12–e20.

Sahoo, S., Padhy, S. K., Ipsita, J., Mehra, A., and Grover, S. (2020). Demystifying the myths about COVID-19 infection and its societal importance. *Asian Journal of Psychiatry, 54*, 102244.

Seto, E., Challa, P., and Ware, P. (2021). Adoption of COVID-19 contact tracing apps: A balance between privacy and effectiveness. *Journal of Medical Internet Research, 23*(3), e25726.

Shen, J. (2021). Measuring the impact of mitigation measures on infection risk of covid-19 in Hong Kong since February 2020. *Cities, 114*, 103192.

Siegrist, M., and Zingg, A. (2014). The role of public trust during pandemics. *European Psychologist, 19*(1), 23–32.

Silver, A. (2021). Covid-19: Why China is sticking to "zero tolerance" public health measures. *British Medical Journal, 375*, n2756.

State Council Information Office of the People's Republic of China. (2020). *White paper on fighting Covid-19 China in action.* english.scio.gov.cn/whitepapers/2020-06/07/content_76135269_5.htm.

Stephenson, J. (2022). COVID-19 deaths helped drive largest drop in US life expectancy in more than 75 years. *JAMA Health Forum, 3*(1), e215286.

Stokes, A. C., Lundberg, D. J., Elo, I. T., Hempstead, K., Bor, J., and Preston, S. H. (2021). COVID-19 and excess mortality in the United States: A county-level analysis. *PLOS Medicine, 18*(5), e1003571.

Tam, V. C., Tam, S. Y., Poon, W. K., Law, H. K. W., and Lee, S. W. (2020). A reality check on the use of face masks during the COVID-19 outbreak in Hong Kong. *EClinicalMedicine, 22*, 100356.

The Government of the Hong Kong Special Administrative Region. (n.d.). *COVID-19 vaccination programme.* Retrieved on 7 February 2022 from www.covidvaccine.gov.hk/en/.

The Government of the Hong Kong Special Administrative Region. (2020). *Summary of results of the Universal Community Testing Programme* [Press release]. 15 September 2020. www.info.gov.hk/gia/general/202009/15/P2020091500931.htm.

The Government of the Hong Kong Special Administrative Region. (2021a). *Hong Kong and Singapore decide not to further pursue bilateral air travel bubble* [Press release]. 19 August 2021. www.info.gov.hk/gia/general/202108/19/P2021081900699.htm.

The Government of the Hong Kong Special Administrative Region. (2021b). *Government enhances virus testing for high-risk and high-exposure groups* [Press release]. 28 October 2021. www.info.gov.hk/gia/general/202110/28/P2021102800454.htm.

The Government of the Hong Kong Special Administrative Region. (2021c). *Measures approved by the Anti-Epidemic Fund Steering Committee.* Retrieved on 7 February 2022 from www.coronavirus.gov.hk/eng/anti-epidemic-fund-new16.html.

The Government of the Hong Kong Special Administrative Region. (2021d). *CS meets with Vice-Governor of Guangdong Province to prepare for resumption of quarantine-free travel* [Press release]. 14 December 2021. www.info.gov.hk/gia/general/202112/14/P2021121400722.htm.

The Government of the Hong Kong Special Administrative Region. (2021e). *COVID-19 thematic website, Together, we fight the virus, home*. Retrieved on 28 December 2021 from www.coronavirus.gov.hk/eng/index.html.

The Government of the Hong Kong Special Administrative Region. (2022a). *LCQ16: Coping with fifth wave of epidemic* [Press release]. 26 January 2022. www.info.gov.hk/gia/general/202201/26/P2022012600382.htm.

The Government of the Hong Kong Special Administrative Region. (2022b). *Government tightens social distancing measures in view of changes in epidemic situation* [Press release]. 9 February 2022. www.info.gov.hk/gia/general/202202/09/P2022020900022.htm.

The Government of the Hong Kong Special Administrative Region. (2022c). *Chief Executive welcomes passage of funding application for sixth round of Anti-epidemic Fund by LegCo* [Press release]. 15 February 2022. www.info.gov.hk/gia/general/202202/15/P2022021500679.htm.

The Government of the Hong Kong Special Administrative Region. (2022d). *Chief Executive thanks Central Government for ceaseless support for Hong Kong to fight epidemic* [Press release]. 19 February 2022. www.info.gov.hk/gia/general/202202/19/P2022021900721.htm.

The Government of the Hong Kong Special Administrative Region. (2022e). *Government continues adopting risk-based testing strategy* [Press release]. 25 February 2022. www.info.gov.hk/gia/general/202202/25/P2022022500816.htm.

The Government of the Hong Kong Special Administrative Region. (2022f). *'Declaration System for Individuals Tested Positive for COVID-19 Using Rapid Antigen Test' launched* [Press release]. 7 March 2022. www.info.gov.hk/gia/general/202203/07/P2022030700768.htm.

The Legislative Council Commission. (2021). Development of telehealth services. *Essentials, 20–21*, ISE14/20-21. www.legco.gov.hk/research-publications/english/essentials-2021ise14-development-of-telehealth-services.htm.

United Nations Sustainable Development Group. (2020). *Policy brief: COVID-19 and the need for action on mental health*. unsdg.un.org/resources/policy-brief-covid-19-and-need-action-mental-health.

Urban Land Institute, Singapore and Centre for Liveable Cities, Singapore. (2013). *Ten principles for liveable high-density cities*. www.clc.gov.sg/docs/default-source/books/10principlesforliveablehighdensitycitieslessonsfromsingapore.pdf.

US Department of Labor. (2020). *Guidance on preparing workplaces for COVID-19*. www.osha.gov/sites/default/files/publications/OSHA3990.pdf.

USA TODAY. (2021). *COVID lockdown: Which states have restrictions in place in 2021?* Retrieved on 31 December 2021 from eu.usatoday.com/storytelling/coronavirus-reopening-america-map/#restrictions.

Wan, K. M., Ho, L. K.-k., Wong, N. W., and Chiu, A. (2020). Fighting COVID-19 in Hong Kong: The effects of community and social mobilization. *World Development*, 134, 105055.

Waszak, P. M., Kasprzycka-Waszak, W., and Kubanek, A. (2018). The spread of medical fake news in social media: The pilot quantitative study. *Health Policy and Technology, 7*(2), 115–118.

Wong, M. C., Wong, E. L., Huang, J., Cheung, A. W., Law, K., Chong, M. K., Ng, R. W., Lai, C. K., Boon, S. S., Lau, J. T., Chen, Z., and Chan, P. K. (2021). Acceptance of the COVID-19 vaccine based on the health belief model: A population-based survey in Hong Kong. *Vaccine, 39*(7), 1148–1156.

Wong, S., and Tin, P. (2022). "Hong Kong's overwhelmed hospitals show up urgent gaps in primary health care." *South China Morning Post.* 27 February 2022. www.scmp.com/comment/opinion/article/3168437/hong-kongs-overwhelmed-hospitals-show-urgent-gaps-primary-health?module=perpetual_scroll_0&pgtype=article&campaign=3168437.

Wong, S. Y., Kwok, K. O., and Chan, F. K. (2020). What can countries learn from Hong Kong's response to the COVID-19 pandemic? *Canadian Medical Association Journal, 192*(19), E511–E515.

Wong, S. Y. S., Tan, D. H. Y., Zhang, Y., Ramiah, A., Zeng, X., Hui, E., and Young, D. Y. L. (2021). A tale of 3 Asian cities: How is primary care responding to COVID-19 in Hong Kong, Singapore, and Beijing? *The Annals of Family Medicine, 19*(1), 48–54.

Woolf, S. H., Chapman, D. A., Sabo, R. T., Weinberger, D. M., Hill, L., and Taylor, D. D. H. (2020). Excess deaths from COVID-19 and other causes, March–July 2020. *JAMA, 324*(15), 1562.

World Health Organisation. (n.d.). *COVID-19 high-risk groups.* Retrieved on 31 December 2021 from www.who.int/westernpacific/emergencies/covid-19/information/high-risk-groups.

World Health Organisation. (2015). *Summary of probable SARS cases with onset of illness from 1 November 2002 to 31 July 2003.* www.who.int/publications/m/item/summary-of-probable-sars-cases-with-onset-of-illness-from-1-november-2002-to-31-july-2003.

World Health Organisation. (2017). *A strategic framework for emergency preparedness.* apps.who.int/iris/bitstream/handle/10665/254883/9789241511827-eng.pdf.

World Health Organisation. (2020a). *Coronavirus.* Retrieved on 24 December 2021 from www.who.int/health-topics/coronavirus#tab=tab_3.

World Health Organisation. (2020b). *COVID-19 global risk communication and community engagement strategy, December 2020–May 2021: Interim guidance, 23 December 2020.* apps.who.int/iris/handle/10665/338057.

World Health Organisation. (2021a). *China: WHO coronavirus disease (COVID-19) dashboard with vaccination data.* Retrieved on 29 December 2021 from covid19. who.int/region/wpro/country/cn/.

World Health Organisation. (2021b). *Living guidance for clinical management of COVID-19.* www.who.int/publications/i/item/WHO-2019-nCoV-clinical-2021-2.

World Health Organisation. (2021c). *Coronavirus disease (COVID-19) advice for the public: Mythbusters.* Retrieved on 29 December 2021 from www.who.int/emergencies/diseases/novel-coronavirus-2019/advice-for-public/myth-busters.

World Health Organisation. (2021d). *WHO coronavirus (COVID-19) dashboard.* Retrieved on 29 December 2021 from covid19.who.int/.

Xiang, Y. T., Yang, Y., Li, W., Zhang, L., Zhang, Q., Cheung, T., and Ng, C. H. (2020). Timely mental health care for the 2019 novel coronavirus outbreak is urgently needed. *The Lancet Psychiatry, 7*(3), 228–229.

Xu, T. L., Ao, M. Y., Zhou, X., Zhu, W. F., Nie, H. Y., Fang, J. H., Sun, X., Zheng, B., and Chen, X. F. (2020). China's practice to prevent and control COVID-19 in the context of large population movement. *Infectious Diseases of Poverty, 9*, 15.

Yang, B., Tsang, T. K., Wong, J. Y., He, Y., Gao, H., Ho, F., Lau, E. H., Wu, P., Sullivan, S. G., and Cowling, B. J. (2021). The differential importation risks of COVID-19 from inbound travellers and the feasibility of targeted travel controls: A case study in Hong Kong. *The Lancet Regional Health – Western Pacific, 13*, 100184.

Yang, F., Heemsbergen, L., and Fordyce, R. (2020). Comparative analysis of China's health code, Australia's COVIDSafe and New Zealand's COVID tracer surveillance apps: A new corona of public health governmentality? *Media International Australia, 178*(1), 182–197.

Yau, B., Vijh, R., Prairie, J., McKee, G., and Schwandt, M. (2021). Lived experiences of frontline workers and leaders during COVID-19 outbreaks in long-term care: A qualitative study. *American Journal of Infection Control, 49*(8), 978–984.

Young, B. E., Ong, S. W. X., Kalimuddin, S., Low, J. G., Tan, S. Y., Loh, J., Ng, O. T., Marimuthu, K., Ang, L. W., Mak, T. M., Lau, S. K., Anderson, D. E., Chan, K. S., Tan, T. Y., Ng, T. Y., Cui, L., Said, Z., Kurupatham, L., Chen, M. I. C., Chan, M., Vasoo, S., Wang, L. F., Tan, B. H., Lin, R. T. P., Lee, V. J. M., Leo, Y. S., and Lye, D. C. (2020). Epidemiologic features and clinical course of patients infected with SARS-CoV-2 in Singapore. *JAMA, 323*(15), 1488.

Yu, B. Y. M., Yeung, W. F., Lam, J. C. S., Yuen, S. C. S., Lam, S. C., Chung, V. C. H., Chung, K. F., Lee, P. H., Ho, F. Y. Y., and Ho, J. Y. S. (2020b). Prevalence of sleep disturbances during COVID-19 outbreak in an urban Chinese population: A cross-sectional study. *Sleep Medicine, 74*, 18–24.

Yu, E. Y., Leung, W. L., Wong, S. Y., Liu, K. S., and Wan, E. Y. (2020a). How are family doctors serving the Hong Kong community during the COVID-19 outbreak? A survey of HKCFP members. *Hong Kong Medical Journal, 26*(3), 176–183.

Zhang, H., Qing, X., Huang, M., and Li, G. (2015). A correlation analysis model for multidisciplinary data in disaster research. *Data Science Journal, 14*, 19.

Zhang, L., Li, H., and Chen, K. (2020). Effective risk communication for public health emergency: Reflection on the COVID-19 (2019-nCoV) outbreak in Wuhan, China. *Healthcare, 8*(1), 64.

Zhu, P., and Tan, X. (2021). Is compulsory home quarantine less effective than centralized quarantine in controlling the COVID-19 outbreak? Evidence from Hong Kong. *Sustainable Cities and Society, 74*, 103222.

The Operation and Practices of Humanitarian and Emergency Logistics in Hong Kong

Simon S. M. YUEN and Calvin CHENG
College of Professional and Continuing Education, The Hong Kong Polytechnic University

Humanitarian and emergency logistics is a sensitive but important issue for most people around the world. With the increasing risk of natural and man-made disasters and viral outbreaks, there is a vital need for Hong Kong to develop comprehensive policies for humanitarian and emergency logistics services. This chapter identifies eight important criteria for efficient humanitarian and emergency logistics, namely, recovery ability, response ability, logistics and operating functions, collaboration and outsourcing capacity, information and information technology (IT) systems, emergency plans, infrastructure and resource inputs, and strategic partnership and social support. The Hong Kong government is recommended to review and consider the introduction of a more well-rounded policy with clear guidelines for humanitarian and emergency logistics. The major limitation of the study presented in this chapter is the use of qualitative research. Further empirical analysis is recommended.

Introduction

According to the World Meteorological Organisation (2021), the number of disasters worldwide has increased fivefold over the past 50 years. A disaster related to a climate, weather, or water hazard happens nearly every day, causing a daily loss of more than US$200 million. On average, 115 people die from disasters every day.

Hong Kong is located off the southeast coast of China. This geographical location has made the city fairly vulnerable to natural disasters like heavy rainfall, storm surges, and tropical cyclones. Given the growing risk of natural and man-made disasters and viral outbreaks like the ongoing coronavirus disease 2019 (COVID-19) pandemic, it is critical for Hong Kong to have more comprehensive policies for humanitarian and emergency logistics services.

The study presented in this chapter focuses on the operations and practices of humanitarian and emergency logistics in Hong Kong, and its objectives include the following:

a. identifying the importance of humanitarian and emergency logistics;
b. examining major criteria influencing the implementation of humanitarian and emergency logistics in Hong Kong;
c. developing successful practices for efficient humanitarian and emergency logistics in Hong Kong;
d. providing policy recommendations to the Hong Kong government and stakeholders for efficient humanitarian and emergency logistics.

Literature Review

Humanitarian Logistics

Humanitarian logistics is a new field in logistics scholarship and has received increasing interest from both researchers and industry practitioners since the 2004 Indian Ocean tsunami and other subsequent natural disasters in different parts of the world. The concept was first proposed by Thomas and Mizushima (2005, p. 60). Thomas was the managing director of the Fritz Institute and Mizushima was its chief logistics officer. They gave a detailed definition of humanitarian logistics: "the process of planning, implementing and controlling the efficient, cost-effective flow and storage of goods and materials, as well as related information, from point of origin to point of consumption for the purpose of meeting the end beneficiary's requirements". Humanitarian logistics involves the movement and storage of commodities and materials from the point of production to the affected area during the initial critical days following a disaster. Thomas and Mizushima (2005) conceived the main functions of humanitarian logistics as planning, preparation, procurement, transportation, warehousing, tracing, tracking, customs clearance, etc. The main participants are the government, the military, volunteers, donors, relief agencies, and other non-governmental organisations (NGOs).

Moreover, humanitarian logistics refers to humanitarian aid, in order to save lives, support the basic needs of all, and uphold human dignity. It is the fair, efficient, and cost-effective flow of relief supplies, equipment, personnel, funds, and information from the point of supply to the affected area in line with the three principles of fraternity, neutrality, and impartiality, and without profit as the primary goal. It is the process of organically combining the functions of planning, preparation, procurement, transportation, storage, handling, distribution, and information to meet the needs of disaster-stricken people.

Humanitarian logistics is central to disaster relief for a number of reasons (Thomas and Kopczak, 2005). First, it is vital to the speed and effectiveness of the responses for major humanitarian programmes, for instance, food, water, shelter, healthcare, and sanitation. Second, humanitarian logistics can be one of the most expensive parts of a relief effort given the procurement and transportation involved. Third, humanitarian logistics is critical to the performance of current and future operations since the logistics data can be utilised to provide post-event learning. Humanitarian logistics data covers all areas of execution, from the effectiveness of transportation providers and suppliers to the timeliness and cost of response, and the management of information and suitability of donated goods.

Humanitarian and Emergency Logistics in Hong Kong

Hong Kong is a city blessed with few natural or man-made disasters. This results in a low level of awareness of and attention to humanitarian and emergency logistics issues among Hong Kong people. Nevertheless, the Hong Kong Special Administrative Region (HKSAR) government and several NGOs play an active role in humanitarian and emergency logistics operations and provide related services.

The Security Bureau (SB) of the Hong Kong government created the Emergency Response System to provide an effective and efficient response to all emergency situations that may threaten public security, life, and property in Hong Kong (Security Bureau, 2021a). The Emergency Response System is a policy and guideline for emergency logistics operations at the government level. It details the emergency response procedures, and roles and responsibilities of different government units and departments concerned in the context of particular incidents. There are six main contingency plans for emergency responses in force at the moment: "Contingency Plan for Dealing with an Aircraft Crash in Hong Kong", "Contingency Plan for the Salvage of Crashed Aircraft", "Contingency Plan for Natural Disasters", "Contingency Plan for Maritime and Aeronautical Search and Rescue", "Daya Bay Contingency Plan", and "Emergency Response Operations Outside the HKSAR".

The Emergency Response System has defined two forms of emergency— emergency and extreme emergency. An emergency (i.e., a lower-level emergency) is a natural or man-made event that requires a rapid response for the protection of life, property, and public security. An extreme emergency (i.e., a disaster) is a very serious event, which usually happens with little or no warning, that disrupts life and causes death or injury on a large scale exceeding the normal response capacity of the public emergency services of Hong Kong. The system emphasises a bottom-up approach in handling emergencies, which limits the number of government departments or agencies involved, limits the communication levels, and delegates all essential responsibility and authority to those on site during the emergency. While most emergencies are to be handled by the Hong Kong Police Force (HKPF) and the Fire Services Department (FSD), there are always other government departments and agencies involved in different circumstances. To ensure that an appropriate response can always be provided, a three-tier emergency response system has been developed and implemented to segment different functions and government departments involved into three different levels: the Tier One response involves the emergency services offered and operated mainly by the HKPF and FSD; the Tier Two response is activated when an incident needs the attention of the Government Secretariat, which monitors the incident via the Emergency Support Unit (ESU); the Tier Three response is activated when an incident requires extensive government emergency response operations managed by the Emergency Monitoring and Support Centre (EMSC), and other security committees may also be convened if deemed necessary. In case of a very large-scale natural disaster (e.g., a super typhoon), a Chief Secretary Steering Committee is set up to oversee the government's emergency responses, supported by the relevant government bureaus or departments. The Government Logistics Department (GLD) plays an important role during emergencies. It is responsible for the provision of emergency transport support and for distributing emergency supplies, such as household bleach, hand towels, and blankets, from its central warehouse at the Government Logistics Centre. The GLD is also responsible for the urgent purchase of supplies or equipment that other government bureaus or departments have difficulties acquiring. The GLD has a land transport division that can provide emergency transport support for the delivery of supplies or equipment to other government departments. In case of emergency, a control centre is also set up in the transport pool to help with the coordination and deployment of different vehicles.

The Contingency Plan for Natural Disasters contains the Hong Kong government's overall strategy, organisational framework, and alert system in response to natural disasters like heavy rain, thunderstorms, storm surges, and tropical cyclones (Security Bureau, 2021b). The plan comprises a proactive and dynamic disaster management strategy that consists of a cycle of preparedness, response, recovery, and post-disaster review. Due to the increasingly strong impacts of different natural disasters, the ESU of the SB and relevant government bureaus/departments adopt a "prior risk assessment" approach, carrying out pre-disaster risk assessment and risk-reduction control measures to reduce any possible risks or threats to the community and important infrastructure in Hong Kong. In the response and recovery phases, one government bureau or department is assigned as the lead coordinator to supervise all those involved. The lead coordinator also rounds up the disaster situation, provides safety tips, and gives recovery information to the media.

Besides the Hong Kong government, NGOs also play important role in humanitarian and emergency logistics in Hong Kong. Local NGOs (e.g., Hong Kong St John Ambulance and the Hong Kong Red Cross (HKRC)) support the government in emergency response and disaster relief. Local NGOs not only provide various training sessions on emergency awareness and self-help knowledge to the Hong Kong community, but also participate in government interdepartmental exercises in order to ensure good cooperation and communication with different government departments in case of emergency or disaster. Many NGOs also arrange territory-wide publicity campaigns to enhance public awareness of emergency preparedness in Hong Kong. NGOs like the HKRC have even set up unique departments or units to provide relief and logistics services during emergency incidents or disasters.

Criteria for Efficient Humanitarian and Emergency Logistics

The literature offers eight important criteria for efficient humanitarian and emergency logistics: recovery ability, response ability, logistics and operating functions, collaboration and outsourcing capacity, information and information technology (IT) systems, emergency plans, infrastructure and resource inputs, and strategic partnerships and social support (Liao et al., 2018; Luis et al., 2021; Yuen and Yu, 2021).

Recovery ability refers to the ability of the humanitarian and emergency logistics network to quickly return to normal operation or its initial state after an emergency situation. The ability to recover is critical in humanitarian and emergency logistics as it can ensure that the supply of emergency supplies and relief services from the government and NGOs is not interrupted for a prolonged time during emergency situations and disasters. Recovery ability depends on the overall quality of the local physical and social infrastructure. It is the foundation for the efficiency of the entire humanitarian and emergency logistics.

Response ability is the ability of the humanitarian and emergency logistics network to respond to emergency situations and disasters, in terms of rapid decision-making and rapid execution. A quick and immediate response with relief resources is essential. Response capability depends largely on early warning systems, emergency plans, logistics levels, material management, and information sharing. The early warning system and emergency plan should be developed in the disaster preparation stage. Together with the logistics level, they represent the technical basis for response ability. Material management and information sharing guarantee response ability from the perspective of logistics and information flow, respectively.

Logistics and operating functions include receiving, handling, inventory and distributing emergency stores, and managing administrative issues related to the emergency situation. During emergency situations and disasters, it is vital to use the most efficient means of transporting and releasing supplies. Locating relief resources and facilities in the best locations at minimal costs and effort is essential in humanitarian and emergency logistics.

Collaboration and outsourcing capacity relates to relief organisations' ability to work together towards a common goal during an emergency and to delegate different logistics activities (e.g., inventory management, transportation, warehousing, reverse logistics, and customer services) to third parties. Close vertical and horizontal collaboration among different parties in humanitarian and emergency logistics can better optimise transport, reduce costs, and improve service levels. Outsourcing can help shorten the lead time and improve the performance of humanitarian and emergency logistics.

Information and IT systems are the data and software systems that support the logistical procedures and processes of humanitarian and emergency logistics. They are the foundation for managing supplies and starting up a logistics supply chain for disaster relief. Effective information and IT systems help to keep track of emergency supplies and materials anywhere and anytime, and reduce transportation errors.

Emergency plans are a set of guidelines and protocols for managing an emergency incident or disaster. They can provide valuable decision-making points of reference for relevant parties in humanitarian and emergency logistics. Scientific and well-designed disaster-relief emergency plans can improve rescue speed and decision-making efficiency, and reduce the impact of breakdowns on rescue operations.

Infrastructure and resource inputs include railways, highways, airports, hospitals, disaster-relief material reserves, and communication facilities. They are important in the operation of humanitarian and emergency logistics. Good infrastructure and resource inputs speed up the delivery of emergency supplies and materials, which means reductions in transportation costs and time.

Strategic partnerships with international couriers, donors, customs, and logistics clusters, and social support from the community, other firms, and government are other critical factors in humanitarian and emergency logistics. As humanitarian and emergency responses can easily be affected by various geographical factors, support from strategic partners and society can greatly strengthen the ability of relief organisations to deal with emergency incidents or disasters.

Case Report from Hong Kong

In this study, a semi-structured interview approach was adopted to collect data. The use of interviews in business research has a number of advantages (Eriksson and Kovalainen, 2016; Jain, 2021; Myers, 2013; Young et al., 2018). Interviews are a popular, practical, and efficient way of collecting data that cannot be found in published forms, such as journal articles, books, magazines, or newspapers. They allow the study of people's experiences from their own point of view. Interviews can also gather specific additional points that are insightful. They are useful in acquiring a deeper understanding of how and why certain things happen.

The semi-structured interview was conducted in January 2022 with a management professional and practitioner from a well-known NGO, the HKRC, providing local and overseas disaster relief and development services based in Hong Kong. The respondent was selected because managerial staff play a critical role in an organisation's operations and give overall business directions. Managerial staff are the ones who identify and evaluate the strategies and practices of humanitarian and emergency logistics in Hong Kong.

The Red Cross (International Committee of the Red Cross) is one of the most well-known international humanitarian organisations, helping with rescue work around the world. The HKRC was established in 1950. It is a highly autonomous branch of the Red Cross Society of China (Hong Kong Red Cross, 2022b) and runs a range of humanitarian services for the underprivileged, such as schooling for children in hospitals, volunteering services in ageing communities, uniform groups for youths and adults, and first-aid courses. In case of disasters in neighbouring regions, the HKRC raises funds and sends relief forces.

The vision of the HKRC is to strive for a world in which people respect and protect human life and dignity, and where people are ready to offer impartial and voluntary aid to help improve the lives of the vulnerable. The HKRC has three major missions, as stated on its webpage: "Protect human life, Care for the health of the vulnerable and Respect human dignity" (Hong Kong Red Cross, 2022b).

At present, the HKRC provides four main social community services: emergency relief and disaster preparedness, community health service and education, humanitarian engagement and education, and special education and rehabilitation. In relation to emergency relief and disaster preparedness, the HKRC established the International and Relief Service Department to handle both local and overseas disaster relief.

The Interview

The interviewee is part of the HKRC International and Relief Service. In general, the interviewee agreed that there is increasing demand for humanitarian and emergency logistics in both local and overseas disaster relief. He shared that there has been high demand for local relief services, such as food and shelter, as well as support services in quarantine centres since the COVID-19 outbreak in early 2020.

The interviewee noted that Hong Kong has developed a systemic framework to handle local disaster relief because the government has long provided related social community services. Departments of the Hong Kong government like the Home and Youth Affairs Bureau, the Health Bureau, the Security Bureau, and the Home and Youth Affairs Department take a leading role in planning, organising, and implementing policy and services to react and respond to different disaster and crisis situations (i.e., typhoon, fire, flooding, pandemic). Local NGOs (like the HKRC and the Salvation Army) and government auxiliary emergency services (like the Auxiliary Medical Service and Civil Aid Service) also provide logistics and support to maintain smooth and efficient humanitarian and emergency services.

Currently, the NGO provides local disaster-relief and project-based relief services. Local disaster-relief services for emergencies require an immediate response and the NGO sends service personnel to disaster-hit areas to carry out aftermath restoration work and distribute supplies. Usually, the relevant services are provided within 6–24 hours of the incident.

Moreover, local disaster relief services provide emergency supplies (such as clothing, daily necessities, etc.) to local people affected or cases referred by government departments and social service organisations, to help them cope with daily necessities. The material handling centre is equipped with clothing bundles, sweaters, jackets, blankets, quilts, toothpaste, toothbrushes, shampoo, adult and child face masks, alcohol hand sanitiser, and other relief materials to ensure effective responses to unexpected incidents and referral cases.

Some NGOs support the Social Welfare Department by providing emergency local disaster relief service. They also provide humanitarian support to residents in high-risk areas that are vulnerable to natural disasters or emergencies. For example, they provide electrical appliances/furniture elevation services before a disaster, restoration after the disaster, and post-disaster clean-up services.

Another category of service is project-based relief, such as the distribution of masks and daily necessities to people sleeping rough, which is carried out on an ongoing basis. With the COVID-19 outbreak in Hong Kong in 2020, various humanitarian and emergency logistics systems saw a huge rise in demand for supplies, manpower, and financial support. Some basic relief services were affected. To enhance the capability and effectiveness of humanitarian and emergency logistics, the interviewee agreed that Hong Kong needs a set of comprehensive criteria and service requirements (like major key performance indicators).

Regarding the criteria and service requirements, the interviewee agreed that all eight factors identified in this study are vital to providing efficient and agile humanitarian and emergency logistics services. First of all, response ability is critical to avoiding further damage and accidents. It is important to make quick decisions and execute quick responses to environmental changes and uncertain events. As the interviewee mentioned, most local relief and related services need to be provided within 6–24 hours of the incident. Moreover, logistics and operating functions can ensure sufficient supply and the smooth operation flow of materials, medical distribution, and aftercare. Efficient use of technology and equipment in relief and rescue by well-trained logistics personnel can ensure appropriate logistics practice and solutions are employed in different disaster conditions.

As noted by the interviewee, is also important to have collaboration and outsourcing capacity during emergencies in Hong Kong, in the pre-disaster or post-disaster stage, from outsourcing manpower to managing relief supplies storage facilities for emergency relief activities, which focuses on distribution and transportation. Using the current network, technology, or ability of contracted third-party logistics, service providers can improve the efficiency of operations, optimise resource allocation, and minimise the risks to the humanitarian relief service provider.

The interviewee also agreed that strengthening information communication and IT systems is one of the best ways to improve rescue efficiency and success rates. As NGOs face many restrictions and limitations (i.e., data privacy, cybersecurity), it is very important to continuously optimise their IT network in humanitarian and emergency logistics services. The dashboard and geodata on novel coronavirus infections in Hong Kong since 2020 (Centre for Health Protection, 2022) are examples demonstrating that well-rounded IT support providing real-time information and alerts for residents can protect public health.

"Prevention is better than cure" (British Red Cross, 2022): recovery ability and emergency plans should be organised in advance. Recovery ability relates to the degree and speed of recovery. Scientific and reasoned disaster relief emergency plans (with a warning system) can improve rescue speed and decision-making efficiency and reduce the interference of emergencies on rescue operations. The interviewee concurred that it is vital to provide plans as guidelines and handbooks for handling different relief situations in Hong Kong. A regular (e.g., annual) review and report can provide holistic reflection and follow-ups as appropriate.

Infrastructure and resource inputs are fundamental in humanitarian and emergency logistics services. A well-planned social infrastructure including road systems and networks, hospitals, disaster relief material reserves (government and NGOs), and communication facilities is required to deal with unexpected events. The interviewee also shared that logistics companies and warehouses in South Korea need to store emergency supplies for use in emergencies. Furthermore, strategic partnerships and social support are another key part of sustainable humanitarian and emergency logistics services. As shown via "Every One Matters", a campaign by the HKRC (2022a), social participation (such as donations, first-aid training, volunteer services) and public awareness of humanitarian and emergency logistics services can not only minimise the impacts of disasters, but also reduce subsequent losses and damage.

Among the eight criteria, the interviewee felt that response ability, logistics and operating functions, and collaboration and outsourcing capacity are the top three for achieving efficient and agile humanitarian and emergency logistics services.

Implications and Recommendations

The interview shows that response ability, logistics and operating functions, and collaboration and outsourcing capacity are the key criteria for efficient and agile humanitarian and emergency logistics. Response and recovery depend on the strength of social infrastructure such as railways, highways, airports, hospitals, disaster relief material reserves, and communication facilities. This is the material basis for the agility of the entire humanitarian logistics system.

Taking the Gansu earthquake in China in 2013 as an example, due to poor local infrastructure, the recovery speed of the humanitarian logistics network was slow, and many victims were not able to obtain relief materials in time (Liao et al., 2018; Luis et al., 2021). Response capability is mainly manifested in the rapid decision-making and action capability of the humanitarian logistics system after a disaster.

Having good infrastructure and resource inputs and well-designed emergency plans in the disaster preparation stage, together with effective information communication and IT systems, can guarantee fast response ability.

Strategic partnerships and social support can uphold quick response capacity and sustainable humanitarian and emergency logistics in the long run. All eight criteria are interrelated and can influence the humanitarian and emergency logistics support among government, NGOs, and other stakeholders.

In addition, comprehensive decision-making capacity is needed at various stages in the disaster management cycle, both pre- and post-incident/disaster. Challenges arise in many areas, such as evacuation, relief distribution, victim transportation, inventory management, resource allocation, traffic control, debris management, and planning and mitigation.

In the pre-disaster context, there is a strong need for strategically focused work and the extension of analysis and decisions to both tactical and operational levels. Humanitarian and emergency logistics management is reactive, such that participation in rescue work can only be undertaken when disaster strikes. There is a need to consider multiple goals and multiple stakeholders even in a common scenario. Comprehensive decision-making capacity (with specific skill sets) is important to achieve efficient and agile humanitarian and emergency logistics practices. Another aspect is support and continuity. It is observed that there is a lack of research and related policy analysing the socioeconomic impacts on affected households in the post-disaster period.

There is little research on public policy settings, humanitarian aid organisations, decision support systems, local data integration, and community responses (like public planning, risk education and training, etc.). Therefore, it is necessary for governments, academics, and professional organisations to conduct practical studies and develop relevant and appropriate policies.

The Hong Kong government should develop more comprehensive policies for humanitarian and emergency logistics services. It should enhance the Emergency Monitoring and Support Centre to provide information and coordination of related humanitarian relief and emergency work and services. It is necessary to establish various subcommittees, task forces, and "one-stop shop" online communication and resource platforms across government, NGOs, and other stakeholders to strengthen their handling and response capability and to create efficient, agile, and resilient humanitarian logistics and emergency services. This would not only protect the lives and property of

Hong Kong residents, but also consolidate Hong Kong as a safe, secure, and prosperous metropolis.

Conclusion

In general, humanitarian and emergency logistics services are important for Hong Kong to react to unexpected events and incidents as well as natural disasters, such as typhoons, diseases, and pandemics. The recent COVID-19 outbreak shows that efficient and agile humanitarian and emergency logistics operation and practices are necessary to avoid anxiety, chaos, and crisis. This chapter has identified eight criteria for efficient humanitarian and emergency logistics services. Based on the empirical analysis of an in-depth interview with a practitioner, response ability, logistics and operating functions, and collaboration and outsourcing capacity are found to be the three major criteria for achieving efficient and agile humanitarian and emergency logistics services.

In addition, well-rounded policy, operation flow, and guidelines are needed to minimise negative consequences and impacts. The major limitation of this study is that it mainly relies on qualitative research and secondary data gathering. An empirical analysis is recommended for future inquiries. More research is needed to investigate the roles of different stakeholders in humanitarian and emergency logistics services and further service collaborations in the Guangdong-Hong Kong-Macao Greater Bay Area region.

References

British Red Cross. (2022). *More health and social care funding.* Retrieved on 27 March 2023 from www.redcross.org.uk/about-us/what-we-do/we-speak-up-for-change/more-health-and-social-care-funding.

Centre for Health Protection. (2022). *Latest situation of coronavirus disease (COVID-19) in Hong Kong.* Retrieved on 27 March 2023 from chp-dashboard.geodata.gov.hk/covid-19/en.html.

Eriksson, P., and Kovalainen, A. (2016). *Qualitative methods in business research: A practical guide to social research.* London: SAGE Publications Ltd.

Hong Kong Red Cross. (2022a). *Every one matters.* Retrieved on 27 March 2023 from www.redcross.org.hk/en/everyonematters.html.

Hong Kong Red Cross. (2022b). *The history of Hong Kong Red Cross*. Retrieved on 27 March 2023 from www.redcross.org.hk/en/rcmovement/history.html.

Jain, N. (2021). Survey versus interviews: Comparing data collection tools for exploratory research. *The Qualitative Report, 26*(2), 541–554.

Liao, H., Tian, X., Feng, C., and Zhang, Y. (2018). Research on factors affecting agility of humanitarian logistics. *China Safety Science Journal, 28*(7), 172–178.

Luis, Y., Cristian, E. C., and Pablo, A. R. (2021). Humanitarian logistics and emergencies management: New perspectives to a sociotechnical problem and its optimization approach management. *International Journal of Disaster Risk Reduction, 52*, 1–19.

Myers, M. D. (2013). *Qualitative research in business and management*. London: Sage.

Security Bureau. (2021a). *Contingency plans*. Retrieved on 27 March 2023 from www.sb.gov.hk/eng/emergency/cp.html.

Security Bureau. (2021b). *Emergency response system*. Retrieved on 27 March 2023 from www.sb.gov.hk/eng/emergency.

Thomas, A., and Mizushima, M. (2005). Logistics training: Necessity or luxury. *Forced Migration Review, 22*(22), 60–61.

Thomas, A. S., and Kopczak, L. R. (2005). From logistics to supply chain management: The path forward in the humanitarian sector. *Fritz Institute, 15*(1), 1–15.

World Meteorological Organisation. (2021). *Weather-related disasters increase over past 50 years, causing more damage but fewer deaths* [Press release]. 31 August 2021. public.wmo.int/en/media/press-release/weather-related-disasters-increase-over-past-50-years-causing-more-damage-fewer.

Young, J. C., Rose, D. C., Mumby, H. S., Benitez-Capistros, F., Derrick, C. J., Finch, T., Garcia, C., Home, C., Marwaha, E., Morgans, C., Parkinson, S., Shah, J., Wilson, K. A., and Mukherjee, N. (2018). A methodological guide to using and reporting on interviews in conservation science research. *Methods in Ecology and Evolution, 9*(1), 10–19.

Yuen, S. M., and Yu, H. (2021). Implementation and practice of humanitarian logistics in Hong Kong. *International Journal of Science Academic Research, 2*(7), 1763–1766.

Part III

Looking Forward: Policy and Technology Systems Thinking

Technology in Disaster Management

Joseph LEUNG

College of Professional and Continuing Education, The Hong Kong Polytechnic University

Natural disasters are disruptive and unexpected incidents that impact people, communities, infrastructure, animals, agriculture, buildings, and environmental assets. The United Nations Office for Disaster Risk Reduction is exploring the use of advanced technologies to tackle climate change and related natural disasters. The goal is not only to control disasters through the adoption of technology, but also to develop appropriate frameworks, as emergency relief and post-disaster scenarios all depend on the magnitude of the disaster. Recent studies compare the emergency response frameworks in well developed countries such as Japan and the United States with those in less developed countries. In order to mitigate these effects, real-time information exchange between responsible organisations and the ability to make coordinated responses and prompt decisions are invaluable, and the usability of disrupted technologies could improve the negative consequences of disaster management. As many timely disasters are competing with time and require timely decision-making, user-friendly disaster information systems could facilitate effective communication and coordination, addressing people's urgent needs and concerns and managing disaster relief. The adoption of technologies may not make it possible to prevent all disasters, but could reduce the magnitude of loss of life and property to a certain extent.

Natural disasters are disruptive and unexpected incidents that impact people, communities, infrastructure, animals, agriculture, buildings, and environmental assets (Chatfield and Reddick, 2018; Wang and Ye, 2018; Yu et al., 2018). In view of natural disasters becoming common around the world, the United Nations Office for Disaster Risk Reduction is now exploring the use of advanced technologies to tackle climate change and related natural disasters (Hickmann et al., 2021). In the past few decades, natural disasters worldwide have tripled and have caused more than eight times the previous economic losses (Wannous and Velasquez, 2017). Building disaster resilience is now a priority around the world. The goal is not only to control disasters through the adoption of technology, but also to develop appropriate frameworks, as emergency relief and post-disaster scenarios all depend on the magnitude of the disaster. For instance, when the 2010 Haiti earthquake occurred, it took more than a year for relief operations to be completed. However, after the 2011 earthquake in Chile, it took only about a month for relief efforts to be completed, despite the differences in the magnitude of the disasters. Recent studies have compared the emergency response frameworks in well developed countries such as Japan and the United States with those in less developed countries (Munawar et al., 2022).

A natural disaster could have enormous impacts across multiple domains (Johar et al., 2022). In order to mitigate these effects, real-time information exchange between responsible organisations and the ability to make coordinated responses and prompt decisions are invaluable, and the usability of disrupted technologies could improve the negative consequences of disaster management (Velev et al., 2018). It has been reported by the Centre for Research on the Epidemiology of Disasters that US$2.9 trillion was lost from 1998 to 2017 in disaster-affected countries (Rehman et al., 2019). Furthermore, as many timely disasters are competing with time and require timely decision-making, user-friendly disaster information systems could facilitate effective communication and coordination, addressing people's urgent needs and concerns and managing disaster relief (Sun et al., 2020). The adoption of technologies may not make it possible to prevent all disasters, but could reduce the magnitude of loss of life and property to a certain extent (Leiras et al., 2014).

In general, disaster management can be divided into pre-event activities, such as mitigation, and post-event activities, such as recovery (Zlatanova et al., 2014). Disaster management consists of four phases: mitigation, preparedness, response, and recovery. In recent years, more studies have explored how data are manipulated in each phase of disaster management (Santos Rocha et al., 2016).

The Role of Technology in Disaster Management

Technology has the potential to transform disaster management, especially if one can successfully integrate emerging technology with existing infrastructure. As technologies such as artificial intelligence, Internet of Things (IoT), big data, and blockchain become even more sophisticated, they can help to drastically improve disaster response and relief capabilities. When powerful ideas and sophisticated machinery come together, they create new advances in disaster management (Poonia et al., 2021). Recent developments in disruptive technologies not only affect the ecosystem in various industries, but also disaster management, especially risk detection and mitigation (Fekete, 2020; Lamanna et al., 2012; Parker, 2020). The innovative use of technologies could facilitate positive development and address the challenges faced city by city. Innovative technologies can also play a major role in climate change adaptability and urban resilience (Yigitcanlar et al., 2020). The adoption of social media can further serve as an efficient and effective form of communication between the government, citizens, and communities in terms of information dissemination and social intervention tools (Yigitcanlar et al., 2022).

The term "disruptive technology" was coined by Clayton M. Christensen (Bower and Christensen, 1995) to refer to technologies that could affect the usual operation of a product or an industry, and also displace an existing product or technology. In recent years, mobile technology (5G), artificial intelligence, big data, the internet, robotics, drone technology, and blockchain have been cited as disruptive technologies (Abid et al., 2021; Amshoff et al., 2015). For instance, artificial intelligence has been adopted to analyse earthquakes and model the weather in order to predict disaster risks (Munawar, 2020; Ovesný et al., 2014), and drones have been deployed to capture images of areas at risk of disaster (Syifa et al., 2019). Recent studies suggest that disruptive technologies could act as a game changer in disaster management; they strengthen our ability to analyse the risk of disasters and assist in policies regarding disaster relief (Munawar et al., 2022). Apart from disruptive technologies, the internet has also played an important role in social communication and social behaviour, which results in new forms of communications. The emergence of social media in the past decade has accelerated information transfer, encouraging users' active engagement and contributions (Dwivedi, Ismagilova, and Rana et al., 2021).

Artificial Intelligence

Artificial intelligence (AI) has integrated computer science and data science to facilitate big data problem solving (McCarthy, 2004). It includes machine learning and deep learning. Machine learning focuses on data-driving via statistical models and human intervention, while deep learning eliminates human intervention and can adopt multiple layers of neural networks (Cendes and McDonald, 2022; McCarthy, 2004).

Since the past decade, artificial intelligence has supported disaster management in many forms, such as the way in which predictive analytics can help to forecast disasters and accelerate recovery and response times. Similarly, image recognition can identify damaged roads and buildings; large call volumes to emergency hotlines can be managed by chatbots and related voice response systems; airborne robots can access disaster areas to inspect the destruction; machine learning can interpret patterns from collected information such as videos, photos, numbers, and words to predict outcomes; sensors can assist with providing disaster information to related rescue platforms for real-time support; and sensors and algorithms facilitate speedier rescue and relief activities (Antoniou and Potsiou, 2020; Canon et al., 2018; Mosavi et al., 2018; Saravi et al., 2019; Wheeler and Karimi, 2020).

Deep learning algorithms can extract features across multiple layers. They are applicable to facial recognition, damage assessment, transportation prediction, and motion detection in relation to supporting disaster management (Sun et al., 2020). Large volumes of disaster-related data, such as satellite and social media images of damaged buildings, could be analysed with computer vision methods, to compare maps and images pre-event and post-event, which could speed up damage assessment. Following masses of social media posts during disasters, Artificial Intelligence for Disaster Response (AIDR) assists in identifying and classifying details from messages into categories (Chae et al., 2014). For example, machine learning successfully classified informative versus non-informative tweets during the 2013 Pakistan earthquake.

Big Data

Big data are considered to be one the most powerful tools available in this context, capable of transforming various industries and businesses, such as retail, manufacturing, and healthcare (Kankanhalli et al., 2016; Marr, 2017). The emergence of digitalisation, with the growing proliferation of digital gadgets such as smartphones and smart watches, has caused the amount of data available to increase at an incredibly fast pace, leading to the growth of big data analytics (Yu et al., 2018). One of the main objectives of big data management is to enhance the value of data, as well as decision-making (Munawar et al., 2022).

Big data are characterised by five "V"s: volume, which refers to the quantity of stored data; variety, which is the type and nature of the data; velocity, which represents the speed at which the data are processed; variability, which refers to dataset inconsistency; and veracity, which is the quality of captured data (Kankanhalli et al., 2016; Marr, 2017; Wamba et al., 2015). The sources of big data can be varied, from devices, sensors, networks, and transactional applications to social media, websites, video, and audio networks. Big data analytics refers to the process used to discover the hidden patterns and correlations in the data (Akter and Wamba, 2019). The collection of high-resolution satellite imagery is an important form of data in disaster management, and is crucial after the occurrence of disasters. Information regarding damaged land areas, buildings, and bridges can assist with the production of three-dimensional (3D) analysis, so as to compare pre- and post-disaster situations. These images are also intensively used for disaster risk reduction, such as in regard to landslides, and flood risk assessment (Raspini et al., 2016).

One of the biggest challenges in disaster management is data quality, as large varieties of heterogeneous data come from various data sources. For instance, sensors might generate various types of data including textural, time series, and semi-structured data. However, noise and false information cannot be avoided when social media and crowdsourcing are involved. With machine learning, data could be integrated and filtered, thus eventually increasing the quality of data (Yu et al., 2018).

Blockchain

Blockchain is an immutable and shared ledger that facilitates the process of recording transactions and tracking assets in a business network. Blockchain networks can help with tracking production, documents, and providing a single view to all associated members, which results in transparent information stored in the ledger (Attaran, 2022).

A decentralised blockchain-based form of disaster management provides a fast, safe, and sustainable response system. Members are free to exchange information, as the system is securely designed (Poonia et al., 2021). Blockchain technology also enables a permanent, searchable, irrevocable public records repository (Dubey et al., 2020). As people might panic during disasters, a great deal of misinformation might be circulated, causing a lack of trust during relief efforts. Blockchain technology could help to mitigate this concern, while managing reliable data, and smart contracting platforms could encode data without amendments, thus accelerating decisions and relieving the pressure on strained rescuers (Dubey et al., 2020).

Cloud Computing

Data constitute one of the most valuable assets in every organisation and data loss could result in irreversible damage to a business (Jadeja and Modi, 2012). Cloud computing is a large-scale distributed form of computing that is driven through economies of scale; the computer sources are delivered as services over the network (Qian et al., 2009). Recent studies suggest that cloud computing is a promising technology due to its flexibility, scalability, and cost-efficiency (Müller et al., 2011).

Traditionally, disaster recovery involves establishing a secondary data centre, to keep all redundant copies of critical data. However, it could be very complex to maintain, and time-consuming and costly to support (Jadeja and

Modi, 2012). With cloud computing, a cloud discovery centre allows storage and recovery to take place within a remote cloud-based platform. Critical workloads might prevent business from resuming and result in downtime during disasters, so cloud computing is especially vital to government authorities and related non-governmental organisations (NGOs), as they need this important information to resume operations (Yang, 2022).

Drone Technology

As drones can cover a 50-mile radius within an hour, rescue organisations can use them to outpace ground-based supply transports, making them especially good options to manage surveillance and damage assessment, and thus accelerating rescue recovery and rebuilding tasks. During disasters, conventional access becomes limited when bridges, airport runways, and roads are clogged with debris; drones could play an important role in these scenarios (Idid, 2022). Drone data could provide high resolution images as supplements to satellite images, to provide a comprehensive analysis of the disaster. The data can be analysed by humans or through machine learning with artificial intelligence technology (Kumar and Sud, 2020).

Geographic Information Systems

Geographic information systems store, manipulate, and display information using a geographic approach. They support spatial data and databases, and other sources of information such as hydrological (water) and socioeconomic (population) data could be embedded into a geo-database (Abbas et al., 2009). Geographic information systems can also capture, store, validate, and display data related to position on the Earth's surface. They can express this information in different ways, such as latitude and longitude (Tomlinson, 2007). These systems assist users in understanding patterns, relationships, and geographic contexts, so as to improve understanding as well as facilitate better management (Koller et al., 1995). Large-scale disasters require extensive amounts of geospatial information (Kapucu et al., 2022). These systems could provide a platform to centralise all visual data during an emergency, and all government authorities and related NGOs could then share information via these databases using data-generated maps (Laituri and Kodrich, 2008).

The Internet of Things

The Internet of Things (IoT) is a term coined by Kevin Ashton at the Massachusetts Institute of Technology (MIT) (Berte, 2018). The IoT connects objects together under the same standard protocols (Atzori et al., 2010) and enables the development of smart objects providing sensing, communication, and actuating capabilities, which allows the fast-growing number of everyday smart devices to connect with the internet and each other (Sinha et al., 2017). The IoT is a network with embedded technologies that can link up objects (things) via the internet, which can then be identified, tracked, and monitored through microchips (Bail et al., 2021).

In the context of disaster risk minimisation and prevention, the IoT could assist in monitoring disaster possibilities via geographic information systems and satellite technology and trigger alarm messages to social media when there is potential danger, and these responses could be generated in real time (Sinha et al., 2017). The interconnection of objects and devices in the network, including mobile devices, computers, satellites, and sensors, could enable risk identification and assessment, and the mapping of affected areas could be supported. For instance, the IoT-based sensors can help detect potentially dangerous situations, movements, forest fires (by measuring carbon dioxide levels), moisture, and temperature. They can also monitor river levels to detect flooding (Bail et al., 2021).

Mobile Technology

Mobile technologies (e.g., 5G) have been rapidly developing over the past decade. According to an International Telecommunication Union report in 2021 (ITU, 2021a), more than 75% of the world's total population has an active mobile broadband subscription, and over 57% of households have internet access at home. Studies on disaster management believe mobile technologies are one of the most effective approaches to managing disasters, due to the instant access to the internet they provide; the use of a Global Positioning System (GPS) could play an important role during natural disasters as a result (Djoumessi and Mbongo, 2022). In addition, the high penetration of mobile technologies can facilitate the collection of big data, such as environmental information and societal interventions, which are important to disaster risk reduction (Paul et al., 2021). In studies of mobile technologies in the field of disaster risk management since the early 2000s, most attention has been paid to the highly visible roles and tangible benefits of adopting mobile phones in emergency responses, such as information dissemination, education for the public (Gething and Tatem, 2011), and swift responses, rather than to traditional broadcast media (Laituri and Kodrich, 2008).

From public safety, security, and emergency perspectives, all governments are looking for resilient, stable, and secure communication infrastructures to support robust and mission-critical communication, in order to minimise the impacts of disasters and emergencies. In recent years, government agencies have been unable to develop proprietary broadband communications infrastructure due to limited interoperability. However, 5G networks could handle critical communication through low latency communication (Völk et al., 2021); information such as videos and images could be transferred and exchanged without delay, which is especially important during natural disasters (Velev et al., 2018).

Robotics

With innovations in computing technology, especially artificial intelligence, robots are used virtually everywhere (e.g., cooking bots and vacuum cleaners), easing human tasks and serving as assistants. They have also replaced employees in industrial workplaces, to manage tasks quickly while reducing human error. Robotics are being adopted in the medical industry, as they can provide 3D views and tenfold enlargement of surgical areas, reducing human error in traditional surgery (Bakshi et al., 2022). During the coronavirus disease 2019 (COVID-19) pandemic, robots have played an important role; they sanitised hospitals, supported frontline medical staff, made deliveries in hospitals and hotels, and monitored patients (Guizzo and Klett, 2020).

When facing disasters, robots could promptly team up through a network of mobile sensors and actuators for the sake of rapid action, and could be equipped with appropriate sensors and cameras to help save victims' lives without endangering rescuers (Chaudhury, 2011). According to the 2019 International Telecommunications Union Report, the emergence of disruptive technologies has successfully reduced risks in disaster management with the use of rescue robots, as it was deemed too dangerous for humans or rescue animals to take up some rescue duties (United Nations, 2021). Robots could enter burning buildings, secure city streets contaminated by poisonous chemicals, or scour avalanche sites, thus enhancing the effectiveness of rescue missions (Massy-Beresford, 2014).

Social Media

Recent studies have investigated how to maximise the use and adoption of social media (Andersson and Wikström, 2017; Bernard, 2016; Bolat et al., 2016; Dwivedi, Ismagilova, Hughes, et al., 2021; Dwivedi, Ismagilova, Rana, et al., 2021). It has been proven that social media could be a useful and effective form of communication in various situations, even during natural disasters (Yigitcanlar et al., 2022). Social media tools, such as Twitter-based warning systems, are a viable alternative for the government to use to disseminate prompt and accessible messages to the public, in order to reduce the risk to life during natural disasters (Chatfield and Reddick, 2018). Apart from collecting data using a traditional approach, the adoption of social media analysis can act as a new source of qualitative data; people share their views and opinions across social media platforms such as Facebook, Instagram, Twitter, and Snapchat, which could represent a significant portion of valuable data. The advantages of social media analysis include its ability to collect a large group of people's views and comments in a real-world setting.

Social media could become a useful communication platform in disaster rescue and relief; it can not only support government authorities to disseminate disaster relief information (Li and Rao, 2010; Takahashi et al., 2015), but can also provide time and geolocation information for developing disaster information systems (Srivastava et al., 2012). Visual analytics via social media provide spatial data to support evacuation planning disaster management (Chae et al., 2014). Social media platforms have also launched disaster response mechanisms. For instance, Facebook provides a safety check feature that could help with identifying which users are safe; another feature helps to connect people through fundraising; and the disaster maps feature facilitates recovery (Domalewska, 2019).

Sentiment and contents analysis have been successfully adopted in marketing (Rambocas and Gama, 2013; Shen and Bissell, 2013) and extended to the study of natural disaster management recently. Research has captured the emotional state of the population during the occurrence of natural disasters, and could help estimate the damage caused by natural disasters for governments and related authorities. The use of social media could be very effective in natural disasters such as earthquakes, floods, and wildfires, through the dissemination of photos, videos, and stylistic messages. For instance, over 177 million related tweets were posted in one day during the 2011 earthquake in Japan (Roslan et al., 2021). As social media data embeds emotional expression through texts, images, time, and geolocation information, it can be useful in identify psychological and healthcare needs (Sun et al., 2020).

Case Studies of Technology Adoption in Disaster Management

Case Study 1: The Use of Social Media in the 2019 Poland Floods

In May 2019, heavy storms and rains resulted in severe flooding in eastern and southern Poland. The flooding was accompanied by tornadoes and the highest flood warning level was issued. The Polish government collected 10,755 Facebook posts and 7,709 Twitter posts and used these to conduct sentiment analysis (Fig. 10.1). The results show that 58% of Facebook posts and tweets were not directly related to the emergency. These unrelated posts included digital marketing messages, such as insurance advertisements and advertisements for cleaning products (Domalewska, 2019).

It was discovered that numerous posts and tweets were related to flooded animal shelters, assistance with evacuating animals, criticisms of dog owners for leaving their chained dogs behind, donation collections, and support for flood victims. A total of 43.5% of comments related to the flood included a negative sentiment, and 1.6% expressed fear or threat. As a result, these messages could provide a picture for related government authorities to follow up (Domalewska, 2019).

Figure 10.1 Sentiment analysis of flood-related discussions on Facebook and Twitter

Sentiment	Distribution
Neutral	48.9%
Positive	2.1%
Compassion toward animals	4.2%
Compassion (other)	0.9%
Negative (fear or threat)	1.6%
Political negative	12.5%
Other topic negative	31%

Case Study 2: Big Data Analytics in Responding to the 2016 Typhoon in the Philippines

The Philippines is located in a typhoon belt and is vulnerable to as many as 20 typhoons per year. In October 2016, the country faced a severe typhoon, Haima, which affected almost five million people and caused catastrophic destruction. The Philippines government cooperated with 510 Global (www.510.global/) in an initiative proposed by the Netherlands Red Cross. The platform has made use of big data analytics to develop a Priority Index, which consists of details related to typhoons, such as precipitation rates and wind speeds. It assisted in predicting the "worst-hit" areas prior to the typhoon, thus providing information to those areas that required urgent support (Murwani, 2018).

Case Study 3: Using AI to Better Understand Natural Hazards and Disasters

In view of protecting countries and communities, artificial intelligence has been adopted by the World Meteorological Organisation, the International Telecommunication Union (ITU), and the United Nations Environment Programme. These groups have explored artificial intelligence to analyse and refine large datasets, so as to accelerate disaster management interventions. With a collection of earth observation data, data on connected devices, and street images, artificial intelligence could aid accessibility, interoperability, and reusability. Machine learning could help detect and respond to extreme events; for example, the study of waveforms could produce probabilistic forecasts to warn affected areas (ITU, 2021b).

Case Study 4: Using Drones in Disaster Management

The advantages of drone technology include drones' ability to fly at low altitudes and better visibility than satellite images, especially when faced with cloud cover. Drones can pinpoint the location of victims, damaged sites, and disaster relief sites. As flooding problems are becoming more frequent all over the world, many governments and authorities are looking for drone technology to revolutionise disaster management efforts. In 2005, drones were used in the United States to search for Hurricane Katrina survivors; drones were used by the Philippines in 2013 to create maps and assess the extent of the damage after Typhoon Haiyan; and South Korea's National Disaster Management Research Institute has been using drones to investigate damage caused by typhoons (Idid, 2022).

Case Study 5: Using Geographic Information System Technology in Disaster Management

Taiwan frequently suffers from natural disasters due to its geographical location, including flooding, earthquakes, and typhoons. To mitigate the loss and damage due to natural disasters, a well-established disaster management system is necessary. Geographic information systems could play an important role, as they could be used in modeling techniques to analyse large volumes of data during disaster prevention, and plan for evacuation routes in disaster warning systems. Moreover, they could organise details about the damage, such as pictures, in the post-disaster stage. The National Disaster Prevention and Protection Commission has coordinated with non-governmental organisations in regard to disaster management phases: mitigation, preparedness, response, and recovery. The development of a National Geographic Information System platform should serve as a common resource that can be used to manage an entire range of spatial and non-spatial data, in order to carry out responsibilities and services during disasters (Hsu et al., 2005).

Case Study 6: The MyDisasterDroid App for Disaster Management

MyDisasterDroid is a smartphone app developed in the Philippines. It can be used to locate victims during disasters in real time. An algorithm has been developed to compute the best route to reach that destination. However, this app strongly depends on a reliable mobile network, as well as GPS (Munawar et al., 2022).

Conclusion

Disaster management is not a one-step process and there is no simple solution available. Every stage of disaster management requires the formulation of public policies, strategies, advanced technologies, and applications to ensure the best possible preparation, reliable warnings, reduced vulnerability, and, ultimately, the mitigation of the disaster's impact. To improve disaster management, continuous reviews of and improvements to appropriate technologies must be made. Undoubtedly, different technologies play an important role in different phases of disaster management; the key is how government authorities maximise their value during disasters. Many recent disasters have already shown that technologies might not assist in avoiding them, but can mitigate the impact and consequences.

Emerging technologies not only assist in predicting potential disasters such as earthquakes and floods, but also support the improvement of related infrastructures. The adoption of innovative technologies can be capitalised on to increase disaster resilience on a global scale. Better management of disasters requires better coordination. To maintain the best quality disaster management, ongoing training programmes, updates, and communication among stakeholders such as government authorities and NGOs are very important. By utilising disaster resilient technology infrastructure, disaster warnings and inter-government authorities' coordination would be greatly improved.

Finally, public awareness programmes delivered via social media could educate and emphasise the importance of disaster management to the public.

The government could consider providing satellite phones and other resilient technologies to residents to enable disaster risk reduction measures in the community. Vulnerable groups are usually the most neglected and government authorities should take additional measures to provide necessities to these groups in particular.

References

Abbas, S., Srivastava, R., Tiwari, R., and Ramudu, P. B. (2009). GIS-based disaster management: A case study for Allahabad Sadar sub-district (India). *Management of Environmental Quality, 20*(1), 33–51.

Abid, S. K., Sulaiman, N., Chan, S. W., Nazir, U., Abid, M., Han, H., Ariza-Montes, A., and Vega-Muñoz, A. (2021). Toward an integrated disaster management approach: How artificial intelligence can boost disaster management. *Sustainability, 13*(22), 12560.

Akter, S., and Wamba, S. F. (2019). Big data and disaster management: A systematic review and agenda for future research. *Annals of Operations Research, 283*(1), 939–959.

Amshoff, B., Dülme, C., Echterfeld, J., and Gausemeier, J. (2015). Business model patterns for disruptive technologies. *International Journal of Innovation Management, 19*(03), 1540002.

Andersson, S., and Wikström, N. (2017). Why and how are social media used in a B2B context, and which stakeholders are involved? *Journal of Business & Industrial Marketing, 32*(8), 1098–1108.

Antoniou, V., and Potsiou, C. (2020). A deep learning method to accelerate the disaster response process. *Remote Sensing, 12*(3), 544.

Attaran, M. (2022). Blockchain technology in healthcare: Challenges and opportunities. *International Journal of Healthcare Management, 15*(1), 70–83.

Atzori, L., Iera, A., and Morabito, G. (2010). The Internet of Things: A survey. *Computer Networks, 54*(15), 2787–2805.

Bail, R. d. F., Kovaleski, J. L., da Silva, V. L., Pagani, R. N., and Chiroli, D. M. d. G. (2021). Internet-of-Things in disaster management: Technologies and uses. *Environmental Hazards, 20*(5), 493–513.

Bakshi, G., Kumar, A., and Puranik, A. N. (2022). Adoption of robotics technology in healthcare sector. In: Dhar, S., Mukhopadhyay, S. C., Sur, S. N., and Liu, C.-M. (Eds.), *Advances in communication, devices and networking* (pp. 405–414). Singapore: Springer.

Bernard, M. (2016). The impact of social media on the B2B CMO. *Journal of Business & Industrial Marketing, 31*(8), 955–960.

Berte, D.-R. (2018). Defining the IoT. *Proceedings of the International Conference on Business Excellence, 12*(1), 118–128.

Bolat, E., Kooli, K., and Wright, L. T. (2016). Businesses and mobile social media capability. *Journal of Business & Industrial Marketing, 31*(8), 971–981.

Bower, J. L., and Christensen, C. M. (1995). Disruptive technologies: Catching the wave. *Harvard Business Review, 73*(1), 43–53.

Canon, M. J., Satuito, A., and Sy, C. (2018). *Determining disaster risk management priorities through a neural network-based text classifier.* Paper presented at the 2018 International Symposium on Computer, Consumer and Control (IS3C), 6–8 December 2018, Taichung, Taiwan.

Cendes, F., and McDonald, C. R. (2022). Artificial intelligence applications in the imaging of epilepsy and its comorbidities: Present and future. *Epilepsy Currents, 22*(2), 91–96.

Chae, J., Thom, D., Jang, Y., Kim, S., Ertl, T., and Ebert, D. S. (2014). Public behavior response analysis in disaster events utilizing visual analytics of microblog data. *Computers & Graphics, 38,* 51–60.

Chatfield, A. T., and Reddick, C. G. (2018). All hands on deck to tweet #sandy: Networked governance of citizen coproduction in turbulent times. *Government Information Quarterly, 35*(2), 259–272.

Chaudhury, S. (2011). Disaster management using mobile robots. In: *ACWR '11: Proceedings of the 1st International Conference on Wireless Technologies for Humanitarian Relief.* New York: Association for Computing Machinery.

Djoumessi, Y. F., and Mbongo, L. d. B. E. (2022). An analysis of information communication technologies for natural disaster management in Africa. *International Journal of Disaster Risk Reduction, 68,* 102722.

Domalewska, D. (2019). The role of social media in emergency management during the 2019 flood in Poland. *Security and Defence Quarterly, 27*(5), 32–43.

Dubey, R., Gunasekaran, A., Bryde, D. J., Dwivedi, Y. K., and Papadopoulos, T. (2020). Blockchain technology for enhancing swift-trust, collaboration and resilience within a humanitarian supply chain setting. *International Journal of Production Research, 58*(11), 3381–3398.

Dwivedi, Y. K., Ismagilova, E., Hughes, D. L., Carlson, J., Filieri, R., Jacobson, J., Jain, V., Karjaluoto, H., Kefi, H., and Krishen, A. S. (2021). Setting the future of digital and social media marketing research: Perspectives and research propositions. *International Journal of Information Management, 59,* 102168.

Dwivedi, Y. K., Ismagilova, E., Rana, N. P., and Raman, R. (2021). Social media adoption, usage and impact in business-to-business (B2B) context: A state-of-the-art literature review. *Information Systems Frontiers.* Published online 2 February 2021.

Fekete, A. (2020). Critical infrastructure cascading effects: Disaster resilience assessment for floods affecting city of Cologne and Rhein-Erft-Kreis. *Journal of Flood Risk Management, 13*(2), e312600.

Gething, P. W., and Tatem, A. J. (2011). Can mobile phone data improve emergency response to natural disasters? *PLoS Medicine, 8*(8), e1001085.

Guizzo, E., and Klett, R. (2020). "How robots became essential workers in the COVID-19 response." *IEEE Spectrum*. 30 September 2020. spectrum.ieee.org/how-robots-became-essential-workers-in-the-covid19-response.

Hickmann, T., Widerberg, O., Lederer, M., and Pattberg, P. (2021). The United Nations Framework Convention on Climate Change Secretariat as an orchestrator in global climate policymaking. *International Review of Administrative Sciences, 87*(1), 21–38.

Hsu, P.-H., Wu, S.-Y., and Lin, F.-T. (2005). Disaster management using GIS technology: A case study in Taiwan. In: *Proceedings of the 26th Asian Conference on Remote Sensing*. Hanoi: Asian Association on Remote Sensing.

Idid, S. N. K. A. S. A. (2022). "Using drones in disaster management." *New Straights Times*. 4 January 2022. nst.com.my/opinion/letters/2022/01/760057/using-drones-disaster-management.

International Telecommunication Union. (2021a). *Measuring digital development: Facts and figures 2021*. www.itu.int/itu-d/reports/statistics/facts-figures-2021/.

International Telecommunication Union. (2021b). *Using AI to better understand natural hazards and disasters* [News release]. 24 March 2021. www.itu.int/hub/2021/03/using-ai-to-better-understand-natural-hazards-and-disasters/.

Jadeja, Y., and Modi, K. (2012). Cloud computing-concepts, architecture and challenges. In: *2012 International Conference on Computing, Electronics and Electrical Technologies (ICCEET)* (pp. 877–880). Nagercoil, India: Institute of Electrical and Electronics Engineers.

Johar, M., Johnston, D. W., Shields, M. A., Siminski, P., and Stavrunova, O. (2022). The economic impacts of direct natural disaster exposure. *Journal of Economic Behavior & Organization, 196*, 26–39.

Kankanhalli, A., Hahn, J., Tan, S., and Gao, G. (2016). Big data and analytics in healthcare: Introduction to the special section. *Information Systems Frontiers, 18*(2), 233–235.

Kapucu, N., Özerdem, A., and Sadiq, A.-A. (2022). *Managing emergencies and crises: Global perspectives*. Burlington, Mass.: Jones & Bartlett Learning.

Koller, D., Lindstrom, P., Ribarsky, W., Hodges, L. F., Faust, N., and Turner, G. (1995). Virtual GIS: A real-time 3D geographic information system. *Proceedings Visualization '95*, 94–100.

Kumar, T. V., and Sud, K (Eds.). (2020). *AI and Robotics in Disaster Studies*. Singapore: Springer.

Laituri, M., and Kodrich, K. (2008). On line disaster response community: People as sensors of high magnitude disasters using internet GIS. *Sensors, 8*(5), 3037–3055.

Lamanna, Z., Williams, K. H., and Childers, C. (2012). An assessment of resilience: Disaster management and recovery for greater New Orleans' hotels. *Journal of Human Resources in Hospitality & Tourism, 11*(3), 210–224.

Leiras, A., de Brito Jr, I., Peres, E. Q., Bertazzo, T. R., and Yoshizaki, H. T. Y. (2014). Literature review of humanitarian logistics research: trends and challenges. *Journal of Humanitarian Logistics and Supply Chain Management, 4*(1), 95–130.

Li, J., and Rao, H. R. (2010). Twitter as a rapid response news service: An exploration in the context of the 2008 China earthquake. *The Electronic Journal of Information Systems in Developing Countries, 42*(1), 1–22.

Marr, B. (2017). "Really big data at Walmart: Real-time insights from their 40+ petabyte data cloud." *Forbes.* 23 January 2017. www.forbes.com/sites/bernardmarr/2017/01/23/really-big-data-at-walmart-real-time-insights-from-their-40-petabyte-data-cloud/?sh=ae7b2386c105.

Massy-Beresford, H. (2014). "Robot rescuers to help save lives after disasters." *Horizon: The EU Research & Innovation Magazine.* 19 March 2014.

McCarthy, J. (2004). "What is artificial intelligence?" Stanford University. www-formal.stanford.edu/jmc/whatisai/.

Mosavi, A., Ozturk, P., and Chau, K.-w. (2018). Flood prediction using machine learning models: Literature review. *Water, 10*(11), 1536.

Müller, G., Sonehara, N., Echizen, I., and Wohlgemuth, S. (2011). Sustainable cloud computing. *Business & Information Systems Engineering, 3*(3), 129–131.

Munawar, H. S. (2020). Image and video processing for defect detection in key infrastructure. *Machine Vision Inspection Systems: Image Processing, Concepts, Methodologies and Applications, 1,* 159–177.

Munawar, H. S., Mojtahedi, M., Hammad, A. W., Kouzani, A., and Mahmud, M. P. (2022). Disruptive technologies as a solution for disaster risk management: A review. *Science of the Total Environment, 806,* 151351.

Murwani, A. (2018). *Technology and disaster manager: Lessons learned from the Philippines.* CfDS Case Studies Series #40. cfds.fisipol.ugm.ac.id/wp-content/uploads/sites/1423/2021/01/40-CfDS-Case-Study-Technology-and-Disaster-Management-Lesson-Learned-from-the-Philippines.pdf.

Ovesný, M., Křížek, P., Borkovec, J., Švindrych, Z., and Hagen, G. M. (2014). ThunderSTORM: A comprehensive ImageJ plug-in for PALM and STORM data analysis and super-resolution imaging. *Bioinformatics, 30*(16), 2389–2390.

Parker, D. J. (2020). Disaster resilience: A challenged science. *Environmental Hazards, 19*(1). Published online 28 December 2019.

Paul, J. D., Bee, E., and Budimir, M. (2021). Mobile phone technologies for disaster risk reduction. *Climate Risk Management, 32,* 100296.

Poonia, V., Goyal, M. K., Gupta, B., Gupta, A. K., Jha, S., and Das, J. (2021). Drought occurrence in different river basins of India and blockchain technology based framework for disaster management. *Journal of Cleaner Production, 312,* 127737.

Qian, L., Luo, Z., Du, Y., and Guo, L. (2009). Cloud computing: An overview. In: Jaatun, M.G., Zhao, G., Rong, C. (Eds.), *Cloud Computing. CloudCom 2009. Lecture Notes in Computer Science, vol. 5931*. Berlin: Springer.

Rambocas, M., and Gama, J. (2013). Marketing research: The role of sentiment analysis. *FEP Working Papers, 489*.

Raspini, F., Bardi, F., Bianchini, S., Ciampalini, A., Del Ventisette, C., Farina, P., Ferrigno, F., Solari, L., and Casagli, N. (2016). The contribution of satellite SAR-derived displacement measurements in landslide risk management practices. *Natural Hazards, 86*(1), 327–351.

Rehman, S., Sahana, M., Hong, H., Sajjad, H., and Ahmed, B. B. (2019). A systematic review on approaches and methods used for flood vulnerability assessment: Framework for future research. *Natural Hazards, 96*(2), 975–998.

Roslan, A. F., Fernando, T., Biscaya, S., and Sulaiman, N. (2021). Transformation towards risk-sensitive urban development: A systematic review of the issues and challenges. *Sustainability, 13*(19), 10631.

Santos Rocha, R. d., Widera, A., Berg, R. P., Albuquerque, J. P. d., and Helingrath, B. (2017). Improving the involvement of digital volunteers in disaster management. In: Murayama, Y., Velev, D., Zlateva, P., Gonzalez, J. (Eds.). *Information Technology in Disaster Risk Reduction. ITDRR 2016. IFIP Advances in Information and Communication Technology*, vol. 501. Cham: Springer.

Saravi, S., Kalawsky, R., Joannou, D., Rivas Casado, M., Fu, G., and Meng, F. (2019). Use of artificial intelligence to improve resilience and preparedness against adverse flood events. *Water, 11*(5), 973.

Shen, B., and Bissell, K. (2013). Social media, social me: A content analysis of beauty companies' use of Facebook in marketing and branding. *Journal of Promotion Management, 19*(5), 629–651.

Sinha, A., Kumar, P., Rana, N. P., Islam, R., and Dwivedi, Y. K. (2017). Impact of Internet-of-Things (IoT) in disaster management: A task-technology fit perspective. *Annals of Operations Research, 283*(1–2), 759–794.

Srivastava, M., Abdelzaher, T., and Szymanski, B. (2012). Human-centric sensing. *Philosophical Transactions of the Royal Society A: Mathematical, Physical and Engineering Sciences, 370*(1958), 176–197.

Sun, W., Bocchini, P., and Davison, B. D. (2020). Applications of artificial intelligence for disaster management. *Natural Hazards, 103*(3), 2631–2689.

Syifa, M., Kadavi, P. R., and Lee, C.-W. (2019). An artificial intelligence application for post-earthquake damage mapping in Palu, central Sulawesi, Indonesia. *Sensors, 19*(3), 542.

Takahashi, B., Tandoc Jr, E. C., and Carmichael, C. (2015). Communicating on Twitter during a disaster: An analysis of tweets during Typhoon Haiyan in the Philippines. *Computers in Human Behavior, 50*, 392–398.

Tomlinson, R. F. (2007). *Thinking about GIS: Geographic information system planning for managers* (Vol. 1). Redlands, Calif.: ESRI, Inc.

United Nations. (2021). *Robots to rescue: Using technology to mitigate effects of natural disasters.* Retrieved on DATE from un.org/en/academic-impact/robots-rescue-using-technology-mitigate-effects-natural-disasters.

Velev, D., Zlateva, P., and Zong, X. (2018). Challenges of 5G usability in disaster management. In: *Proceedings of the 2018 International Conference on Computing and Artificial Intelligence* (pp. 71–75). New York: Association for Computing Machinery.

Völk, F., Schwarz, R. T., Lorenz, M., and Knopp, A. (2021). Emergency 5G communication on-the-move: Concept and field trial of a mobile satellite backhaul for public protection and disaster relief. *International Journal of Satellite Communications and Networking, 39*(4), 417–430.

Wamba, S. F., Akter, S., Edwards, A., Chopin, G., and Gnanzou, D. (2015). How 'big data' can make big impact: Findings from a systematic review and a longitudinal case study. *International Journal of Production Economics, 165,* 234–246.

Wang, Z., and Ye, X. (2018). Social media analytics for natural disaster management. *International Journal of Geographical Information Science, 32*(1), 49–72.

Wannous, C., and Velasquez, G. (2017). United Nations Office for Disaster Risk Reduction (UNODRR): UNODDR's contribution to science and technology for disaster risk reduction and the role of the International Consortium on Landslides (ICL). In: Sassa, K., Mikoš, M., Yin, Y. (Eds.), *Advancing Culture of Living with Landslides.* WLF 2017. Cham: Springer.

Wheeler, B. J., and Karimi, H. A. (2020). Deep learning-enabled semantic inference of individual building damage magnitude from satellite images. *Algorithms, 13*(8), 195.

Yang, W. (2022). Research on risk intelligent assessment method of IT operation and maintenance based on cloud computing. In: *2022 IEEE 2nd International Conference on Power, Electronics and Computer Applications (ICPECA)* (pp. 900–913).

Yigitcanlar, T., Desouza, K. C., Butler, L., and Roozkhosh, F. (2020). Contributions and risks of artificial intelligence (AI) in building smarter cities: Insights from a systematic review of the literature. *Energies, 13*(6), 1473.

Yigitcanlar, T., Regona, M., Kankanamge, N., Mehmood, R., D'Costa, J., Lindsay, S., Nelson, S., and Brhane, A. (2022). Detecting natural hazard-related disaster impacts with social media analytics: The case of Australian states and territories. *Sustainability, 14*(2), 810.

Yu, M., Yang, C., and Li, Y. (2018). Big data in natural disaster management: A review. *Geosciences, 8*(5), 165.

Zlatanova, S., Ghawana, T., Kaur, A., and Neuvel, J. (2014). Integrated flood disaster management and spatial information: Case studies of Netherlands and India. *The International Archives of Photogrammetry, Remote Sensing and Spatial Information Sciences, 40*(8), 147.

11

Disaster Risk Reduction, Sustainability, and Systems Thinking

Wang-kin CHIU
College of Professional and Continuing Education, The Hong Kong Polytechnic University

Jocelyn R. TONG
College of Professional and Continuing Education, The Hong Kong Polytechnic University

Ben Y. F. FONG
College of Professional and Continuing Education, The Hong Kong Polytechnic University

Vincent T. S. LAW
College of Professional and Continuing Education, The Hong Kong Polytechnic University

The Asia-Pacific region has witnessed some extremely serious disasters in the past two decades. The Hyogo Framework for Action was introduced in 2005 to build the resilience of nations and communities in the face of disasters. The United Nations (UN) then formulated the Sendai Framework for Disaster Risk Reduction 2015–2030 as a global policy, with explicit reference to health, development, and climate change. About the same time, the UN also suggested mobilising collective actions and sharing information in order to achieve the Sustainable Development Goals (SDGs) it had adopted with respect to water, energy, climate, the oceans, urbanisation, transport, science, and technology, particularly in developing countries. Some SDGs aim to resolve and manage disasters through disaster risk reduction, while enhancing resilience to natural and man-made hazards. In 2019, the World Health Organisation (WHO) established the Health Emergency and Disaster Risk Management Framework (HEDRM) to consolidate contemporary approaches and practice in disaster management and prevention. In this chapter, systems thinking is promoted as a suitable policy approach for governments to implement response and recovery services by providing effective tools and methodology for appropriate decision-making and actions in disaster management.

Major Disastrous Incidents in the Asia-Pacific Region

Over the past few decades, the frequency and severity of disasters appear to be rapidly increasing. Tragically, they are causing a drastic rise in damage to communities and loss of life around the world. Hong Kong, and the Asia-Pacific region, has witnessed a number of critical events. After the devastating Garley Building fire that killed 41 and injured 81 people in November 1996, Hong Kong was later haunted by the outbreak of severe acute respiratory syndrome, commonly known as SARS, in 2003, which killed 299 people in three months (Lee, 2003). In addition, the city has been hit hard by the coronavirus disease 2019 (COVID-19) pandemic which began in January 2020. As of 14 July 2022, this global disaster has had a devastating impact, with over 560 million confirmed cases, a figure representing 7% of the world's population. The pandemic has also led to a death toll of over 6 million, and "no light is seen at the end of the tunnel" (World Health Organisation, n.d.).

The Indian Ocean earthquake and tsunami in 2004, also known as the Boxing Day Tsunami, a powerful undersea earthquake that struck off the coast of Sumatra, Indonesia, on the morning of Sunday 26 December 2004, was yet another disaster in the Asia-Pacific. The magnitude 9.1 quake ruptured a 900-mile stretch of fault line where the Indian and Australian tectonic plates meet. It was a powerful megathrust quake, causing the ocean floor to suddenly rise by as much as 40 metres and triggering a massive tsunami. According to a report by World Vision (n.d.), more than 100,000 people were killed and cities were pounded into rubble. Then, successive tsunami waves rolled over coastlines in Thailand, India, and Sri Lanka, killing tens of thousands more. Eight hours later and 5,000 miles from its Asian epicenter, the tsunami claimed its final casualties on the coast of South Africa. It has also been reported that nearly 230,000 people were killed when the tsunami hit coastal regions in Indonesia, Thailand, Sri Lanka, and India, making it one of the deadliest natural disasters in modern history (Satake, 2014.).

In China, the 2008 Sichuan earthquake, also known as the Great Sichuan Earthquake or Wenchuan earthquake, occurred on 12 May 2008 in southwestern China, only weeks before the 2008 Beijing Olympics. The earthquake, felt over 932 miles away in both Beijing and Shanghai, ruptured the fault line for over 149 miles, causing ground surface displacements of several metres. The subsequent geohazards were devastating. Tremors were also triggered in Bangkok, Thailand, and Hanoi, Vietnam. There were about 200,000 landslides, and more than 800 quake lakes were created (Xu, Xu, Yao, and Dai, 2014). The 2008 Sichuan earthquake was considered the deadliest earthquake to hit China since the 1976 Tangshan earthquake, which killed at least 242,000 people (Britannica, n.d.).

Japan is located in the Pacific Ring of Fire and, because of its extreme climate variations and topography, has become the developed country most affected by natural disasters. Japan experiences countless natural disasters of different levels, such as earthquakes, volcanic eruptions, and mudslides which have direct economic, development, and social impacts on the country (National Geographic, n.d.). The Great East Japan Earthquake occurred on 11 March 2011 on the east coast of Honshu Island, and caused a large tsunami resulting in vast damage, involving a death toll of more than 15,000, with over a million buildings completely or partly destroyed (World Nuclear Association, 2021).

Since the 1960s, Japan has been working hard to implement measures to stock sufficient materials and install safeguards to fight against disasters, with emphasis mainly on prevention. It established a well-planned, comprehensive administrative system for disaster prevention under the Disaster Countermeasures Basic Act in 1961. The Act is divided into five categories: (a) research into the scientific and technical aspects of disaster prevention; (b) reinforcement of the disaster prevention system; (c) construction projects to strengthen the ability of the country to defend itself against disasters; (d) setting up emergency measures and recovery operations; and (e) the improvement of information and communication systems. Each year 1 September is designated as Japan's official annual Disaster Prevention Day to educate the public on the most up-to-date disaster prevention knowledge, and to raise awareness of how they can protect themselves from critical events (Ministry of Foreign Affairs of Japan, n.d.).

Disaster Risk Reduction

International Day for Disaster Risk Reduction

The International Day for Disaster Risk Reduction was officially inaugurated in 1989 after the United Nations (UN) General Assembly resolved to mark a day to build a global culture of raising risk awareness and disaster reduction (UN, n.d.a). 13 October is designated as a day to acknowledge the progress being made toward the recuction of disaster risk and losses in lives, livelihoods, and health, as well as the reduction of the number of disasters occurring in all countries. It also reminds the general public not to forget the importance of reducing risks. There is a different theme or slogan every year. In 2021, the main theme was "International cooperation for developing countries to reduce disaster risk and losses due to disasters", corresponding to the sixth target of the Sendai Framework for Disaster Risk Reduction 2015–2030 (see below).

The Sendai Framework for Disaster Risk Reduction 2015–2030

To address the complexity of the various risks posed by disasters, a well-planned disaster risk reduction (DRR) policy provides guidelines to formulate practical strategies for closer collaboration among all sectors in the community to prepare, prevent, respond to, and recover from disasters and emergencies. After the introduction of the Hyogo Framework for Action 2005–2015: Building the Resilience of Nations and Communities to Disasters at the UN World Conference on Disaster Reduction in 2005, the Sendai Framework for Disaster Risk Reduction 2015–2030 was launched by the UN in 2015 in Sendai, Japan, as a global policy with an explicit focus on health, development, and climate change (Aitsi-Selmi, Egawa, Sasaki, Wannous, and Murray, 2015). The Sendai Framework was a call to action over the 15 years up to 2030 to make the world a safer place and to reduce the risk of man-made and natural hazards by substantially reducing disaster risk and thus losses in lives, livelihoods, and health. The Sendai Framework set four priorities: (a) understanding disaster risk—to ensure that policies and practices for disaster risk management are based on a clear understanding of vulnerability and exposure to hazards; (b) strengthening disaster risk governance—to have a clear strategy, for example, strong institutions, laws, and budget, to ensure the efficient management of disaster risks; (c) investment in DRR for resilience—to include public and private investment in measures for the prevention and reduction of losses; and (d) the importance of strengthening disaster preparedness and building a better environment after a disaster.

There are seven targets to measure progress toward the achievement of substantial reduction of disaster risk and losses by 2030 at the global level (UN Office for Disaster Risk Reduction, n.d.):

Target 1: To reduce global disaster mortality substantially;

Target 2: To reduce the number of people affected globally, embracing all Sustainable Development Goals (SDGs) for a universally safer world;

Target 3: To reduce direct disaster economic loss in relation to global gross domestic product (GDP), aiming at ending poverty and promoting sustainable economic growth and decent work to save for response and recovery costs;

Target 4: To reduce disaster damage to critical infrastructure and disruption of basic services, including health and educational facilities, and to make human settlements sustainable and safe through developing resilience structures;

Target 5: To increase the number of countries with national and local DRR strategies that aim to make habitats safer internationally and help to end poverty and hunger;

Target 6: To enhance international cooperation in developing countries through adequate and sustainable support, covering all SDGs, to complement their national actions for implementation of the Framework; and

Target 7: To make available to the public multi-hazard early warning systems and disaster risk information and assessments, specifically about combating climate change and its impact on disaster risk.

The Sendai Framework was a critical global direction of the post-2015 development agenda and was followed by the 2030 development agenda, which identified 17 SDGs to eradicate poverty and make such goals a reality by 2030.

Disaster Risk Reduction and Sustainable Development for All Nations

Disaster risk reduction is an integral part of social and economic development, and is essential if development is to be sustainable for the future. The UN developed 17 SDGs with 169 targets in 2015 to address unpleasant life events, including disasters and critical events that threaten people in all countries (UN, n.d.b). The Division for SDGs at the UN provides support to build capacity by mobilising collective actions and sharing information for the achievement of the SDGs, with respect to issues concerning water, energy, climate, the oceans, urbanisation, transport, science, and technology, particularly in developing countries. The Division also investigates relevant policy design and responses to these priority issues, and ensures that they incorporate the objective of strengthening the science-policy interface. All 17 SDGs aim to end poverty and hunger, to achieve equality within and among countries, to build peaceful societies, to safeguard human rights, and to protect dwindling natural resources from climate change. Some SDGs therefore aim to resolve and manage disasters through DRR while enhancing resilience to natural and man-made hazards. This is particularly the focus of Target 13.1, "Strengthen resilience and adaptive capacity to climate-related hazards and natural disasters in all countries", and Goal 11, "Make cities and human settlements inclusive, safe, resilient and sustainable". There are 25 targets related to DRR in 10 of the 17 SDGs that direct the role of DRR as a core development strategy toward sustainability for all nations (UN, n.d.c).

Personal Development

Sustainable reduction of global poverty is one of the major objectives of the SDGs, and its dynamics are closely related to resilience building and coordinated governmental interventions (Li, Wu, and Wang, 2021). It is proposed to end poverty, to build resilience, and reduce the exposure to events due to extreme climate variation, social and environmental shocks, and disasters for the poor and vulnerable. Lifelong equitable, quality education to acquire knowledge and skills is important in the development of sustainable lifestyles for the promotion of global citizenship. The goal is to provide safe, nonviolent, inclusive, and effective learning environments for all. Public education on and awareness of climate change can be enhanced by integrating relevant issues related to its impact reduction, adaptation, and early warning as important components into the school curriculum at primary, secondary, and tertiary levels (UN, n.d.b).

Policy

Holistic disaster risk management is to be achieved at all levels by adopting the Sendai Framework through integrated policies and plans. Resilience and adaptive capacity to combat climate-related hazards and natural disasters should be strengthened by integrating relevant and effective measures into national policies, strategies, and planning. All nations should also have systems for early warning and the reduction and management of health risks. The Mainstreaming, Acceleration, and Policy Support approach was adopted by the UN Development Group in 2015 to favour policy implementation in relation to the SDGs (UN Development Operations Coordination Office, 2016). This initiative has introduced risk governance and considerations from policymakers into the design and implementation agenda of policy interventions in 18 countries, among which disaster and climate risks are recognised as key impediments to achieving the SDGs and building resilience, and the important goals of enhancing risk-informed development and accelerating the progress of achieving SDGs at the national level (Issar, 2019).

Environment

To achieve the SDGs, the capacity for adaptation to climate change, extreme weather, drought, flooding, and other disasters should be strengthened by ensuring sustainable food production and agricultural practices, and improving land and soil quality. Water-related ecosystems have to be protected to ensure the availability and sustainable management of water and sanitation. Quality, reliable, sustainable, and resilient infrastructure, and innovation, should also be established to support economic development with the objective of affordability and equitable access for all. Financial, technological, and technical support to African countries and the least developed countries will then be improved. Cities and other human settlements should be inclusive, safe, resilient, resource-efficient, and sustainable, and be able to protect people from disasters.

Marine and coastal ecosystems must be protected from adverse impacts and managed sustainably to achieve healthy and productive oceans for sustainable development of marine resources (UN, n.d.b). The terrestrial ecosystems of forests, wetlands, mountains, and other types of land such as grassland must be protected with conservation and sustainable use. Overall, the degradation of environmental quality will lead to increasing exposure to disasters, and so policy interventions for a sustainable environment are important factors contributing to the reduction of disaster risk (Uitto and Shaw, 2016).

Risks and Development

Development can be a risk in itself. For example, hotels and restaurants near a coastline are at a higher risk of destruction when an earthquake strikes an island. This means that development can be affected by risks, but development also creates its own risks. Risk-informed development requires planners and decision makers to apply all available information on the various kinds of risk in a given location in planning, budgeting, and project implementation (Issar, 2019).

Health Emergency and
Disaster Risk Management Framework

Disasters, whether natural or caused by human activity, often result in setting back development in the affected community and country, particularly regarding the health of the population. Health systems can be overwhelmed by such events, which also severely hamper the local economy and the associated funding. In response, the World Health Organisation (WHO) has pledged to reduce these impacts and made this one of its top priorities alongside achieving universal health coverage, health security, and health for all, by establishing the Health Emergency and Disaster Risk Management (HEDRM) Framework in 2019 (WHO, 2019). The HEDRM Framework is a document incorporating contributions from member states and staff of different WHO programmes around the world. It consolidates contemporary approaches and practices in disaster management and prevention. It is the wish of the WHO that member states implement the HEDRM Framework effectively in the utilisation and management of resources to prepare for all kinds of unpredictable emergencies and to reduce associated risks with the aim of creating a safer and healthier world for all.

All communities are subject to the risks of emergencies and disasters. Without effective management of such risks, other factors like climate change, unplanned urbanisation, and population growth will result in more frequent, more severe, and more hazardous events causing emergencies and disasters, an example of which is the COVID-19 pandemic, which at time of writing has affected everyone worldwide for over two years since early 2020. Therefore, assuring health security, building community resilience, and local and national health systems are vital to all countries. In addition to the HEDRM Framework, the WHO suggests that governments and agencies should have competent risk management for the development and implementation of the SDGs that are instrumental in setting the path to universal health coverage with reference to the Sendai Framework, International Health Regulations (2005), the Paris Agreement on climate change, health system building blocks, good practices, and other related global, regional, and national models and frameworks.

The HEDRM Framework is a comprehensive guide with an integrated approach to managing health risks and building resilience and capacities in a common language, so that all health workers and persons from other sectors can work together to assess, communicate, and mitigate risks to health and consequences arising from disastrous incidents in different settings and geographical locations. The Framework emphasises the importance of prevention, preparedness, readiness, response, and recovery in handling disasters, saving lives, protecting health, safeguarding property, and building the resilience of the community in a continuum. The Framework also calls for different sectors across health systems to work together, paying special attention to vulnerable groups that will be most badly affected. Optimal development outcomes, particularly for public health with a focus on the well-being of the affected population, cannot be achieved if approaches to hazardous events are fragmented, or if there is a lack of coordination in the system and among related sectors (WHO, 2019).

Apart from risk management, emergency medicine, disaster management, epidemic preparedness and response, and health system strengthening are represented in the HEDRM Framework by multisectoral and multidisciplinary approaches to steering policies and actions in disaster management for the improvement of universal health through reduction of risks and humanitarian action as well as sustainable development. Communities and countries will have enhanced capacity to face and handle disasters and emergencies, taking inclusive and ethical considerations to protect the population.

In functional terms, the HEDRM Framework entails the following components: (a) policies, strategies, and legislation; (b) planning and coordination; (c) human resources; (d) financial resources; (e) information and knowledge management; (f) risk communications; (g) health infrastructure and logistics; (h) health and related services; and (i) monitoring and evaluation. Joint efforts and actions by governments, disaster management agencies, professional bodies, the private sector, and community organisations will determine the effectiveness and success of HEDRM. Community participation must be solicited to nurture resilience and lay the foundations of the disaster management cycle for optimal prevention, preparedness, response, and recovery in handling unexpected crises. Moreover, a systemic approach is recommended in the consideration of risks, capacities, and available resources when HEDRM measures are being implemented at various levels of government and in various settings. Past experiences and events are useful sources of learning for the planning and development of appropriate strategies and for setting the priorities of associated tasks.

Surveillance, early warning and alert systems, preparedness for response, including operational readiness and mass casualty management systems, and resilient hospitals and healthcare facilities form the foundations of a comprehensive disaster management strategy. Facilities must be secure, safe, and sustainable, so that they can continue to operate in emergencies or disasters. The health sector should participate in national and international meetings, including those organised through the national disaster management agency, to ensure that the health of the population is considered in multisectoral policy, planning, and discussion of resources allocation. After all, effective management of the risks of emergencies and disasters by all stakeholders across the world will make a great contribution to the strengthening of resilience, health security, equity, and sustainable development, and achieve the highest possible standards of health and well-being (WHO, 2019).

Adoption of Systems Thinking in Disaster Management Policy

Systems thinking has been widely applied across different disciplines including public health and population policy (Haynes, Garvey, Davidson, and Milat, 2020; Peters, 2014; Van Mai and To, 2015). In recent years, systems thinking has also played an emerging role in disaster studies due to the growing complexity and increasing frequency of disasters (Ismail, Halog, and Smith, 2017). Systems thinking is a holistic, interdisciplinary approach applied to understand the interconnections between different systems and to analyse the complex relationships involved (Van Mai and To, 2015). Unlike the traditional reductionist approach, which focuses on separate linear causal relationships within specialised disciplines, systems thinking aims to achieve systems modeling, systems exploration, and effective problem-solving through a comprehensive analysis of system components and the interacting effects of associated factors (Xia, Zhou, and Liu, 2017).

Government policies and measures to mitigate the impact of disasters usually focus on specific aspects and neglect the interconnections between different systems. Sometimes, predefined approaches and frameworks for disaster preparedness and early warning systems may not be able to consider the complex interdependent risks, especially as most DRR approaches tend to be linear in nature. On the other hand, systems thinking emphasises achieving a comprehensive understanding of the complex interactions between systems and the underlying rationales and root causes. It also focuses on the cyclical impact of variables in a system, instead of merely adopting linear approaches that deal with direct cause-and-effect relationships (Chen, Neal, and Zhou, 2013). Moreover, systems thinking aims to recognise known and unknown risks as well as closing the loop between policy, society, and institutions through a thorough analysis of the interconnectivity of different systems. Policymakers, as well as key players and institutions providing disaster response and recovery services, need effective tools and methodology for appropriate decision-making and actions. It is imperative that policymakers are capable of visualising complex systems, and aware of the relevant structures and policies that are responsible for the dynamic nature of performance regulation in the event of a disaster. Therefore, studies related to the application of systems thinking in the critical aspects of disaster research are particularly valuable to policymakers. It is suggested that nonlinear and holistic approaches such as systems thinking should be applied because of disaster risk complexity and dynamic interactions between systems and subsystems such as people, organisations, various physical and virtual infrastructures, political leaders, and many other decision makers and stakeholders in the different stages of disaster events (Mutanga and Lunga, 2021; Riden, Felt, and Pinkerton, 2021).

In recent decades, the increasing frequency of various types of disasters, both man-made and natural, further necessitates systems thinking to deal with the uncertainty in a disaster situation, as there is no single, absolute way to conduct effective disaster management due to the complexity of disasters and the associated impacts. Sustainable disaster management requires a broad and complete understanding of the nonlinear socioeconomic, natural, and constructed systems, and the complex interconnections between them. Regulations, laws, and policies are the main focus of socioeconomic systems, while natural systems are concerned with the global commons or the physical environment, and constructed systems are characterised by physical infrastructure including public facilities, transport systems, electricity, water supply, and drainage (Mutanga and Lunga, 2021; Riden et al., 2021). By working on different timescales encompassing various processes as parts of a whole, systems thinking acts as a diagnostic tool and enables different stakeholders to deal with the complex and interacting nonlinear systems in disaster management and risk reduction (Simonovic, 2015). Considering the promise of systems thinking, an overview of studies investigating how it can be applied to different types of disasters can shed light on ways to reduce risk and provide important insights into the development of related policy frameworks to enhance community resilience. The following will review relevant studies on selected major disasters, and discuss how the findings shape new research directions and provide policy implications from the lessons learnt.

Tropical Cyclones

Due to ongoing climate change, the frequency of extreme weather events and the associated costs, including loss of life and property, will inevitably increase. The devastating nature of tropical cyclones poses a serious threat to sustainable development (Zhang, Gu, Shi, and Singh, 2017). In 2019, Tropical Cyclone Idai and the subsequent floods caused extensive destruction across several countries in the Southern African Development Community (SADC), including Mozambique, Madagascar, Malawi, and Zimbabwe. Disaster preparedness levels were found to be uneven across and within the SADC countries. A low level of disaster preparedness and ineffective early warning systems in some communities which were already under-resourced and unprepared, together with the uniqueness of a series of foreseeable and unforeseeable risks, have further highlighted the need for the application of systems thinking to unpack the whole structure of complex disaster situations and to achieve sustainable realisation of the uncertainty involved in DRR (Mutanga and Lunga, 2021). Furthermore, the efforts of most SADC countries to enhance DRR were considered to be minimal in comparison with other more developed countries, and the disaster policies in the majority of these countries were reported to focus primarily on reactive approaches more than proactive ones (Davis and Vincent, 2017; Mavhura, 2016).

Under these circumstances, the systems thinking approach is expected to enhance disaster preparedness and management, as well as DRR, by providing a model to critically link the important elements, including vulnerability, risk analysis, and risk assessment (Chen et al., 2013; Xia et al., 2017). Mutanga and Lunga (2021) recently reported field observations and impact assessment of Tropical Cyclone Idai in Zimbabwe based on empirical research. The framework of study was a systems thinking approach using causal loop diagrams, as well as situational analysis from a systems perspective. The application of qualitative systems thinking analysis was demonstrated in aspects of disaster management and risk reduction based on the experience of the disastrous impact of the cyclone, which severely disrupted most districts in Zimbabwe. Destruction of food production systems, one of the most serious impacts of the cyclone, was used as an example in the systems analysis. This substantial destruction led to acute food security problems in the affected areas. The situation in the Chimanimani communities of Zimbabwe was analysed and a simplified causal loop diagram was used to illustrate the impact of the cyclone on food security within the affected zones. Key variables for inclusion were identified and the analysis revealed the linkage between cyclone events and increased incidence of supply disruption during and after the disaster, which also had a potential nationwide impact of catastrophic food loss and insecurity.

Moreover, Mutanga and Lunga (2021) extended the application of systems thinking to three nonlinear systems working differently through various processes in consideration of timeframe and scale. They constructed a simplified causal loop diagram in an attempt to achieve a comprehensive understanding of nonlinear systems in DRR by linking the socioeconomic, physical, and political systems, based on insights gained from the experience of Tropical Cyclone Idai (Mutanga and Lunga, 2021). They analysed the complexity of relationships, and different factors such as governance structure and transparency, vulnerable populations, humanitarian support, disaster impact, and resilience capacity, through the lens of systems thinking. Their research identifies a number of benefits of systems thinking in the formulation of an integrated framework to deal with the many uncertainties involved in DRR. The results are in line with a study conducted by Joakim et al. (2016) which also demonstrated the promising use of systems thinking for the build-up of dynamic community resilience and the development of a holistic climate change impact assessment tool for urban policymakers with regard to the increasing frequency of natural hazards induced by climate change.

Flooding

In addition to cyclones, large-scale floods due to extreme climate change and rapid urbanisation have also been frequently observed in recent decades. Flooding is a natural disaster that has a devastating impact on infrastructure, agriculture, and human lives, particularly in developing countries (Qasim et al., 2016). Furthermore, the recurring phenomenon of devastating flooding is of particular concern for developing countries on the Asian continent, which are vulnerable to natural disasters. Drawing insights from the experience of the 2010 floods in Pakistan, Deen (2015) revealed the inadequacy of flood preparedness and relevant mechanisms of risk management, as well as policy gaps and weak regulatory measures observed in disaster response and management. To address these issues, policy recommendations have been made regarding institutional reform and capacity building, taking into account the important aspects of public health service provision, the establishment of sustainable shelters, public administration, agricultural restoration, infrastructure, and education services in the affected regions, as well as increased investment in disaster-prevention interventions combined with disaster preparedness. Furthermore, mere reliance on technical problem-solving approaches is insufficient for the mitigation of disastrous flooding situations. It is noted that structural measures corresponding to flood disaster management have a high cost for developing countries. The planning and implementation of relevant measures and policies require the engagement of all relevant stakeholders in the public and private sectors. At the same time, the significance and necessity of socioeconomic viability and environmental feasibility should also be considered. Substantial collaborative efforts at community and institutional levels, guided by a comprehensive understanding of all the systems and dynamic interactions involved, are required through effective empowerment, enhanced capacity, and coordination among stakeholders.

Accordingly, systems thinking has been suggested for the efficient implementation of integrated strategies for flood management to address the complexity of the systems and processes involved (Rehman, Sohaib, Asif, and Pradhan, 2019). In their study, Rehman, Sohaib, Asif, and Pradhan (2019) analysed the flooding situations and problems in Pakistan with a systems thinking approach, adopting the Drivers-Pressures-States-Impacts-Responses (DPSIR) Framework (Kristensen, 2004). The DPSIR Framework was adopted as a diagnostic tool to establish and understand the causal relationships between different elements of the environment and society. Factors leading to the flooding problems in Pakistan were identified and grouped under several main categories, including natural factors, technical and infrastructural factors, institutional factors, and socioeconomic factors. They were considered in combination with the various driving forces and elements identified in the DPSIR Framework to construct a comprehensive causal loop diagram. The diagram facilitates understanding of the relationships between public communities, the media, non-governmental organisations (NGOs), and government departments. It also demonstrates how existing systems can better facilitate interaction and cooperation among all components of the community to achieve flood reduction, based on relevant policies in technological, social, institutional, and environmental contexts. Overall, the application of a systems thinking approach is supported by analysis of primary data and review of existing research, and has led to the identification of key risk factors of flooding and associated impacts. Based on these findings, Rehman, Sohaib, Asif, and Pradhan (2019) made recommendations for the federal government, provincial governments, and international and local NGOs on how to address flooding in Pakistan, with the aim of achieving a sustainable design for long-term disaster-response strategies.

Pandemic

Systems thinking has also been considered a useful approach to understanding the complexity of disease dynamics. It provides a comprehensive perspective, unrestricted by confined boundaries of specific disciplines, for analysing the infectious disease transmission process with emphasis on structural complexity and behavioural entirety of the system. After different components and their interactions are considered, various impact factors and their interactions can be identified for the exploration and implementation of effective intervention measures. In addition to biological factors such as genetic mutation of disease pathogens or parasites, it is found that human socioeconomic and behavioural factors, as well as environmental and ecological factors, are important for the characterisation of disease transmission dynamics and the mitigation of infectious diseases (Walters, Meslé, and Hall, 2018; Xia et al., 2017). Systems thinking is crucial in combating infectious diseases and assessing strategies to reduce spread, especially in a pandemic. During the emergent situation when a disease is spreading rapidly, scientific findings and the information gathered and disseminated must be reliable, and the derived measures must be feasible and practical for both the government and the public (Rybniker and Fätkenheuer, 2020). Overall, health is significantly affected by policies outside the health sector and policymakers need to systematically consider and thoroughly take into account the health implications of their decisions.

The outbreak of the COVID-19 pandemic in 2019 and its substantial worldwide impact has called for researchers to apply systems thinking to analyse important issues related to health management and policy in the context of the evolving pandemic situation (Cristiano and Zilio, 2021; Zieba, 2021). Gonella, Casazza, Cristiano, and Romano (2020) proposed a stock-flow diagram based on a systems thinking approach for illustrating the complex interacting relationships linking different components for the effective communication and management of health services, and interventions with regard to COVID-19. The stock-flow diagram is valuable to both policymakers and the general public since it serves as an analytical and communication tool with regard to critical issues. It also provides potential protocols for effective health management and policy implementation, enabling the visualisation of complicated causes leading to the malfunctioning or even failure of health interventions and systems. Furthermore, there are reports of lessons learnt from the COVID-19 pandemic. One example is the revisiting and realisation of much-needed changes in the design of built environments, further acknowledging the critical role of public health in the development of urban planning (Pinheiro and Luís, 2020). More collaboration between urban planning and public health is desirable with the ultimate goals of strengthening the capability of the built environment to promote well-being and the development of effective policies to make cities more sustainable, healthier places to live (Lovasi, Roux, and Kolker, 2020). It should be noted that urban policies have a close relationship with environmental health, affecting the quality of the air we breathe, the water we drink, and the food we consume. The sustainability of a green environment is a key factor for better overall health, and it plays a significant role in contributing to the well-being of all, in particular ageing populations (Fong, Chiu, Chan, and Lam, 2021; Chiu and Fong, 2022). Since the onset of COVID-19, the research community has encouraged scientific and policy research to realise the links between urban environments and public health through the application of systems thinking, as exemplified by a recent study which adopted the systems approach to evaluate sustainable, healthy urban planning and related management strategies (Cristiano and Zilio, 2021).

Planning for Disaster Preparedness, Major Community Events, and Emergencies

Disaster preparedness is an essential element of disaster management, no matter how the process is affected by government policies. It relates to the capability of the healthcare system and the community to prevent risks and protect against emergencies, as well as to take immediate actions in response to events and to initiate recovery from impacts. It is a well-coordinated and ongoing process of planning and implementation through appropriate actions. While individuals are responsible for maintaining their own health and well-being, the general population, social resources, community organisations, and the administration are the key components of any emergency preparedness programme.

The most important steps in the process of disaster preparedness are (a) the evaluation of the level of risk posed by a disaster to the country or a particular community; (b) the coordination of information and warning systems, and the availability of appropriate response mechanisms; and (c) measures to ensure that adequate financial and other resources are available for increased readiness and can be mobilised in disaster situations (Page, 1999). The government should also set up public education programmes to inform the population of actions to be taken and coordinate information sessions with the news media. Disaster simulation exercises should also be organised to test response mechanisms to ensure their appropriateness for the country or community, and to explore improvements for a better disaster management system.

Governments

Governments are the most important stakeholders in the disaster management and risk-reduction process. They steer the major development and implement the policy in relation to DRR. They have three main roles in the implementation of the disaster management policy. First, governments coordinate and sustain a multilevel and multi-stakeholder platform to prevent specific hazards. They engage stakeholders to take charge of the efforts and provide them sufficient support and assistance so that everything can operate smoothly and successfully. Secondly, governments are in a strategic position to effectively engage the general public to participate in risk-reduction activities such as education programmes, risk-reduction seminars in schools, and the production of advertisements for social media to educate the community and to raise awareness of the prevention of hazards and self-protection when facing a disaster. Thirdly, governments strengthen their own institutional capacity in order to effectively engage in practical actions to avoid or lessen the adverse impacts of disasters on the community. This is done by putting in place an organisational structure for all sectors to deal with DRR.

Schools

There are three main areas in which schools can prepare for disasters. The first is to ensure that students can enjoy their academic studies in a safe learning environment. Continual monitoring of school premises is very important and maintenance should be carried out immediately if there is a need to minimise both structural and nonstructural risks. The infrastructure of school premises should allow for smooth evacuation. The second is to establish a feasible system for school disaster management. Schools should have the most up-to-date and detailed policies and guidance on emergency planning, risk reduction, and response preparedness. Lastly, students and staff need to be trained in DRR and resilience, and fully engaged in real-life disaster management activities such as fire and other hazard drills. Relevant information should be included in the learning materials for students to provide guidelines on disaster response and important messages on safety and preparedness. Training should be given to teachers to equip them with the principles and methodologies of risk reduction. All education and training can be conducted in the context of formal teaching or as extracurricular activities.

Conclusion

The UN's Sendai Framework for Disaster Risk Reduction 2015–2030 set out a global policy to assist the design and planning of DRR in the areas of health, social, and economic development, and climate change. The UN has also developed a number of SDGs concerning water, energy, climate, the oceans, urbanisation, transport, science, and technology, and some of these SDGs focus on DRR. The WHO's HEDRM Framework suggests contemporary approaches and practices to solve problems in disaster management and prevention. This chapter has discussed these policies and approaches to DRR in detail, and proposes that systems thinking be promoted as a policy approach for governments to implement response and recovery services, using effective tools and methodology for appropriate decision-making and actions in disaster management. The systems thinking approach to disaster management is illustrated with local and worldwide examples.

References

Aitsi-Selmi, A., Egawa, S., Sasaki, H., Wannous, C., and Murray, V. (2015). The Sendai Framework for disaster risk reduction: Renewing the global commitment to people's resilience, health, and well-being. *International Journal of Disaster Risk Science, 6*, 164–176.

Britannica. (n.d.). *Sichuan earthquake of 2008*. Retrieved on 20 February 2022 from www.britannica.com/event/Sichuan-earthquake-of-2008.

Chen, C., Neal, D., and Zhou, M. (2013). Understanding the evolution of a disaster: A framework for assessing crisis in a system environment (FACSE). *Natural Hazards, 65*(1), 407–422.

Chiu, W. K., and Fong, B. Y. F. (2022). Chemical pollution and healthy ageing: The prominent need for a cleaner environment. In: Law, V. T. S., and Fong, B. Y. F. (Eds.), *Ageing with dignity in Hong Kong and Asia – Holistic and humanistic care* (pp. 277–288). Singapore: Springer.

Cristiano, S., and Zilio, S. (2021). Whose health in whose city? A systems thinking approach to support and evaluate plans, policies, and strategies for lasting urban health. *Sustainability, 13*(21), 12225.

Davis, C. L., and Vincent, K. (2017). *Climate risk and vulnerability: A handbook for Southern Africa* (2nd edition). Pretoria: CSIR. hdl.handle.net/10204/10066.

Deen, S. (2015). Pakistan 2010 floods. Policy gaps in disaster preparedness and response. *International Journal of Disaster Risk Reduction, 12*, 341–349.

Fong, B. Y., Chiu, W. K., Chan, W. F., and Lam, T. Y. (2021). A review study of a green diet and healthy ageing. *International Journal of Environmental Research and Public Health, 18*(15), 8024.

Gonella, F., Casazza, M., Cristiano, S., and Romano, A. (2020). Addressing COVID-19 communication and management by a systems thinking approach. *Frontiers in Communication, 5*, 63.

Haynes, A., Garvey, K., Davidson, S., and Milat, A. (2020). What can policy-makers get out of systems thinking? Policy partners' experiences of a systems-focused research collaboration in preventive health. *International Journal of Health Policy and Management, 9*(2), 65.

Ismail, F. Z., Halog, A., and Smith, C. (2017). How sustainable is disaster resilience? An overview of sustainable construction approach in post-disaster housing reconstruction. *International Journal of Disaster Resilience in the Built Environment, 8*(5), 555–572.

Issar, R. (2019). "Integrating disaster and climate risk into the SDGs." *United Nations Development Programme.* 25 April 2019. www.undp.org/blog/integrating-disaster-and-climate-risk-sdgs.

Joakim, E. P., Mortsch, L., Oulahen, G., Harford, D., Klein, Y., Damude, K., and Tang, K. (2016). Using system dynamics to model social vulnerability and resilience to coastal hazards. *International Journal of Emergency Management, 12*(4), 366–391.

Kristensen, P. (2004). *The DPSIR framework.* Paper presented at a workshop on a comprehensive/detailed assessment of the vulnerability of water resources to environmental change in Africa using river basin approach, 27–29 September 2004, UNEP Headquarters, Nairobi, Kenya.

Lee, S. H. (2003). The SARS epidemic in Hong Kong: what lessons have we learned? *Journal of the Royal Society of Medicine, 96*(8), 374–378.

Li, Y., Wu, W., and Wang, Y. (2021). Global poverty dynamics and resilience building for sustainable poverty reduction. *Journal of Geographical Sciences, 31*(8), 1159–1170.

Lovasi, G. S., Roux, A. V. D., and Kolker, J. (Eds.). (2020). *Urban public health: A research toolkit for practice and impact.* New York: Oxford University Press.

Mavhura, E. (2016). Disaster legislation: A critical review of the civil protection act of Zimbabwe. *Natural Hazards, 80*(1), 605–621.

Ministry of Foreign Affairs of Japan. (n.d.). *Disaster prevention.* Retrieved on 20 February 2022 from www.mofa.go.jp/policy/disaster/21st/2.html.

Mutanga, S. S., and Lunga, W. (2021). Uncertainty in disaster risk management: A reflection on cyclone Idai using the systems thinking approach. In: Nhamo, G., and Dube, K. (Eds.), *Cyclones in Southern Africa* (pp. 179–192). Cham: Springer.

National Geographic. (n.d.). *Ring of fire.* Retrieved on 20 February 2022 from www.nationalgeographic.org/encyclopedia/ring-fire/.

Page, J. A. (1999). When disaster strikes: First steps in disaster preparedness. *The Serials Librarian, 36*(3–4), 347–361.

Peters, D. H. (2014). The application of systems thinking in health: Why use systems thinking? *Health Research Policy and Systems, 12*(1), 1–6.

Pinheiro, M. D., and Luís, N. C. (2020). COVID-19 could leverage a sustainable built environment. *Sustainability, 12*(14), 5863.

Qasim, S., Qasim, M., Shrestha, R. P., Khan, A. N., Tun, K., and Ashraf, M. (2016). Community resilience to flood hazards in Khyber Pukhthunkhwa province of Pakistan. *International Journal of Disaster Risk Reduction, 18*, 100–106.

Rehman, J., Sohaib, O., Asif, M., and Pradhan, B. (2019). Applying systems thinking to flood disaster management for a sustainable development. *International Journal of Disaster Risk Reduction, 36*, 101101.

Riden, H. E., Felt, E., and Pinkerton, K. E. (2021). The impact of climate change and extreme weather conditions on agricultural health and safety in California. In: Pinkerton, K. E., and Rom, W. N. (Eds.), *Climate change and global public health* (pp. 353–368). Cham: Humana.

Rybniker, J., and Fätkenheuer, G. (2020). Importance of precise data on SARS-CoV-2 transmission dynamics control. *The Lancet Infectious Diseases, 20*(8), 877–879.

Satake, K. (2014). Advances in earthquake and tsunami sciences and disaster risk reduction since the 2004 Indian Ocean tsunami. *Geoscience Letters, 1*, 15.

Simonovic, S. P. (2015). Systems approach to management of disasters: A missed opportunity? *IDRiM Journal, 5*(2), 70–81.

Uitto, J. I., and Shaw, R. (2016). Sustainable development and disaster risk reduction: Introduction. In: Uitto, J., and Shaw, R. (Eds.), *Sustainable development and disaster risk reduction* (pp. 1–12). Tokyo: Springer.

UN Development Operations Coordination Office. (2016). *MAPS – A common approach to the UNDG's policy support to the SDGs – An update on implementation.* www.un.org/ecosoc/sites/www.un.org.ecosoc/files/files/en/qcpr/doco-summary-brief-on-maps-march2016.pdf.

UN Office for Disaster Risk Reduction. (n.d.). *The Sendai Framework.* Retrieved on 20 February 2022 from www.undrr.org/implementing-sendai-framework/what-sendai-framework.

United Nations. (n.d.a). *International day for disaster risk reduction.* Retrieved on 20 February 2022 from iddrr.undrr.org/.

United Nations. (n.d.b). *Sustainable development goals.* Retrieved on 20 February 2022 from sdgs.un.org/goals.

United Nations. (n.d.c). *SDGS with targets related to disaster risk.* Retrieved on 20 February 2022 from www.preventionweb.net/sustainable-development-and-drr/sdgs-targets-related-disaster-risk.

Van Mai, T., and To, P. X. (2015). A systems thinking approach for achieving a better understanding of swidden cultivation in Vietnam. *Human Ecology, 43*(1), 169–178.

Walters, C. E., Meslé, M. M., and Hall, I. M. (2018). Modelling the global spread of diseases: A review of current practice and capability. *Epidemics, 25*, 1–8.

World Health Organisation. (n.d.). *WHO Coronavirus (COVID-19) dashboard.* Retrieved on 20 February 2022 from covid19.who.int/.

World Health Organisation. (2019). *Health emergency and disaster risk management framework.* Geneva: World Health Organisation. www.who.int/publications/i/item/9789241516181.

World Nuclear Association. (2021). *Fukushima Daiichi accident.* Retrieved on 20 February 2022 from world-nuclear.org/information-library/safety-and-security/safety-of-plants/fukushima-daiichi-accident.aspx.

World Vision. (n.d.). *2004 Indian Ocean earthquake and tsunami: Facts, FAQs, and how to help.* Retrieved on 20 February 2022 from www.worldvision.org/disaster-relief-news-stories/2004-indian-ocean-earthquake-tsunami-facts.

Xia, S., Zhou, X. N., and Liu, J. (2017). Systems thinking in combating infectious diseases. *Infectious Diseases of Poverty, 6*(05), 57–63.

Xu, C., Xu, X., Yao, X., and Dai, F. (2014). Three (nearly) complete inventories of landslides triggered by the May 12, 2008 Wenchuan Mw 7.9 earthquake of China and their spatial distribution statistical analysis. *Landslides, 11*(3), 441–461.

Zhang, Q., Gu, X., Shi, P., and Singh, V. P. (2017). Impact of tropical cyclones on flood risk in southeastern China: Spatial patterns, causes and implications. *Global and Planetary Change, 150*, 81–93.

Zięba, K. (2021). How can systems thinking help us in the COVID-19 crisis? *Knowledge and Process Management, 29*(3), 221–230.

About the Editors and Contributors

Editors

Kenneth N. K. FONG, PhD, MSc(OT), PgD(Biomech.), BSc, PD(OT), PD(OSH), Cert(CMH), OTR

Kenneth Fong is a Professor in the Department of Rehabilitation Sciences and Director of the Research Centre for Assistive Technology, The Hong Kong Polytechnic University. Currently he is the coordinator of the assistive technology laboratory in the Department of Rehabilitation Sciences, management committee member of the Research Institute in Artificial Intelligence of Things, chairman of the University Ethics Committee, member of the Senate, The Hong Kong Polytechnic University, and Editor-in-Chief, *Hong Kong Journal of Occupational Therapy*. He is a registered occupational therapist in Hong Kong, the United States, and the United Kingdom. He has received the individual and team teaching awards from the department and the Faculty of Health and Social Sciences. In the last 10 years, he has received competitive public research grants as chief investigator, among them, the Research Impact Fund, General Research Fund, Hospital and Medical Research Fund, Innovation and Technology Fund—Midstream Programme for the Universities, Beat Drugs Fund, etc. from the Research Grants Council, University Grants Committee, and the government, in order to develop innovative technology and rehabilitation intervention for people with disabilities. He serves as an honorary advisor of several non-government and self-help organisations for people with chronic diseases and disabilities in Hong Kong.

Ben Y. F. FONG, MPH (Syd), FHKCCM, FHKAM

Ben Fong is a specialist in community medicine, holding Honorary Clinical Associate Professorship at the two local medical schools in Hong Kong. He is currently the Professor of Practice (Health Studies), Associate Division Head and Director of the Centre for Ageing and Healthcare Management Research of the College of Professional and Continuing Education, The

Hong Kong Polytechnic University, and President of the Hong Kong College of Community Health Practitioners. He was formerly Senior Assistant Commissioner (Medical) of the Auxiliary Medical Service, former President of the Hong Kong Disaster Medicine Association, and former Medical Director of the Standard Chartered Hong Kong Marathon.

Contributors

Sandra Wing Yi CHAN, MN, BN(Hons), RN, APN, NCHK

Ms Sandra Wing Yi Chan is a senior lecturer at the School of Nursing and Health Studies, the Hong Kong Metropolitan University. Before joining the Hong Kong Metropolitan University, she was an advanced practice nurse at Pamela Youde Nethersole Eastern Hospital of the Hospital Authority. She was responsible for infection control in the department and deployed to an isolation ward during the COVID-19 pandemic. Sandra has always shown an interest in infection control.

Sunshine CHAN, RN, RM, MSc, DHSc

Sunshine Chan is a nurse consultant at the School of Nursing, The Hong Kong Polytechnic University.

Lu CHEN, BSc

Lu Chen is a PhD candidate at the School of Nursing, Beijing Capital Medical University in Beijing, China. After graduating from Guangzhou University of Chinese Medicine with a bachelor's degree, she participated in a research project on disaster education needs for undergraduate nursing students.

Shaohua CHEN, BSc, PhD

Shaohua Chen is a PhD graduate from the School of Nursing, Beijing Capital Medical University in Beijing, China. She is now a lecturer at the School of Nursing, Fujian Medical University.

Calvin CHENG, BA, MEcon, DBA, ACIM, MHKIM

Calvin Cheng is a Senior Lecturer and Award Leader of the Bachelor of Arts (Honours) in Marketing Management at the College of Professional and Continuing Education, The Hong Kong Polytechnic University. He is a Research Fellow of the Hong Kong College of Community Health Practitioners. His research interests include consumer behaviour, services marketing, green advertising, brand management, relationship marketing, learning and teaching in higher education, strategic management, supply chain management, entrepreneurship, and healthcare. His research has been published in reputable peer-reviewed international journals and conferences. He has also obtained a number of external and internal research funds with his research teams.

Wang-kin CHIU, BSc, PhD

Wang-kin Chiu is a Senior Lecturer, Assistant Programme Leader of the Associate in Health Studies, and Assistant Award Leader of the Bachelor of Science (Honours) in Applied Sciences (Health Studies) at the College of Professional and Continuing Education at The Hong Kong Polytechnic University. He received his Bachelor of Science (first class honours) and PhD in chemistry from The Chinese University of Hong Kong. He is currently the Hon. Secretary of the Hong Kong College of Community Health Practitioners.

Hao DAI, BSc

Hao Dai is a nursing officer in the Emergency Department of Chengdu No. 2 People's Hospital. At present, he is studying for a master's degree in disaster nursing and has become a national disaster team member providing supporting care for the affected community during the COVID-19 pandemic.

Thomas M. C. DAO, MSc, LLM (Distinct – MEL), FHKCFP, FRACGP, FHKAM

Thomas Dao is a specialist in family medicine and a doctor-in-charge of a government-funded primary care clinic in Hong Kong. He is also a part-time lecturer in the School of Chinese Medicine at The Chinese University of Hong Kong (CUHK) and an honorary clinical assistant professor in the Department of Family Medicine and Primary Care at The University of Hong Kong (HKU). He obtained a Master of Science degree in Diagnostic Ultrasonography from CUHK and a Master of Laws degree in Medical Ethics and Law with distinction from HKU. His research interests include chronic disease management and point-of-care ultrasonography in primary care.

Bean S. N. FU, PhD, FHKCFP, FRACGP, FHKAM

Bean Fu is a family medicine specialist and a Consultant in the Kowloon West Cluster of the Hong Kong Hospital Authority, Deputy Coordinator in the Specialist Exit Examination Board of the Hong Kong College of Family Physicians, and an Honorary Associate Professor and Assistant Professor at The Chinese University of Hong Kong and The University of Hong Kong, respectively. She obtained a Doctor of Philosophy from the Department of Medicine, University of Hong Kong. Her research interests include care of primary care patients with type 2 diabetes mellitus, hypertension, and chronic obstructive pulmonary disease.

Billy Shing Hin HO, BSc (Hons)

Billy Ho received a Bachelor of Science (Honours) in Applied Science (Health Studies) at The Hong Kong Polytechnic University. He is a research assistant at the Hong Kong Institute of Integrative Medicine at The Chinese University of Hong Kong, and was a research intern at the Hong Kong College of Community Health Practitioners and an intern at the Centre for Ageing and Healthcare Research.

Percy Wing Tung HO, BSc (Hons), MPH

Percy Ho obtained her Bachelor of Science (Honours) in Applied Science (Health Studies) with first class honours from The Hong Kong Polytechnic University and Master of Public Health at The Chinese University of Hong Kong. Upon graduation, she qualified as an international practitioner of the UK Faculty of Public Health, and a fellow member of the Hong Kong College of Community Health Practitioners. With keen interest in health promotion and clinical research, Percy has served in universities, private and public healthcare sectors, and non-profit organisations, as well as contributed to numerous publications. Percy is currently a senior public health programme manager at the Department of Health.

Kin-kwan LAM, FHKCEM, FHKAM

Kin-kwan Lam is a specialist in emergency medicine, holding Honorary Clinical Associate Professorship at the two local medical schools in Hong Kong. He is currently a Consultant in Emergency Medicine for the Hospital Authority, the Deputy Commissioner (Human Resources) of the Auxiliary Medical Service, the Assistant Commissioner (Medical) of Hong Kong St John Ambulance, the Chairman of the Hong Kong Disaster Medicine Association, and the Chairman of the Resuscitation Council of Hong Kong. He was formerly the Chief Medical Officer of the Hong Kong ePrix 2016; the Medical Director of the Standard Chartered Hong Kong Marathon 2019, 2021, and 2023; the former Chairman of the Pre-hospital Care Subcommittee of the Hospital Authority; and the former Chairman of the Pre-hospital Medicine Subcommittee of the Hong Kong College of Emergency Medicine.

Simon Ching LAM, PhD, RN, FHKAN

Prof Simon Lam is currently the Associate Dean (Research) and Professor of the School of Nursing at Tung Wah College. He has over 16 years of teaching experience as an academic in both University Grants Committee and self-financing tertiary institutions in Hong Kong. Prof Lam has published over 90 peer-reviewed articles and book chapters in the fields of infection control, psychometric testing, and public health. He received the 2021 Emerging Nurse Researcher/Scholar Award for the Asia Region from the Sigma Theta Tau International Honor Society of Nursing and has been recognised by Stanford University's List of the World's Top 2% Scientists recently.

Yukie Yuk Ki LAM, MBChB, MRCP (UK)

Yukie Lam is a resident doctor in the Adult Intensive Care Unit, Queen Mary Hospital, The University of Hong Kong. She was previously a resident in the Department of Medicine and Therapeutics, The Chinese University of Hong Kong.

Derrick K. W. LAW, BSc (Hons)

Derrick Law is an intern at the Centre for Ageing and Healthcare Management Research, College of Professional and Continuing Education, The Hong Kong Polytechnic University, and a research intern at the Hong Kong College of Community Health Practitioners.

Vincent T. S. LAW, BSc, MBA, DBA

Vincent Law is a senior lecturer, and also the Founding Member and Deputy Director of the Centre for Ageing and Healthcare Management Research in the College of Professional and Continuing Education at The Hong Kong Polytechnic University. His research fields include public policy, management, health, Chinese philosophy, etc. As an experienced researcher in public policy, Vincent has participated in some large-scale consultancy and research projects on public policy and public engagement with the Hong Kong government in recent years. He has authored a few academic journal papers, co-edited the book *Primary Care Revisited— Interdisciplinary Perspectives for a New Era* published by Springer, authored a few book chapters on health care and sustainability, and published four books in Chinese on Chinese philosophy and wisdom.

Alan K. T. LEUNG, BSc (Hons)

Alan Leung is an intern at the Centre for Ageing and Healthcare Management Research, College of Professional and Continuing Education, The Hong Kong Polytechnic University, and a research intern at the Hong Kong College of Community Health Practitioners.

Joseph LEUNG, DBA, MBA, MEd, MMgt, PgDipArb, PgDipBPsy, PgCertMPsy

Joseph Leung is a lecturer at the College of Professional and Continuing Education, The Hong Kong Polytechnic University. Joseph is currently Honorary Research Associate of the Hong Kong Institute of Asia-Pacific Studies, The Chinese University of Hong Kong; Reviewer of *Computer Science and Information Technology*; Vice Chairman of the Hong Kong Internet Forum; Vice Chairman of the Chartered Institute of Marketing (HK); and Panel Member of the Asian Domain Name Dispute Resolution Centre. He is also a Fellow Member of the British Computer Society, Hong Kong Computer Society, Singapore Computer Society, Chartered Institute of Marketing, Hong Kong Institute of Directors; an Accredited Mediator, Arbitrator, Certified Business Psychologist, Certified Behavioural Consultant; and a columnist for various newspapers and magazines.

Peng LIAO, BSc, MOT(China)

Peng Liao is a lecturer in Rehabilitation Medicine at Kunming Medical University in Yunnan, China.

Leon Wai LI, BSc (Hons), MPH

Leon Li completed his Bachelor of Science (Honours) in Applied Science (Health Studies) at The Hong Kong Polytechnic University and subsequently obtained a Master of Public Health at The Chinese University of Hong Kong. Afterwards, he has published journal articles and book chapters related to public health issues on behalf of the Hong Kong College of Community Health Practitioners. He is also actively working in the public health field as a public health programme manager and is currently serving as a research officer in the Department of Health to continuously contribute to the community.

Sijian LI, BSN, MPhil, PhD

Dr Sijian Li got her MPhil from the Department of Social Work and Social Administration, The University of Hong Kong, and her PhD from the School of Nursing, The Polytechnic University of Hong Kong. She received her nursing education from the post-graduate Medical School of Wuhan. Since 2013, she has been working as programme leader for the Master of Science in Disaster Nursing, School of Nursing, The Hong Kong Polytechnic University. Her research interest is in programme development in nursing education in disaster preparedness, response, and recovery.

Cecilia Wai-Ping LI-TSANG, PD(OT), PhD

Prof Li-Tsang has more than 30 years of academic teaching and research experience in the field of physical rehabilitation including paediatrics, orthopaedics, work-related injuries, and hand and burns injuries. She is the senior editor of the *Journal of Burn and Trauma*, and an associate editor of the *Hong Kong Journal of Occupational Therapy* and *WORK*. She also holds positions as the Vice-chairman, Board of Directors, Wai Ji Christian Services; Executive Committee member, Hong Kong Rheumatology and Arthritis Foundation; consultant, Hong Kong Christian Service; Honorary Advisor, SAHK; and consultant, IDEAL (parents organisation). Since the 2008 Sichuan earthquake, she has actively promoted rehabilitation training and services for quake survivors in China. She continues to serve as a visiting professor after retirement and provides training for occupational therapy students in mainland China. Recently, she has been working to promote community rehabilitation in rural areas of China in collaboration with Keswick Foundation.

Wei Kwang LUK, MBChB, FRCPA, FHKAM

Wei Kwang Luk is a medical microbiologist and Clinical Associate Professor (Honorary) at The Chinese University of Hong Kong. He is Deputy Commissioner (Sup) of the Auxiliary Medical Service, Vice-President of the Hong Kong Disaster Medicine Association, and an Examiner of The Hong Kong College of Pathologists.

Jocelyn Rosemary TONG, BSc (Hons)

Jocelyn Tong is a research intern at the Hong Kong College of Community Health Practitioners, and an intern at the Centre for Ageing and Healthcare Management Research, College of Professional and Continuing Education, The Hong Kong Polytechnic University.

Cynthia Ka-Cheong WAI, MBBS, FHKAM, FRCSEd (ORL), FHKCORL

Dr Cynthia Wai graduated from The University of Hong Kong and obtained her fellowship in otorhinolaryngology in 2016. She is currently the Consultant in the Department of Otorhinolaryngology, Head and Neck Surgery at Yan Chai Hospital, serving the Kowloon West Cluster. She also joined the Auxiliary Medical Service (AMS) in 2009 as a volunteer, and is currently a Deputy Regional Commander of the AMS. She has actively participated in medical support for various major events, such as serving at the Standard Chartered Hong Kong Marathon every year.

Jonathan Heung-On WAI, MBBS, DLO (RCS England), DFM, MSc Sports Medicine and Health Science

Dr Jonathan Wai is currently the Medical Superintendent of Precious Blood Hospital, Honorary Clinical Associate Professor at The Chinese University of Hong Kong, and President of the Hong Kong Disaster Medicine Association (HKDMA), with a private practice in otorhinolaryngology. He was a former President of the Hong Kong Society of Otorhinolaryngology, Head and Neck Surgery and former Deputy Commissioner of the Auxiliary Medical Service (AMS). Dr Wai has great proficiency and extensive experience in coordinating and providing medical first-aid support for major sports events in Hong Kong. He has been assigned as the medical coordinator and Deputy Medical Director to the Standard Chartered Hong Kong Marathon. He also worked as a team physician for the Hong Kong team in many national games outside Hong Kong. He is actively involved in the promotion of disaster awareness, preparedness, and emergency response at the community and pre-hospital level through disaster field trainings, workshops, and symposia with his roles in HKDMA and AMS.

Cong WANG, BSc, MOT(China)

Cong Wang is a lecturer in the Occupational Therapy Department, School of Rehabilitation at Kunming Medical University in Yunnan, China.

Qian WANG, MD, PhD

Dr Qian Wang is a consultant in the Department of Rehabilitation Medicine, West China Hospital, Sichuan University. His main research interests are regenerative medicine for musculoskeletal disorders, stem cells and gene therapy, scoliosis and posture rehabilitation, and minimally invasive techniques for myofascial pain syndrome. He has 30 peer-reviewed publications in journals such as *Bone, Quality of Life Research, Stem Cells and Development, Journal of Medical Internet Research, Disability and Rehabilitation,* and *Disaster Medicine and Public Health Preparedness,* etc. He is the Associate Head of the Youth Committee of Physical Medicine and Rehabilitation of the Sichuan Medical Association.

Qiuyun WANG, BSc, MOT(China)

Qiuyun Wang is a lecturer at Yunnan Medical Health College in Kunming, Yunnan, China.

M. S. WONG, CPO, PhD, FHKSCPO, FISP

Dr M. S. Wong is an Associate Professor (Prosthetics and Orthotics) in the Department of Biomedical Engineering at The Hong Kong Polytechnic University with both a clinical and engineering background. He has been involved in Prosthetics and Orthotics programme developments, various clinical research studies on prosthetics and orthotics outcome measures, posture and spinal deformities, and learning and teaching projects including the development of peer tutoring, online learning materials, student critical thinking attributes, community services, and student internationalisation.

Brendan C. Y. WU, MB ChB, FRACGP, FHKCFP, FHKAM, MSc PD, MSc Mental Health, MSc Diagnostic Ultrasonography

Brendan Wu serves in the Assure Health Medical Centre in Victoria, Australia, as a family medicine specialist. He is also an honorary assistant professor at both The University of Hong Kong and The Chinese University of Hong Kong. Brendan has a special interest in primary care dermatology, mental health, and point-of-care ultrasonography. He attained a Master of Science in Practical Dermatology from Cardiff University and Masters of Science n Mental Health and Diagnostic Ultrasonography from The Chinese University of Hong Kong. Brendan is keen on medical education and has contributed to the Royal Australian College of General Practitioners as a journal reviewer.

Danli WU, BSc, MOT(China)

Danli Wu is a lecturer at Yunnan University of Chinese Medicine in Kunming, Yunnan, China.

Nana WU, BSc, MSc

Nana Wu is a nursing officer and a neonatal advanced nursing practitioner in the Neonatal Intensive Care Unit, Chengdu Women's and Children's Central Hospital. She graduated from the Master of Science in Disaster Nursing programme at the Institute for Disaster Management and Reconstruction, The Hong Kong Polytechnic University, in 2021.

Rui XIA, BSc, MSc

Rui Xia is a nursing officer in the Emergency Department of Chengdu No. 2 People's Hospital in Chengdu, Sichuan, China.

Alfred P. H. YIP, BSc (Hons)

Alfred Yip is an intern at the Centre for Ageing and Healthcare Management Research, College of Professional and Continuing Education, The Hong Kong Polytechnic University, and a research intern at the Hong Kong College of Community Health Practitioners.

Simon S. M. YUEN, BSc, PhD, CMILT, FSTLA, MIPSHK, PMHKLA

Dr Simon S. M. Yuen is a senior lecturer and scheme leader at the College of Professional and Continuing Education, The Hong Kong Polytechnic

University. He has published papers and articles in international journals, professional magazines, and academic conferences. His research areas include operations and supply chain management, strategic management and practices, aviation logistics, e-business, and learning and teaching in higher education. Moreover, Dr Yuen participates and is involved in several activities of local and international professional bodies such as honorary chairman of the younger managers' club in the Hong Kong Management Association, and Council member of the Hong Kong Logistics Management Staff Association and the Institute of Purchasing and Supply of Hong Kong.

Hong ZHU, BSc, MOT(China)

Hong Zhu is an occupational therapist in private practice in Chengdu, Sichuan, China.